AF506268

Thought Leadership in Advancing International
Business Research

Thought Leadership in Advancing International Business Research

Edited by

Arie Y. Lewin
Duke University, USA

S. Tamer Cavusgil
Georgia State University, USA

G. Tomas M. Hult
Michigan State University, USA

and

David A. Griffith
Michigan State University, USA

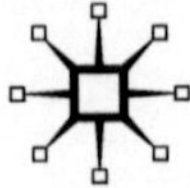

First published 2008 by
PALGRAVE MACMILLAN
Houndmills, Basingstoke, Hampshire RG21 6XS and
175 Fifth Avenue, New York, N.Y. 10010
Companies and representatives throughout the world

PALGRAVE MACMILLAN is the global academic imprint of the Palgrave Macmillan division of St. Martin's Press, LLC and of Palgrave Macmillan Ltd. Macmillan® is a registered trademark in the United States, United Kingdom and other countries. Palgrave is a registered trademark in the European Union and other countries.

ISBN-13: 978–0–230–21777–5 hardback
ISBN-10: 0–230–21777–X hardback

This book is printed on paper suitable for recycling and made from fully managed and sustained forest sources. Logging, pulping and manufacturing processes are expected to conform to the environmental regulations of the country of origin.

A catalogue record for this book is available from the British Library.

Library of Congress Cataloging-in-Publication Data
Thought leadership in advancing international business research / edited by Arie Y. Lewin . . . [et al.].
        p.   cm.
Includes bibliographical references and index.
ISBN 0–230–21777–X (alk. paper)
1. International business enterprises—Research. 2. International business enterprises—Management. 3. International trade—Research.
4. Business—Research. I. Lewin, Arie Y., 1935–
HD2755.5.T57 2008
338.8′8072—dc22   2008016147

10   9   8   7   6   5   4   3   2   1
17 16 15 14 13 12 11 10 09 08

Printed and bound in Great Britain by
CPI Antony Rowe, Chippenham and Eastbourne

Contents

List of Tables

List of Figures

Notes on Contributors

Ruth V. Aguilera is Associate Professor at the Department of Business Administration at the College of Business and at the Institute of Labor and Industrial Relations at the University of Illinois at Urbana-Champaign. She received her Ph.D. in Sociology from Harvard University and works in the fields of comparative corporate governance, cross-border alliances, social networks, and corporate social responsibility.

Christian Geisler Asmussen is Assistant Professor of International Business and Strategic Management at Copenhagen Business School's Center for Strategic Management and Globalization. His research is about the globalization of multinational corporations, focusing on the interaction of geographic scope and competitive advantage.

Gabriel R.G. Benito is Professor of International Strategy at BI Norwegian School of Management, Oslo, Norway. His research has particularly dealt with foreign direct investment and divestment, the structure and behavior of multinational enterprises and their foreign subsidiaries, and foreign operation methods.

Lance Eliot Brouthers is Professor of Management, Michael J. Coles College of Business, the Kennesaw State University, Kennesaw. He has won or been a finalist for numerous research and teaching awards including the Igor Ansoff Award for business strategy, an international award sponsored by Coopers and Lybrand and given only once every two years. Professor Brouthers has published over 80 authored articles, proceedings, and book chapters on international business strategy, the international business environment, and/or international entrepreneurship.

S. Tamer Cavusgil is Fuller E. Callaway Professorial Chair and Director of the Institute of International Business at Georgia State University. He serves as an elected Fellow of the Academy of International Business. His areas of interest include emerging markets, international marketing strategy, and early internationalization. Cavusgil is the author of several books and over 100 refereed articles. His most recent book, *International Business: Strategy, Management, and the New Realities*, co-authored with Gary Knight and John Riesenberger, has just been published by Prentice-Hall. He is also the author of several computer-aided diagnostic tools for managers, including CORE V, Company

Readiness to Export. He served as the inaugural Editor-in-Chief of the *Journal of International Marketing*, published by the American Marketing Association. Cavusgil edits the Elsevier book series, *Advances in International Marketing*.

Craig Crossland is Assistant Professor of Management at University of Texas at Austin. He received his Ph.D. in Strategic Management from the Pennsylvania State University. His research interests lie in the areas of managerial discretion, national institutions, and social networks. Craig is quietly hopeful that this article heralds the start of a long and productive academic career.

John C. Dencker is Assistant Professor in the Institute of Labor and Industrial Relations at the University of Illinois at Urbana-Champaign. He received his Ph.D. in sociology from Harvard University. His research examines the effects of corporate restructuring, mergers and acquisitions, and public policy initiatives on labor markets and the employment relationship.

Sidney J. Gray is Professor of International Business and Associate Dean International in the Faculty of Economics and Business at the University of Sydney, Australia. He was formerly a professor at the Universities of Glasgow, Warwick, and New South Wales. He is Associate Editor of the *Journal of International Financial Management and Accounting* and a member of the Editorial Boards of a number of leading international journals including *Journal of International Business Studies, Management International Review*, and *Journal of International Management*. He is a founder and immediate Past President of the Australia and New Zealand International Business Academy. He is also currently Vice President – International of the American Accounting Association. In 2006, he was elected as a Fellow of the Academy of the Social Sciences in Australia.

David A. Griffith is Associate Professor of Marketing at the Eli Broad Graduate School of Management at Michigan State University, where he also serves as Director of the Ph.D. Program. He is also the John W. Byington Endowed Chair in Global Marketing at Michigan State University. He specializes in marketing strategy and international marketing with a focus on intra- and inter-organizational governance. His research has been published in numerous journals including the *Journal of Marketing, Journal of International Business Studies, Journal of Operations Management, Journal of Advertising,* and the *Journal of Retailing*. He teaches marketing theory, marketing strategy, and international business. He has served on faculty at the *University of Hawai'i at Manoa*, the *Japan-America Institute of Management Science, Wirtschaftsuniversität Wien*, and *University of Oklahoma*. He currently serves as Editor-in-Chief (2008–2010) of the American Marketing Association's *Journal of International Marketing* and on the Board of Directors (2000–present) of the AMA Global Marketing Special Interest Group.

John Hadjimarcou has a Ph.D. from the Kent State University and has been a part of the UTEP family since 1994. He is currently the chairman of the Department of Marketing and Management. He teaches classes in marketing such as international marketing, principles of retailing, and principles of marketing.

John Holt is a management consultant. He was formerly a senior Lecturer in Organization and Management at the University of New South Wales, Sydney, Australia.

G. Tomas M. Hult is Director of the Broad International Business Center and Professor of Marketing and International Business in the Eli Broad Graduate School of Management at the Michigan State University. He is also Executive Director of the Academy of International Business (aib.msu.edu). He has published more than 70 articles on marketing management, strategic marketing/management, supply chain management, and international marketing/business.

David J. Ketchen received his Ph.D. from the Pennsylvania State University. He is Lowder Eminent Scholar in Entrepreneurship and a Professor of Management at Auburn University. He previously taught at the Louisiana State University and the Florida State University. His research interests include entrepreneurship and franchising, methodological issues in organizational research, strategic supply chain management, and the determinants of superior organizational performance. He has published his works in journals such as the *Academy of Management Journal*, the *Academy of Management Executive*, *Strategic Management Journal*, *Journal of Operations Management*, and *Journal of Management*, among others. He has served or is serving on the editorial review boards for the *Academy of Management Journal*, the *Academy of Management Review*, and the *Strategic Entrepreneurship Journal*, among others. He has completed terms as an associate editor for the *Journal of Management, Organizational Research Methods, Journal of Operations Management*, and *Journal of International Business Studies* and has served as a guest co-editor for special issues of the *Academy of Management Review, Journal of Operations Management, Organizational Research Methods*, and *Journal of Management*.

Ahmet H. Kirca is Assistant Professor in the Department of Marketing at the Eli Broad College of Business at the Michigan State University. He previously taught at the George Washington University, Washington, DC. He received his Ph.D. in International Business/Marketing from the University of South Carolina, Columbia. He has published his articles in various academic journals, including *Journal of Marketing* and *Journal of Services Marketing*. In addition, he is the author or co-author in numerous national and international proceedings and invited presentations. Professor Kirca had extensive work experience in textile and tourism industries before he joined academia.

Arie Y. Lewin is Professor of Business Administration and Sociology at the Fuqua School of Business, Duke University. He is the Director of the Center for International Business Education and Research (CIBER). His primary research interests involve the co-evolution of new organization forms and management of strategy and organization change in times of increasing disorder. He leads a cross-national (Denmark, Japan, Korea, the Netherlands, Sweden, Switzerland, the United Kingdom, and the United States) research consortium – New Organization Forms for the Information Age (NOFIA) – involving a longitudinal comparative study of strategic re-orientations and organization restructurings and international competitiveness.

Matthew B. Myers is the Nestlé Professor of Marketing and Associate Professor, Marketing & Logistics and the Director of the Global Business Institute at the College of Business Administration, University of Tennessee. He teaches global marketing and business strategy at the undergraduate, MBA, Executive, and doctoral levels. Dr Myers earned his Ph.D. in Business from the Eli Broad Graduate School of Management, Michigan State University and his Masters of International Business Studies at the Moore College of Business, University of South Carolina. Prior to academia, he worked with both Merrill-Lynch and IBM-Argentina. He has studied, taught, and worked in Central America, South America, Europe, Central and East Asia and has acted as a consultant to organizations in the global distribution, chemical, insurance, pharmaceutical, and marketing research industries.

Torben Pedersen is Professor of International Business at the Copenhagen Business School's Center for Strategic Management and Globalization. He has published over 50 articles and books concerning the managerial and strategic aspects of globalization. His research has appeared in prominent journals such as the *Strategic Management Journal*, the *Journal of International Business Studies*, and the *Journal of Corporate Finance*. His latest book entitled *Managing Global Offshoring Strategies – A Case Approach* has been well received among academics, students, and practitioners.

Bent Petersen is Professor of International Business at the Center for Strategic Management and Globalization, Copenhagen Business School (CBS). He received his Ph.D. from CBS and holds an M.Sc. in Business Economics from the same institution. For five years he worked as an economist at the Carlsberg Research Center, Department of Biotechnology and Business Diversification. His primary research interests are in IT and firms' internationalization (including offshoring) and dynamics of foreign operation methods. He has published in *Journal of Business Research, Managerial Decisions and*

Economics, Journal of International Marketing, Management International Review, Long Range Planning, International Studies of Management & Organization, International Business Review, World Development and *Journal of International Management,* among others. He is a member of the Academy of International Business and the European International Business Academy and serves currently as a reviewer for *International Business Review, Management International Review, Journal of World Business, Journal of International Business Studies,* and *International Marketing Review.*

William R. Purcell is Pro Vice-Chancellor International at the University of Newcastle, Australia. He was formerly Head of the Newcastle Graduate School of Business and Associate Professor of International Business at the University of New South Wales, Sydney, Australia.

Saeed Samiee is the Collins Professor of Marketing and International Business at the University of Tulsa and the Director of the Institute of International Business Education in Moscow, Russia, a joint project between the University of Tulsa and the Moscow Institute of Electronics Engineering. He has served as a visiting professor and has lectured at business schools in over a dozen countries. Prior to joining TU as the Director of the International Management Center, he was a member of the faculty at the University of South Carolina. He received his Ph.D. from the Ohio State University.

Charles C. Snow is the Mellon Foundation Professor of Business Administration in the Smeal College of Business at the Pennsylvania State University. He is on the editorial board of *Strategic Management Journal, Journal of Management,* and *Journal of World Business.* He has published widely on management topics, including co-authoring or co-editing eight books. His research interests are in strategic management, international business, and new organizational forms. He is a member of the advisory board of Syndicom, a firm founded on the principles of an open collaborative community.

Dr Sc (IB) Minna Söderqvist has a Ph.D. from Helsinki School of Economics, Finland. She is now a Senior Adviser in the Rector's Development Unit at TKK, the Helsinki University of Technology, Finland. Her current work includes preparing strategic decisions and projects regarding development of internationalization, coordinating TKK's participation to international networks, preparing contracts between universities and being responsible for evaluation, and reporting TKK's international activities.

John W. Story is Professor in the marketing department at Idaho State University. He holds BBA and MS degrees from Texas A&M University and earned his Ph.D. at the University of Colorado, Boulder. He has published his works in numerous academic journals and in a variety of practitioner-oriented publications. His primary research focus is building value at the customer-firm interface in a global marketing environment.

Brian Toyne (retired) Dr Toyne is Fellow of the Academy of International Business. He taught at the University of South Carolina, St Mary's University, and was Visiting Professor at the University of Auckland, New Zealand, University of Hawaii and the Helsinki School of Economics and Business, Finland. Dr Toyne was the recipient and director of six US Department of Education grants and a consultant to 12 business schools on their internationalization programs. He has authored, co-authored, and edited 11 books and authored and co-authored more than 60 peer-reviewed papers in such journals as the *Journal of International Business Studies*, *Academy of Management Review*, *Management International Review*, *Journal of Management*, *Columbia Journal of Business*, and *Journal of Teaching in International Business*. His research interests include international business education, cross-cultural management, and strategic options.

Peter G.P. Walters B.Sc. (Econ), MBA, Ph.D. He is currently Associate Dean, College of Professional and Continuing Education, Hong Kong Polytechnic University, Hong Kong. He was educated at the London School of Economics, University of Liverpool and the Institute of International Business, Georgia State University. Prior to coming to Hong Kong, he worked at universities in the United States and Norway – primarily University of South Carolina and the Norwegian School of Management. His research focus is in the areas of international marketing and international management, and he has published in the *Columbia Journal of World Business*, *Journal of International Business Studies*, *Journal of the Academy of Marketing Science*, *Strategic Management Journal*, *Journal of International Marketing*, *Entrepreneurship Theory and Practice*, and other refereed journals.

Lawrence S. Welch is Professor at Melbourne Business School and has published extensively on issues pertaining to internationalization and international business operation methods and is a member of the editorial boards of a number of international business journals. His research has involved extensive collaboration with Nordic colleagues over more than three decades. Also, he has spent long periods undertaking research and teaching in Nordic business schools, particularly at the Norwegian School of Management BI, Helsinki School of Economics, and Copenhagen Business School.

Zeynep Yesim Yalabik is a Ph.D. candidate at the Institute of Labor and Industrial Relations, University of Illinois at Urbana-Champaign. Her dissertation focuses on the role of organizational socialization in the mergers and acquisitions context. Her interests lie in the area of strategic human resource management, high performance work systems, and management of human resources in the mergers and acquisitions.

Eden Yin is University Lecturer in Marketing at the Judge Business School, Cambridge University and Fellow of St Edmund's College, Cambridge University. He received his Ph.D. from the Marshall Business School, University of Southern California, Los Angeles. His principal research interests are within new product growth in high-tech industries, internationalization strategies for firms from emerging economies, global business ethics, and managing art and cultural products. He has published his work in *Marketing Science, Journal of Marketing Research, Management International Review*, and others. He is the recipient of a number of awards, which include the ERIM Award for Impact on Management Practice, ISBM Business Marketing Doctoral Support Award, and he was also the winner of *Academy of Marketing Science* 2000 Jane K. Fenyo Student Paper Competition. He is a member of the American Marketing Association, AIB, INFORMS and the Academy of Marketing Science. He has taught marketing management, high-tech marketing, and global marketing at both undergraduate and graduate levels in the United States, the United Kingdom, Australia, Finland, Denmark, Argentina, Brazil, and China.

Leslie Yip lectures on retailing and merchandising, e-marketing, and marketing management for undergraduate and postgraduate programs which include China EMBA. His current research focuses on studying "consumer's shopping mall experience." He is also an academic researcher of the Asian Centre for Brand Management (ACBM), the Department's strategic area research unit. ACBM has been conducting longitudinal research on shoppers' perceived value and the performance of Hong Kong retailers. ACBM serves as a global platform which connects academics and practitioners and facilitates brand knowledge transfer through research, consultancy, training, seminar, and an annual international conference. He has published his work in the *International Journal of Advertising, Entrepreneurship Theory and Practice, Industrial Marketing Management, Journal of Business Research, International Marketing Review, European Journal of Marketing*, and *Journal of Retailing*. Before joining PolyU, he worked in textile and fashion manufacturing and trading businesses.

Introduction

*Arie Y. Lewin, S. Tamer Cavusgil, G. Tomas M. Hult,
and David A. Griffith*

The field of international business (IB) has recently arrived at a point in its development where its search for knowledge has focused on significant, seminal themes able to drive the advancement of the field forward. This call has been heralded in the literature. For example, the *Journal of International Business Studies* has recently published a series of articles where leading scholars have pondered the future development of international business as a scholarly discipline (e.g., Buckley, 2002; Buckley and Ghauri, 2004; Peng, 2004; Shenkar, 2004). Buckley (2002) argued that the field of international business may have run out of steam. He noted that to advance the field scholars need to identify the key factors in the global economy to be explained and then search out a tractable means of explication within a coherent theoretical framework. Peng (2004), responding to Buckley, identified notable areas that can be addressed to drive the IB agenda forward.

At a larger level, these calls build on Sullivan's (1998) critical evaluation of the field in which he contended that the advancement of IB research has been constrained in its ability to develop due to its reliance on a singular approaches. It can be argued that reliance on a single methodological or philosophical approach ignores metatheoretical implications thus hindering theoretical advancement. With this issue at the fore, the *Academy of International Business*, jointly with the *Journal of International Business Studies*, advanced the idea of the Frontiers conference aimed at directly addressing the future of the field. The primary aim of the Frontiers conference was to allow for radical innovation within the literature stimulating researchers to explore issues that could substantially push the boundaries without the standard controls built into the journal review process. The following chapters are an outcome of the second annual Frontiers conference held in the Fall of 2004 at Michigan State University.

Extending our understanding of international business: Thought leadership

In response to the growing seminal issues in the field, this book is devoted to areas that can advance our understanding of international business. This book includes ten excellent contributions that extend our knowledge in the area of international business and IB research. The chapters presented cover a range of IB topics tested via diverse methodologies providing unique insights into the issues raised.

The lead chapter, by Minna Söderqvist and Brian Toyne, titled "A Discourse Analysis of Knowledge Creation in International Business Research: JIBS 1970–2005," focuses on how and how consciously IB scholars see their way of knowledge creation in IB research. By using one of the many existing discourse analysis approaches, this chapter explores the articles published in the *Journal of International Business Studies* between 1970 and 2005. The authors find that 49 articles published in the *Journal of International Business Studies* include ontological, epistemological, and methodological discussions covering three discourses: (1) the validation of international business as a research field; (2) the focus of IB research; and (3) the "right" type of IB research. As such, this chapter provides a thoughtful analysis of the extant literature of the field and therefore sets the stage for detailed topical research presented through the remainder of this book.

The second chapter, by Ahmet H. Kirca, titled "Multinationality of the Firm: Conceptualization and Measurement," drawing upon the Uppsala model of the internationalization of the firm, distinguishes between the state and process aspects of the internationalization and proposes a multidimensional conceptualization of the extent of firm internationalization (i.e., firm multinationality). Then, using meta-analytic data collection procedures, the author identifies existing measures of multinationality in the extant literature culminating in the proposal of an alternative scale development procedure for the construction of a multinationality index.

In the third chapter, by Bent Petersen, Gabriel R.G. Benito, Lawrence S. Welch, and Christian Geisler Asmussen, titled "Mode Configuration Diversity: A New Perspective on Foreign Entry Mode Choice," a framework is developed which describes how firms arrange their value activities in foreign markets. The authors argue that in order to keep the theory testing manageable, entry (or operation) mode researchers have tended to focus on one, or a few, broadly defined value activities, such as production or marketing. As an alternative mode, choice is offered as a configuration of all identifiable value activities of the entrant firm where governance form and location are attached to the individual value activity. When analyzing the number of potential configurations of firms' value activities in foreign markets, the authors find the number to be immense, suggesting that the diversity of foreign operation modes is much greater than usually presented in the literature. As such, the authors argue that mode configuration diversity is an important strategic factor of its own. A series of propositions as to the determinants and the performance implications of mode configuration diversity are presented thus providing a strong foundation for the advancement of the field.

Maintaining the value orientation, the fourth chapter, by Saeed Samiee, Peter G. P. Walters, and Leslie Yip, titled "Value Creation in International Electronic Markets: A Conceptual Framework," explores value creation in supply chain systems within the context of international electronic markets. The authors leverage the resource-based view of the firm as well as theories and concepts in relationship and international marketing to offer a framework for examining value creation and performance within supply chain systems. Their efforts culminate in a proposed model where knowledge and, hence, joint learning, is a critical resource that can be shared and collectively deployed in international electronic markets to achieve greater efficiencies and create or enhance value in supply chain systems. A series of propositions are developed and several preliminary observations are offered suggesting how researchers can employ this framework to gain finer grain insights into this important area of interantional commerce.

The fifth chapter, by John Holt, William R. Purcell, Sidney J. Gray, and Torben Pedersen, titled "Decision Factors Influencing MNEs' Regional Headquarters Location Selection Strategies," identifies the underlying dimensional nature of the range of decision variables that MNEs generally associate with making regional headquarters (RHQ) location choices and also examines the extent to which MNEs, when grouped according to contextual characteristics, use discernibly different decision criteria when making RHQ location selection decisions. Using a sample of respondents from 57 RHQs in Europe and the Asia-Pacific (specifically Australia), principal components analysis yielded nine interpretable factor dimensions, underlying 39 location decision variables, which were then used to compare decision schema groups. Three contextual classifications, "strategic purpose of RHQ establishment," "nationality of company origin," and "industry sector," were hypothesized and used to categorize the sample. The analysis indicated that while subgroups within these grouping categories were associated with distinctive location selection priorities, those RHQs established in order to be responsive to regional markets appeared to use significantly different selection criteria compared to those RHQs established to facilitate global coordination. Similarly, the selection criteria US-based MNEs used to make RHQ location decisions were found to be significantly different to the selection criteria Asian-based MNEs used when making their RHQ location decisions. Finally, location decision priorities were also found to vary across industry sector.

In the sixth chapter, by Lance Eliot Brouthers, John W. Story, and John Hadjimarcou, titled "A Signaling Theory Investigation of How to Overcome Negative Country-of-Origin Effects," the authors employ signaling theory's definition of a brand to suggest that country of origin (COO) labels lack a bonding component and therefore, actually represent "static" in the system. This hypothesis is tested through a series of experiments. Specifically, three salient strategies Chinese firms might use to address the negative impact of COO stereotypes in first world markets (i.e., reducing the noise caused by negative COO stereotypes, strengthening the signal by utilizing brands, and by using familiar brands and multiple COOs) are investigated. The results demonstrate that the three strategies improve consumer product evaluations, thus providing substantially new insights to reinvigorate COO research in the field of international business.

In the seventh chapter, by Ruth V. Aguilera, John C. Dencker, and Zeynep Y. Yalabik, titled "Institutions and Organizational Socialization: Integrating Employees in Cross-Border Mergers and Acquisitions," the authors develop a theoretical framework to help maximize effectiveness of the integration during post-acquisition. The authors primarily focus on how value can be created by understanding and managing the socialization process of *acquired employees* more effectively in the post-acquisition integration stage. By addressing this specialized area of IB research the authors provide a new perspective and unit of analysis for researchers addressing international mergers and acquisitions.

In the eighth chapter, by Craig Crossland, David J. Ketchen, Jr, and Charles C. Snow, titled "Multi-Firm Collaboration and International Competitive Dynamics," the authors describe the multi-firm collaborative network as a new organizational form that is emerging in the IB arena. They argue that this new type of network organization enables a group of collaborating firms to pursue a business strategy of continuous innovation, helping it to efficiently develop businesses outside their existing industries and country markets. They contend that such an organization will have major implications for both network theory and international competitive dynamics and as such they discuss research opportunities in both areas, including the transformation of multi-firm networks into global supply chains and newer forms of international competition such as multi-point competition, co-opetition, and virtual clustering.

In the ninth chapter, by Eden Yin, titled "Establishing the Moral Basis of Global Capitalism: Implications for MNEs in Emerging Markets," the authors investigate the moral basis of global capitalism. Specifically, they argue that the lack of a solid moral basis for modern global capitalism, in the face of recent global business scandals such as *Enron, Arthur Anderson, Worldcom, Global Crossing*, may not only dispel its materialistic gain, but also undermine its long-term survival, and even lead to the clash of civilization depicted in Huntington's work (1996). By endorsing and arguing for the pursuit of "responsible global capitalism," especially in emerging economies, the authors argue that a moral basis for business is not an option but a necessity. The authors use a highly successful multinational enterprise in China, *Xi'an Janssen* Pharmaceutical Ltd, to illustrate their key arguments. Based on their study, the authors believe that morality and global business ethics should draw serious attention from IB scholars who strive to conduct relevant and important academic research.

In the final contribution, by Matthew B. Myers and David A. Griffith, titled "The Study of Fit in International Business Research: Methodological and Substantive Issues," the authors demonstrate the complex issues of fit measurement in IB research. The authors argue that fit has become a central theme of IB research as in this context firms operate in diverse environments and with a diversity of partners. They argue given the importance of fit research in IB research it becomes incumbent upon IB researchers to employ appropriate fit methods to accurately address the phenomena under investigation enhancing substantive inference, as alternative fit measures result in differing conclusions.

Evolving opportunities

The chapters published in this book note a number of important topics that can set the stage for discourse in the field and the advancement of the understanding of international business and IB research. Beyond these topics, central themes related to international business continue to present opportunities for researchers in this area. In the following section some of these opportunities are highlighted.

Globalization

Trade liberalization policies, brought about by international and regional cooperation efforts, have drawn the international community into heightened competition. The increase in trade and participation in international agreements has not only brought forth heightened competition in markets, but also has spawned new form of organization, as noted by Crossland, Ketchen, and Snow, and consumerism, as suggested by Yin and Choi. Future research should be conducted to help understand the effects of globalization at macros and micro firm levels as well as on societies and consumers. Research questions could ponder the interaction of trade liberalization and consumer welfare, the degree of trade liberalization on firm and customer homogenization and strategic effects of backlash to globalization, and the influence of globalization movements on organizational structures and strategies.

New perspectives on seminal topics

Although Buckley (2002) called into question whether or not the field has exhausted the prior seminal IB research, the chapters presented in this book clearly indicate that these questions remain unfulfilled. Specifically, the chapters presented in this book speak to the need for reconceptualizations of key issues for the furtherance of knowledge in the field of international business. For example, Kirca not only calls for the need for reconceptualizing firm internationalization as a multidimensional construct, but furthers our understanding of how the failure to employ a multidimensional approach to firm internationalization may confound prior work. Similarly, the work of Petersen, Benito, Welch, and Asmussen, as well as by Samiee, Walters, and Yip speak to the importance of incorporating the value perspective when investigating traditional multinational issues, as through varied lenses theoretically divergent outcomes may result, potentially at odds with extant findings. The issue of potential variance in extant findings is also touched on by Myers and Griffith in noting that the employment of alternative fit methods results in contradictory findings. The central theme under these studies is that by employing alternative lenses we can enhance our understanding of important issues in the field of IB. As such, an appropriate approach to the extant literature is to examine the boundary constraints and contexts of studies to determine whether changes in these boundary constraints and contexts would shift theoretical outcomes.

Global strategic networks

The ability of firms to strategically build inter-organizational value networks for the mutual benefit of members of their networks and to reduce dysfunctional relational outcomes has been the underlying strategy of many organizations globalizing their operations. A central driver to effective global operations is the coordination of the firm's network of suppliers and distributors. Through the employment of network theory path dependent relationships can be identified to optimize cycle time and maximize value delivery. The chapter by Petersen, Benito, Welch, and Asmussen, as well as the chapter by Samiee, Walters, and Yip, speak to issues of global network influences on value delivery in multinational firms. Future research should be conducted to help understand the elements of a firm's value network, inclusive of firm centrality, strength of network ties, strategic fit of structure and strategy to environment, and so on that facilitate successful operations in a wide variety of firm contexts.

The culture of effectiveness

Organizational culture is the pattern of shared behaviors, values, and beliefs that provide a foundation of understanding of the organizational functioning processes and norms directing employee behavior. Organizational culture can be viewed as a valuable strategic resource in the process of global operations and partnering as it provides the organizational impetus for not only the supportive organizational structure but also the strategic motivation for global effectiveness. The chapters by Aguilera, Dencker, and Yalabik and Crossland, Ketchen, and Snow address aspects of organizational culture in changing IB forms. Future research should focus on better understanding of differing elements of organizational culture which promote successful integration of global operations under new organizational forms as well as the process (such as socialization) by which organizations can effectively transform existing organizational cultures to support effective global mandates.

The importance of human capital

It is important to note that underlying the majority of the chapters presented in this book is the issue of human capital. Firms are globally competitive when they possess and configure the appropriate unique combinations of tangible and intangible resources. This argument, while well founded, often proceeds without consideration of the fundamental unit of analysis (i.e., the human capital employed by the firm) which embodies the firm's capabilities. Human resources are one of a firm's most common means to build and maintain firm capabilities. This fact is more important today when firms compete in global markets where the complexities of business have increased due to trade liberalization and where a firm's employees are challenged to work within complex and dynamically evolving organizational forms (as suggested by Crossland, Ketchen, and Snow). As such, it is important that the professionals responsible for firm global operations be given ardent research efforts. Future research in this area should help to understand the types of human capital required to effectuate global strategy and structure decisions, the types of capital most appropriate at different stages and approaches to international business, as well as how a professional's mindset (domestic, international, global) influences the type and effectiveness of firm IB operations.

Conclusion

The global economy is becoming increasingly interconnected. Greater integration among economies has revolutionized the competitive landscape. As such, competitive advantage in today's marketplace increasingly relies on effective management of international operations for corporate survival. The chapters in this book provide a significant advancement in knowledge relating to this highly complex topic area. The chapters presented not only build on strong literature foundations to advance our understanding of international business and IB research, but also provide new ideas and research directions which can serve as the basis of new studies to further our understanding of this complex area. More broadly, investigation of the areas of globalization, new perspectives on seminal topics, global strategic networks, and the culture of effectiveness and human capital should be helpful to our understanding of effectively structuring and operating global organizations.

References

Buckley, P.J. (2002), "Is the International Business Research Agenda Running Out of Steam?" *Journal of International Business Studies*, 33(2): 365–373.

Buckley, P. J. and Ghauri, P. N. (2004), "Globalisation, Economic Geography and the Strategy of Multinational Enterprises," *Journal of International Business Studies*, 35(2): 81–98.

Huntington, S. (1996), "The West Unique, Not Universal," *Foreign Affairs*, 75: 28–46.

Peng, M. W. (2004), "Identifying the Big Question in International Business Research," *Journal of International Business Studies*, 35(2): 99–108.

Shenkar, O. (2004), "One More Time: International Business in a Global Economy," *Journal of International Business Studies*, 35(2): 161–171.

Sullivan, D. (1998), "Cognitive Tendencies in International Business Research: Implications of a 'Narrow Vision,'" *Journal of International Business Studies*, 29(4): 837–862.

1
A Discourse Analysis of Knowledge Creation in International Business Research: JIBS 1970–2005

Minna Söderqvist and Brian Toyne

Many of the fields of inquiry from which international business (IB) inquiry can trace its origins have histories of exploring different paradigms and methodologies, and their value in increasing our understanding of the phenomena studied. For example, the literatures of economics, sociology, management, and marketing are replete with conversations regarding the conceptualizations, paradigms, and methodologies they have used and are currently using (e.g., Hunt, 1983, 2003; Donaldson, 1985; Swedberg, 1990; Grant et al., 1998). These disciplines also hold annual meetings that include presentations and discussions on the merits of newly developed conceptualizations and research methodologies, all with the purpose of enriching their understanding of the phenomena and relationships explored by their scholars and how these scholars use and value different methods of knowledge creation. That is, the scholars are made aware of what was, what is, and how it might evolve.

In addition to debating models of reality (see, e.g., Denzin and Lincoln, 2000a) and the methodologies employed, these fields of inquiry periodically debate both domains of their inquiry and the wisdom of entering into partnerships with other disciplines in order to enhance their understanding of human behavior and human expression in its broadest sense (e.g., Dunning's (1997) call for including culture in economic analysis, and Casson's (1997) call for the joining of economics and sociology).

There are, of course, several benefits from such a dialog. First, it brings to light the disparate perspectives that can exist among a field's scholars regarding their topic of study (see, e.g., Hunt 2003: 3). It also results in a discussion and examination of the reasons for any disparities. Such a dialog is beneficial since it often enriches and deepens our understanding, for example by introducing new conceptualizations, new paradigms, and new methodologies (Denzin And Lincoln, 2000).

Second, the discussion helps make clear the implicit and often-conflicting assumptions underpinning the various paradigms used by a field's scholars. Often because of different backgrounds and training, scholars bring different conceptualizations, different paradigms, and different methodologies to a field's attention, and they are adopted in many cases without a deep understanding of their origins, or the assumptions upon which they are based (Toyne and Nigh, 1997). Thus, the discussions provide opportunities to learn from one another while improving on the field's inquiry.

Third, the dialog insures that the field's scholars are aware of any advances that have been made in their field of inquiry and the directions in which it may or may not advance. As such, these dialogs play a critical role in building acceptance, if not consensus, regarding the field's domain, paradigms, theories, and methodologies. Vargo and Lusch (2004: 15), for example in the field of marketing, hint at this salutary outcome by concluding that "...the emerging service-centered dominant logic of marketing will have a substantial role in marketing thought."

In summary, such analysis stimulates thoughtful discussion of the fundamental issues underpinning a field's search for knowledge. All that this actually says is that the painter must occasionally step back from the canvas to critically review what he/she is creating and why.

Interestingly, these wholesome traditions of discourse do not appear to be readily evident in the field of IB, even though there seems to be a change in the contents of the articles having been published in *Journal of International Business Studies* (JIBS) since 2003 (see Table 1.3) IB research is discussed and its contents seem to be expanding, as requested by many. The articles published since 2003 discuss a wider variety of phenomena than just MNE-related issues; for example, frontiers between business and industries as well as between regions and global broadening of many fields of study have been in the frontline since Buckley's (2002) questioning if the IB research agenda was running out of steam. However, because of the benefits derived from such dialog, we thought it would be both interesting and beneficial to use discourse analysis (DA) based on a social constructionist paradigm, and explore what type of discourses exist and what they entail. Thus, using a discourse analytical approach (Potter and Wetherell, 1987; Jokinen et al., 1993, 1999; Lehtonen, 1996, 2000; Potter, 1996), this chapter explores the dialog that has occurred among IB scholars concerning their ontological, epistemological, and methodological discussions.

Being the major academic journal for the field, the *Journal of International Business Studies* was chosen to be the analyzed. According to the logic of DA it is better to have less material than more in order to be able to acquire a depth in the analysis (Potter and Wetherell, 1987; Jokinen et al., 1999, 1993). This is different from the dominant nomothetic or positivistic thinking dominant in IB, but a valid scientific method in business sciences (see, e.g., Keso, 1999; Vaara, 1999; Lehtimäki, 2000; Moisander, 2001; Pietiläinen, 2002; Söderqvist, 2002; Tuusjärvi, 2003).

The chapter is presented in two parts. The first part presents a brief overview of DA, one possible approach to be used under social constructionism (Denzin and Lincoln, 2000). The second part presents the results of the DA of articles in JIBS. Three discourses were identified and are presented in the second part of the chapter. They are (1) the validation of international business as a research field; (2) the focus of IB research; and (3) the "right" type of IB research. The chapter concludes with a discussion of the findings and their implications for the future of IB inquiry as either a separate field of study or an extension of the traditional study of business functions.

Discourse analysis – a loose theoretical framework

A recent major development in the social sciences is the generalization of different types of studies by examining the language used in presenting the studies (see, e.g., Fairclough, 1999/1995). As a result, several methods have been developed that assume language does not mirror reality, but rather constructs it. Examples are narrative, rhetoric, discourse, or conversation analytic methods (Potter and Wetherell, 1987; Nikander, 1998; Matikainen, 1999; Willman, 2001).

Fairclough (1999/1995) provides four reasons why a textual analysis has an important role to play in social research. First, texts constitute an important form of social action. There is a misperception of language as transparent, not recognizing that social analysis of discourse entails going beyond this perception towards language in order to reveal the precise mechanisms and modalities of the social and ideological work of language. Second, texts are a major source of evidence for grounding claims about social structures, relations, and processes. Third, texts are sensitive barometers of social processes, movements, and diversity, and textual analysis provides particularly good indicators of social change. Fourth, texts provide a mechanism for social control and domination.

Discourse analysis is an approach to understanding how truth is constructed. It is not a single distinct method, but rather a loose theoretical framework (Potter and Wetherell, 1987; Jokinen et al., 1993). In DA, similarities and integrity are sought on the one hand, diversity and different meanings on the other (Potter and Wetherell, 1987; Jokinen et al., 1993; Fairclough, 1999/1995). The point is simply that reality cannot be mirrored by the human observer; the human observer must use the language of the culture of which they are part to make sense of what is before them and to talk about it – reality is their own construction (Watson, 2000). It is through the process of differentiating, fixing, naming, labeling, classifying, and relating that social reality is systematically constructed. Discourses work to create some sense of stability, order, and predictability to organize social reality in order to produce a sustainable, functioning, and liveable world (Chia, 2000). Discourses can be defined as systems of meanings constructed in the text.

The object of study in DA is any type of text – speeches, interviews, conversations, meetings, memos, e-mails, and other different documents. The level of analysis is the discourse, not the respondent/informant/participant. Rhetoric becomes essential as it legitimates discourses. Since reality is constructed in texts, texts are understood to be active participants, not just stationary objects. People as actors exist through the subject position concept, the user of the discourse, and the self. The self is constructed through the discourses (Potter and Wetherell, 1987; Lehtonen, 1996, 2000; Jokinen et al., 1999, 1993). Discourses do not exist as such, but some parts of them are only hinted at and are the results of the researchers' interpretations (Jokinen et al., 1993).

To summarize with Lehtonen's (1996, 2000) words, characteristics of discourses are as follows: (1) Discourses are a way to construct reality, one form of knowledge; (2) Discourses help to analyze the concrete and changing ways that people use language to give meanings to it; (3) Discourses are always bound to time and situation as they are produced in social, historical, and institutional contexts. Also, owing to the possibilities of connecting and disconnecting, a discourse cannot be a static enterprise, but is subject to mutations (Xu, 2000).

Contrary to positivist methods, where an attempt is made to eliminate the influence of the researcher, in DA the interaction between the researcher and the informants is taken into consideration in the analysis. As a result, the interpretation of meanings is always partial (Eskola and Suoranta, 1998), and may result in different meanings, depending on the texts' examiners (Lehtonen, 1996, 2000).

To sum up, Söderqvist's (2002: 80) summary of the advantages of the DA as a method is shown in Table 1.1.

Positioning the discourse analysis used in this study amongst the other ways of doing discourse analysis

Different researchers classify language-based analysis in different ways. Nikander (1998), for example, presents four types of language-based analysis and two schools of DA. The four types of analyses are narrative studies, rhetoric, discourse analysis, and conversation analysis. This study is a DA.

The two schools of DA presented by Nikander (1998) are the Loughborough School and the Manchester School. The emphasis in the Loughborough School, represented, for example, by Potter and Wetherell (1987), whose way of seeing DA is used in this study, is on the variation and functions of the language and how language is used in the creation of reality. Interpretative repertoires are used as means of analysis. The critique of the Loughborough School is that it presents individualism and does not pay attention to political

Table 1.1   Advantages of the use of discourse analysis as a method

Why?	What?	Results
Texts and talks important forms of social action, they exercise social control and domination, open space for action, and are sensitive barometers of social processes	Language used to study meanings and systems of meanings New types of data possible to be used	(a) Source for evidence for claims about social structures, relations, and processes (b) Historical evidence from the evolution of meanings and systems of meanings (c) Critical awareness
To understand how the truth is constructed	Analysis of how the interactional and interpretative resources available are used	

Source: Söderqvist (2002).

and power issues. The Manchester School, represented by Burman and Parker (1993), studies the cultural, ideological, and dominating systems of meanings. No tools are given, but some principles through which the deconstruction of discourses is possible are presented. The critique is that this school emphasizes power questions and omits a consideration of individual action.

Fairclough (1997) is maybe one of the most known discourse analysts. He divides DA into seven categories, of which he prefers critical discourse analysis. Critical discourse analysis seeks to deconstruct power relations and constructive influences into social identities and ideologies. In contrast, uncritical discourse analysis emphasizes the description of discourses and their richness. His other six categories of DA are linguistic and socio-linguistic analysis, conversation analysis, semiotic analysis, critical linguistic and social semiotics analysis, social-cognitive analysis, and culture-generic analysis. As power issues were not the focus of this study, critical discourse analysis was not used as a method in this study.

Jokinen compared DA with four other types of text analysis in Jokinen et al. (1999): the new ethnographic approach, conversation analysis, new rhetoric, and semiotics. These four other ways are beyond the scope of this study. From this analysis, Jokinen suggests that the focus of DA is on the textual practices and the relation of meanings to the practices that build these meanings. This focus is followed in this study. The analysis also includes a study of the different cultural meanings within the text and the processes producing these meanings.

Another distinction of DA is to present two wide categories: language and socially oriented traditions (Nikander, 1998; Willman, 2001). In the more linguistically oriented analysis, discourse/speech/parole is at the centre of the analysis without a larger context, whereas in the second category the attention is on cultural processes and social action related to the use of language (Willman, 2001). In this study we are interested in IB scholars' ways of seeing IB research methodology–related issues, which makes this study belong to the category of socially oriented discourse traditions. The focus is not conversation but joint ways of seeing things socially.

Matikainen (1999) divides DA in organizational research into four categories. First is the social psychology–based discourse analysis, which is a large theoretical–methodological framework. The second category is conversation analysis, which is more exact as a method and strives towards empirical generalization. The third is rhetoric social psychology, which emphasizes the argumentative characteristics of social life. The fourth category is the one emphasizing linguistic processes of organizing, in which the main emphasis is on social and psychological processes evident in the text, but does not examine how language is used. This study belongs to the first category in this conceptualization. However, argumentative characteristics of social life are also seen as important.

To sum up, the DA approach based on Potter and Wetherell (1987) was chosen since it focuses on how language is used in the creation of social reality and not on issues of power. The focus is also on textual practices and on the relation of meanings to the practices that build these meanings (Jokinen et al., 1999). Science is understood to be a social reality presented by members of the scientific community. Social reality, like MNEs, is understood to be the focal point of IB research. DA is one valid method of studying social reality. In this study, we are interested in IB scholars' ways of seeing knowledge creation in IB research.

Discourse analysis approach followed in this study

The approach followed here, proposed by Potter and Wetherell (1987), is briefly presented in this section, together with its application to this study. According to Potter and Wetherell (1987), even though the questions asked by discourse analysts can be many and varied, they are always broadly related to construction and function – how discourse is put together and what is gained by this construction. This study seeks to answer the following question: What meanings do IB researchers ascribe to "good research"? The answer to this question is sought with the help of the following sub-questions: (1) Does JIBS discuss ontological, epistemological, and methodological issues? If so, what are the shared meanings of the authors who have addressed these issues? (2) How do these meanings, that is discourses, influence IB knowledge creation?

Discourse analysis differs radically from the traditional methods concerning the sample size. DA is an extremely labor-intensive approach. If one is interested in discursive forms, ten texts might provide as much valid information as several hundred responses to a structured opinion poll. For DA, success is not at all dependent on sample size (Potter and Wetherell, 1987).

It is also not the case that a large sample indicates a more worthwhile or valid piece of research. Quite the contrary, more texts can often simply add to the labor involved without adding anything to the analysis. The amount of texts in DA need not be very extensive in order to ensure the depth of analysis (Jokinen et al., 1993, 1999; Lehtonen, 1996, 2000; Eriksson and Lehtimäki, 2001). The data for the study were the articles stored in the JIBS archives from 1970 to 2005. The depth of the analysis was the reason to concentrate on the flagship of IB research, namely the JIBS. Even though a lot of IB research is published elsewhere, JIBS is ranked the number one IB journal. Even when concentrating on JIBS articles, the amount of data for the DA was quite large.

The DA involved four steps. In DA, the coding is quite distinct from doing the analysis itself. It is an analytic preliminary step preparing the way for a much more intensive study of the material culled through the selective coding process. The first step is to simply select out from the body of texts all references to criteria, however oblique. Coding has the pragmatic rather than analytic goal of collecting instances for examination. It is quite different from the standard techniques of content analysis, where coding data into categories and looking at the frequency of occurrence is simply equivalent to the analysis (Holsti, 1968; Berelson, 1971; Mostyn, 1985 quoted by Potter and Wetherell, 1987).

First, in this study, the JIBS archives were searched using the key words shown in Table 1.2 to find all the articles that included mention of ontology, epistemology, methodology, and methods or words derived from these concepts. Archives were accessed on May 2002 and April 2006 at http://aib.jibs.net and www.jibs.net.

The chosen articles that mentioned the desired words were then read carefully to determine if they addressed the knowledge-creating process on the ontological, epistemological, methodological levels, or on the level of method. If they, for example, discussed the assumptions of IB knowledge creation in data selection, analysis, or interpretation of results, they were classified to be on the methodological level. In some cases, for example, the word "methodology" was just used in a reference and not at all discussed in the article text. All those types of articles were excluded. As a result of this review, 49 were chosen for detailed analysis.

Second, the 49 articles were classified according to four themes: "ontology," "epistemology," "methodology," and "methods," as shown in Table 1.3. Some articles are found in several categories, since they discuss many of these levels of the knowledge-creation process.

Table 1.2 The number of articles found in the JIBS archives containing the search words

The Search Word or Concept	Number of Articles/Number of Articles:Number of Years (1970–2002)	Number of Articles/Number of Articles:Number of Years (2003–2005)	Change from Period 1 to Period 2
Ontolog*	4/0,12	2/0,67	5.6 times more recently
Epistemol*	8/0,24	2/0,67	2.8 times more recently
Methodolog*	509/15	78/26	1.7 times more recently
Method*	774/24	118/39	1.6 times more recently
Qualitative method*	112/3.4	33/11	3.2 times more recently
International business research	71/2.2	49/16	7.2 times more recently

*means that any letters after the sign are implied to be included; for example, epistemology, epistemological, and so on.

Table 1.3 Classified JIBS sources for the discourse analyses of IB's extant literature (1970–2005)

Theme	Authors	Title of article in JIBS
Ontology	Sullivan, Daniel. 1998, 29(4) 877–886	The Ontology of International Business: A Comment on International Business: An Emerging Vision
	Sullivan, Daniel. 1998, 29(4): 837–862	Cognitive Tendencies in International Business Research: Implications of a Narrow Vision
	Toyne, Brian. 1989, 20(1): 1–17	International Exchange: A Foundation for Theory Building in International Business
	Toyne, Brian and Nigh, Douglas. 1998, 29(4): 863–876	A More Expansive View of International Business
Epistemology	Adler, Nancy J. 1983, (Fall): 29–47	A Typology of Management Studies Involving Culture
	Au, Kevin Y. 1999, 30(4): 799–812	Intra-Cultural Variation: Evidence and Implications for International Business
	Brewer, Thomas L. 1998, 29(1): iv–v	A Letter from the New Editor
	Caves, Richard E. 1998, 29(1): 5–19	Research on International Business: Problems and Prospects

	Chandy, P.R. and Williams, Thomas G.E: 25(4): 715–727	The Impact of Journals and Authors on International Business Research: A Citational Analysis of JIBS Articles*
	Daniels, John D. 1991, 22(2): 177–186	Relevance in International Business Research: A Need or More Linkages
	Dubois, Frank L. and Reeb, David M. 2001, 32(1): 197–199	Ranking the International Business Journals: A Reply*
	Dubois, Frank L. and Reeb, David M. 2000, 31(4): 689–704	Ranking the International Business Journals*
	Inkpen, Andrew C. and Beamish, Paul. 1994, 25(4): 703–713	An Analysis of 25 years of Research in the Journal of International Business Studies
	Jacque, Laurent L. 1981, (Spring Summer): 81–101	Management of Foreign Exchange Risk: A Review Article
	Lenartowicz, Tomasz and Roth, Kendall. 1999, 30(4): 781–798	A Framework for Culture Assessment
	Lylek, Marjorie and Salk, Jane. 1996, 27(5): 877–903	Knowledge Acquisition from Foreign Parents in International Joint Ventures: An Empirical Examination in the Hungarian Context
	Morrison, Allen J. and Inkpen, Andrew C. 1991, 22(1): 143–153	An Analysis of Significant Contributions to the International Business Literature
	Negandhi, Anant R. 1983, 14(2): 17–28	Cross-Cultural Management Research: Trend and Future Directions
	Pierce, Barbara and Garven, Ganeth. 1995, 26(1): 69–89	Publishing International Business Research: A Survey of Leading Journals
	Robinson, Richard D. 1981, 12(1): 13–21	Background Concepts and Philosophy of International Business from World War II to the Present
	Wright, Richard W. 1970, (1): 109–123	Trends in International Business Research
	Wright, Richard W. and Ricks, David A. 1994, 25(4): 687–701	Trends in International Business Research: 25 years Later
Methodology or Method	Adler, Nancy J. 1983, (Fall) 29–47	A Typology of Management Studies Involving Culture
	Albaum, Gerald and Peterson, Robert A. 1984, (Spring/Summer): 161–173	Empirical Research in International Marketing 1976–1982
	Beamish, Paul W. and Calof, Jonathan L. 1989, (Fall): 553–564	International Business Education: A Corporate View

Table 1.3   (Continued)

Theme	Authors	Title of article in JIBS
	Boddewyn, Jean J. 1981, (Spring/Summer): 61–79	Comparative Marketing: The First 25 Years
	Brewer, Thomas L. 1998, 29(1): iv–v	A Letter from the New Editor
	Brewer, Thomas L. 1983, (Spring/Summer): 161–164	Political Sources of Risk in the International Money Markets: Conceptual, Methodological, and Interpretive Refinements
	Caves, Richard. 1998, 29(1): 5–19	Research on International Business: Problems and Prospects
	Daniels, John D. 1991, 22(2): 177–186	Relevance in International Business Research: A Need or More Linkages
	Dunning, John. 1989, 20(3): 411–436	The Study of International Business: A Plea for a More Interdisciplinary Approach
	Dymsza, William A. 1984, 15(3): 9–12	Ten Years of JIBS at Rutgers Graduate School of Management
	Dymsza, William A. 1981, (Spring/Summer): 11–12	JIBS at Rutgers University
	Ervin, Marlene and Toyne, Brian. 1987, 18(2): 89–100	The AIB Membership: Who We Are, What We Are Interested in?
	Guisinger, Stephen and Brewer, Thomas L. 1998, 29(1): 1–3	Introduction to the Symposium
	Hawkins, Robert G. 1984, 15(3): 13–18	International Business in Academia: The State of the Field
	Hermel, Philippe. 1999, 30(4): 649–653	Introduction to the Symposium
	Hofstede, Geert. 1983, 14 (Fall): 75–89	The Cultural Relativity of Organizational Practices and Theories
	Hui, Michael, Au, Kevin, Fock Henry. 2004, 35(1): 46–60	Empowerment Effects Across Cultures
	Inkpen, Andrew C. 2001, 32(1): 193–196	A Note on Ranking the International Business Journals
	Iyer, Gopalkrishan R. 1997, 28(3): 531–561	Comparative Marketing: An Interdisciplinary Framework for Institutional Analysis
	Kwok, Leung, Bhagat Rabi, Buchan Nancy, Erez Miriam, Gibson Christina. 2005, 36(3): 357–378	Culture and International Business: Recent Advances and Their Implications for Future Research

Lenartowicz, Tomasz and Roth, Kendall. 1999, 30(4): 781–798 — A Framework for Culture Assessment

Lylek, Marjorie and Salk, Jane. 1996, 27(5): 877–903 — Knowledge Acquisition from Foreign Parents in International Joint Ventures: An Empirical Examination in the Hungarian Context

Mullen, Michael. 1995, 26(3): 573–596 — Diagnosing Measurement Equivalence in Cross-National Research

Negandhi, Anant R. 1983, 14(2): 17–28 — Cross- Cultural Management Research: Trend and Future Directions

Phene, Anupama and Guisinger, Stephen. 1998, 29(3): 621–632 — The Stature of the JIBS

Ricks, David A. 1985, 16(2): 1–4 — International Business Research: Past, Present and Future

Robinson, Richard. 1981, 12(1): 13–21 — Background Concepts and Philosophy of International Business form WWII to the Present

Safarian, Edward. 2003, 34(2): 116–124 — Internationalization and the MNE: A Note on the Spread of Ideas

Sekaran, Uma. 1983, (Fall): 61–73 — Methodological and Theoretical Issues and Advancements in Cross-Cultural Research

Shenkar, Oded. 2004, 35(2): 161–171 — One More Time: International Business in a Global Economy

Singh, Jagdip. 1995, 26(3): 597–619 — Measurement Issues in Cross-National Research

Sivakumar, K. and Nakata, Cheryl. 2001, 32(3): 555–574 — The Stampede toward Hofstede's Framework: Avoiding the Sample Design Pit in Cross-Cultural Research

Sullivan, Daniel. 1998, 29(4): 837–862 — Cognitive Tendencies in International Business Research: Implications of a Narrow Vision

Terpstra, Vern. 1973, 4(1): 67–78 — The Future of the IB Professor, Presidential Address

Venaik, Sunil, Midgley, David, Devinney, Timothy. 2005, 36(6): 655–675 — Dual Paths to Performance: The Impact of Global Pressures on MNC Subsidiary Conduct and Performance

Wright, Richard W. 1970. (1): 109–123 — Trends in International Business Research

Wright, Richard W. and Ricks, David A. 1994, 25(4): 687–701 — Trends in International Business Research: 25 Years Later

Zhao, Hongxin, Luo, Yadong and Suh, Taewoo. 2004, 35(6): 524–544 — Transaction Cost Determinants and Ownership-Based Entry Mode Choice: A Meta-analytical Review

After 2003 there was a clear difference in the published articles. All articles having empirical material also had an explanation for the methods used. An extra criterion was used in articles published during 2003–2005 – only those who discussed the knowledge creation in more general terms were included in further analysis.

Third, the articles were then analyzed in order to identify their shared articulated or unarticulated meanings concerning "good IB research." Potter and Wetherell (1987) say analysis is made up of two closely related phases. First, there is the search for a pattern in data. This pattern will be in the form of both variability, that is differences in either the content or the form of accounts, and consistency, that is identification of features shared by accounts. Second, there is the concern about function and consequence. The basic theoretical thrust of DA is the argument that people's words fulfil many functions and have varying effects. The second phase of analysis consists of forming ideas on these functions and effects and searching for the linguistic evidence. There is no analytic method, but rather a broad framework which focuses attention on the constructive and functional dimensions of discourse, coupled with the researcher's skill in identifying significant patterns of consistency and variation. There are several stages of validation: some are an extension of the analysis, others intrinsic to the presentation of findings.

In this phase, the parts of the articles in which the authors discussed ontological, epistemological, methodological, or method-related issues were first highlighted and chosen to be the focus of the analysis. Then, the chosen texts were read several times in order to internalize how and why the authors discussed these issues. The analysis went on to find shared meanings in these texts. Shared meanings were searched for by focusing on similarities and differences in the texts and in their meanings. The similarities show what issues are included in a discourse and the differences show the boundaries of a discourse. Some words representating or summarizing the meanings were written next to the chosen parts of texts. These were read and reread again and again.

Next, these shared meanings were given names. The result of this step was the identification of three dominant meanings considered by the authors of these 49 articles as "good research in IB." Essentially, the analysis of the 49 articles indicates that knowledge creation in IB research can be grouped under three discourses: (1) the validation of IB as a research field; (2) the focus of IB research; and (3) the "right" type of IB research. The articles discussing knowledge creation started the discourse by presenting the lack inherent in more traditional sciences like management and marketing concerning business across the national frontiers (first discourse). They also stated that the focus of IB research is in business that crosses national frontiers (second discourse). The right type of IB research was identified to be, for example, positivistic, nomothetic, and rigorously using quantitative methods (third discourse).

Since most texts discussed methodology- or method-related issues, it was possible to analyze further that part of the texts. That analysis was to determine the social construction of the meanings concerning "the right type of approaches in good research in IB."

As Jokinen et al. (1999) have noted, the main result of analytic DA is a detailed outline of reality as experienced by the social group under scrutiny. Discourses are part of action, they define what is justified and legitimate, and they both reflect and reconstruct what knowledge creation in IB research means. Texts are perspectives of the past that constitute conditions for the present – asking questions backward allows us to think forward. Although the meanings of the identified discourses are not explicitly stated, the meanings nevertheless identify and organize the life of the examined social group (Lehtonen, 1996, 2000). That is, the identified discourses explain the current actions of the group. In addition, it is important to remember that the discourses are both a societal product and a societal change producer (Berger and Luckmann, 1994/1966).

The fourth and final step was the reporting of the analysis. As integrity and transparency are essential in DA, the DA is presented in considerable detail. If a DA report sometimes looks less rigorous than a report of content analysis, this is probably more to do with the rhetorical effectiveness of tables and numbers than any lack of stringency. In fact, the reporting phase of this study constitutes one part of the confirmation and validation procedure itself (Potter and Wetherell, 1987). That is, reflection on the findings and a discussion of their context is essential. Of course, interpretation may differ depending on age, social position, education, or gender of the reader. As authors we are quite different from each other regarding these characteristics, and hope that it helps to pay attention to relevant issues in reporting.

In practice the analytic section of a discourse article is often considerably longer than the corresponding sector of more traditional empirical reports. The extracts are not characterizations or illustrations of the data, they are examples of the data. Or, in ethnomethodological terms, they are the topic itself, not a resource from which the topic is rebuilt.

Discourses are always time, location, and context related. Moreover, discourses are discussed in relation to other scientific research literature. Potter and Wetherell (1987) also emphasize that researchers should pay a lot of attention to the application of the results. They propose two ways: popularization and opening up a dialogue with the people who have been researched. In this study the results have been used as teaching material on the IB paradigm for undergraduate and postgraduate students. They have also been presented on scientific occasions for discussion. To validate the discourses, their coherency was also sought, and insightful and novel explanations provided as recommended by Potter and Wetherell (1987). The identified discourses are presented in detail to give the reader a possibility to evaluate the results of the analysis.

Evaluation criteria for discourse analysis

We propose that three points should be kept in mind when evaluating a DA. First, five assumptions need to be remembered when characterizing a discourse: (1) language creates reality; (2) there are different competing discourses; (3) the discourses are context-specific; (4) the actors are connected to the discourses; and (5) the use of language produces action and consequences (Jokinen et al., 1993). From this follows that the generally known positivist or nomothetic evaluation criteria cannot be used in a study based on other ontological ideas (Morgan and Smircich, 1980; Morgan, 1984a,b; Lincoln and Guba, 1995).

Second, Moisander (2001) suggested that to improve on the quality and empirical validity of the study, it is important to analyze how and to what extent interpretations of the data reflect the situational factors specific to the context of data generation.

Third, Moisander (2001) further argued that analytic integrity is a central goal of the study. That is, the researcher needs to show how specific aspects of the text produce or shed light on particular facets of the discourse. In other words, the relevancy of categorization and the procedural consequentiality of context are to be demonstrated by focusing on particular features of the text.

Validation of international business as a research field

The first of the discourses identified concerning the knowledge creation in IB was named "the validation of international business as a research field." In this discourse, most of the scholars reviewed have tried to refute the articulated and unarticulated criticism that IB is not a valid area of research. This was a very dominant discourse (Lehtonen, 1996, 2000), which was surprising as IB had already existed as a research field for more than 50 years, and in the northern European context such a discourse does not exist. For one of the explicit examples of the existing discourse, Daniels (1991: 181) has argued that " . . . the international business field . . . still faces some credibility problems." And, even ten years later, explicit examples still existed: Inkpen (2001: 193) has argued "that a debate about IB as a legitimate field of issue is an irrelevant issue and that journals like JIBS should focus on publishing cutting-edge research on IB problems regardless of the author's orientation to a particular field of study."

One possible explanation for this continuing discourse of validation can be that as a consequence of the stage of development of IB there are a lot of explicit and implicit arguments that seek to refute the articulated and unarticulated criticism that IB is not a valid area of research. IB research is a fledgling field when compared to the social sciences in general, and to the functional areas of business, such as management and marketing, in particular. The first IB studies were published about 50 years ago – in the

1950s – by international marketing scholars. Soon after, in the 1960s, the issues of human resource management and foreign direct investment were included in the IB agenda (Wright and Ricks, 1994). International economics was then left out, whereas IB strategy and structure, as well as cultural studies, have gained increasing interest.

Another possible reason why this discourse still exists in the JIBS articles could be the almost nonexistence of IB chair holders in the United States. In the Nordic countries the institutionalization development of IB has been different. For example, in Finland, there are several IB professors in different universities, and due to that fact the dominance of this discourse of validation is rather amazing from a Finnish point of view.

However, today, dozens of subareas in IB research show that international business is an extensive field of study (e.g., Ricks et al., 1990; Wright and Ricks, 1994; Toyne and Nigh, 1997). There is an emerging consensus that a considerable amount of study has been generated from this multidimensional and complex phenomenon (e.g., Luostarinen, 1979; Toyne and Nigh, 1997; Inkpen, 2001).

The focus of international business research

The second identified discourse concerning the knowledge creation in IB was about the focus of IB research. Discourses are evolving all the time (Lehtonen, 1996, 2000). During the early days, it was clear that *"IB research is concerned with firm level activities crossing national boundaries."* This working definition was given by Nehrt et al. (1970) and Wright (1970), who, after discussions with a number of leading scholars and business leaders, established and published this definition. It was one of the first mandates of the International Business Research Institute (founded in 1965) of the Graduate School of Indiana University to prepare an inventory of recent and current research on IB and recommendations for future studies. The same definition was still more or less valid in the 1990s (see Wright and Ricks, 1994). For example, the JIBS publishing policy adopted by Ricks (1985) was highly traditional, asserting as it did that IB was "...a firm level activity that extends from one country to another."

This relatively "narrow" policy, however, was expanded under the editorship of Brewer (1998: iv) to include "...inter-disciplinary scholarship and commentaries that challenge the paradigms and assumptions of individual disciplines or functions." Under the editorship of Lewin (2003–)the editorial policy has been expanded to also include

> multinational and transnational business activities, strategies and managerial processes that cross national boundaries, joint ventures, strategic alliances, mergers and acquisitions, interactions of such firms with their economic, political and cultural environments, as well as cross national

research involving innovation entrepreneurship, knowledge based competition, judgement and decision making, bargaining, leadership, corporate governance and new organizational forms.

(Statement of Editorial Policy, JIBS,2005: 6, 2006: 2)

In order to identify the existence of a discourse, "rebuttal" can be studied (Jokinen et al., 1993; Lehtonen, 1996, 2000). It means that even though scholars do not name the dominant discourse, they present arguments against it, pretending that other scholars know that particular discourse as well as they do, even without presenting it. An example of this was the rebuttal of the discourse of IB research concentrating on studies of phenomena concerning MNEs, namely the discussion of the extension of the IB field.

Already in the 1980s the working definition presented above was questioned. Adler (1983: 43) has called for the extension of the firm view, by calling for "...new research based on solutions to existing management problems." And even before, Robinson (1981: 21) argued that "...little research is being done on the internal dynamics of international business" (see also Terpstra, 1973, and Dymsza, 1984, for interdisciplinary research not concentrating on firms crossing borders).

This discussion went on in JIBS later as well. Toyne and Nigh (1998: 871; see also Toyne, 1989) were among the few scholars who explicitly stated in JIBS that IB research is a part of the social sciences, and because IB involves "businesses in society...such fields of study as sociology, political science, and business, government, and society have excellent potential to contribute to IB understanding." Sullivan's (1998b: 837) comment in the end of the 1990s was part of this discourse when he said, "Some scholars have suggested that international business research suffers from a narrow vision." The direction of today's IB research (e.g., Buckley, 2002, 2005; Verbeke, 2003; van den Bulcke, 2004; Peng, 2004; Shenkar, 2004) can be claimed to be part of this discourse as well.

Already earlier, interdisciplinary research that draws upon different disciplines and does not concentrate on the study of firms crossing national borders has been called for by many IB scholars (e.g., Dunning, 1989; Toyne, 1989; Daniels, 1991; Wright and Ricks, 1994). Söderqvist's (2001a,b,c, 2002) studies of the internationalization of higher-education institutions in Europe and their management are but some examples of such interdisciplinary, expansionary research. After 2003 there seems to be a clear change in the contents of articles published in JIBS as already referred to earlier. Organization learning, values, trust, social questions, and knowledge are examples of the themes manifesting this change. As well, even more critical voices have been heard to awake the IB scholars: Daniels (1991) has noted that "Specialists are seldom the first to develop and apply the new theories and methodologies to business." And, he has also argued that well-known scholars who take an interest in IB research can often be called "closet-internationalists," since they do not come out to fight for the field before it becomes acceptable (Daniels, 1991).

According to the principles of social constructionist research, in DA it is essential to place the findings in a context. This discourse of focus of IB as a research field has also existed elsewhere than in JIBS articles among IB scholars. For example, a debate between Boddewyn (1997), Wilkins (1997), and Toyne (1997b), with comments by Schollhammer (1997), Behrman (1997), and Hench (1997), directly addresses the issue of what IB's field of inquiry is. Their collective comments on the issue indicate that the domain of IB inquiry remains open to differing views.

For example, Boddewyn, Wilkins, and Schollhammer loosely agree that the focus of IB research should be on the firm. Behrman, on the other hand, considers the domain of IB to be indefinable in an absolute sense. Toyne states that there are multiple conceptual domains of IB inquiry, each of which seeks a particular body of knowledge. Finally, Hench introduced the thought that the views presented by Boddewyn, Wilkins, and Schollhammer are grounded in a fundamentally different model (or paradigm) of society than are those espoused by Toyne and Behrman. Hench continues by suggesting that the difference between domestic business and international business is that international business involves qualitatively higher levels of complexity and ambiguity. This view suggests that a single-paradigm approach to the study of IB is probably too restrictive. As Toyne and Nigh (1997: 674) note,

> The history of science suggests that we gain new awareness and new understanding by enlarging on the number of paradigms, or conceptualizations, that underpin and guide our work. As a result of deductive, specialized reasoning we verify and more fully describe this progress. The history of science also teaches us that our horizons remain unnecessarily narrow and our insights unnecessarily shallow when we refuse to consider and examine alternative conceptualizations of reality to those already acknowledged, accepted, and well entrenched.

In 1989, Toyne proposed an exchange, defined as the collective result of political, social, and economic forces, as a unit of study that would provide analytical boundaries and linkages permitting the accumulation of complementary findings, thus producing different ways of developing questions, theories, and methods. About ten years later, Toyne and Nigh (1998: 863) discussed this by introducing the "evolving (or emerging) interaction paradigm," and proposed that " . . . attention should be shifted from the firm as the central unit of analysis to a more comprehensive, multilevel, hierarchical view of the international business process." A recent example of the debate on the need to move to a more comprehensive view of the IB process is that between Boddewyn (1999) and Martinez and Toyne (2000). While

Boddewyn argued that international management scholars should focus on the challenges associated with the management of the multinational firm, Martinez and Toyne (2000) challenged this view by suggesting that international management is a much broader subject, and should include research on any management situation that crosses national boundaries and on any topic that is being investigated by management scholars in general (e.g., international NGOs, World Bank, leadership, decision-making, etc.).

Toyne and Nigh (1997, 1998) also called for cooperation that would generate increased understanding of the researched phenomenon, as well as multiple perspectives that could be used as potential knowledge generators. For example, they (1998: 874) assert that the trend in management, marketing, and finance research is "...clearly expansionary because of their movement toward higher levels of abstraction. These functional disciplines...acknowledge that the phenomena and the relationships of their inquiries are much more extensive than what simply occurs in economic enterprises (e.g., hospitals, government agencies, ad hoc assemblies)."

The "right" type of international business research

To really answer the research question of this study – What meanings do IB researchers ascribe to "good research"? – an examination of the IB discipline's ontology, epistemology, and methodology was required, since these are the attributes of the paradigm accepted by the majority of the discipline's scholars. As Guba (1990), Kuhn (1970), Reynolds (1971), and others have noted, paradigms, even when not stated explicitly, suggest the research strategy, including the questions raised and the methodologies employed.

Ontological issues

Burrell and Morgan (1979/1994) state that assumptions of the ontological nature of the social world can be either that reality is "out there" or that "it is a product of one's mind." In this study, it was identified that in IB research the view that reality is "out there" was shared. According to Neilimo and Nasi (1994), in that type of research the question of reality need not even be discussed. Based on the analysis, we claim that ontological issues were very seldom mentioned. In addition to those articles where the word "ontology" or some of its derivatives (see, e.g., Table 1.3) were mentioned, only a few scholars discussed the contents of ontology, and all of them quite recently.

Lenartowicz and Roth (1999: 795) state explicitly in their JIBS article that "...it is important to recognize these assumptions explicitly." Toyne and Nigh (1998: 873–874) share this idea when they state that "...research questions depend on the assumptions," and continue by asking later, "what knowledge we seek, for what purpose for whose benefit and why?"

Au (1999) and Lyles and Salk (1996) write about their premises as examples in the descriptions of their research results. Au (1999) discusses the antecedents and consequences of intra-cultural variation, but on the level of methodological questions. He (1999: 809) states "...that researchers do not always systematically report the standard deviations of their measures and systematic studies are rare or that identifying factors that determine the ICV of managerial variables across the cultures is needed." Lyles and Salk (1996) write, "...this research was based on two premises. The first was that knowledge acquisition takes place in IJVs..."

Epistemological issues

Epistemological issues are assumptions about the grounds of knowledge, about how one might begin to understand the world and communicate this as knowledge to others. These assumptions entail ideas about what forms of knowledge can be obtained and how one can sort out what is to be regarded as "true" or "false." The epistemological assumptions determine whether knowledge can be acquired or whether it is something that has to be personally experienced. Assumptions about human nature are also important, whether human beings are regarded as products of the environment or whether man is regarded as the creator of his environment (Burrell and Morgan, 1979/1994: 1–2).

There is some more discussion related to epistemological issues than to ontological issues. Positivist arguments (see also Söderqvist, 2002, ch. 3.3) are most evident and present in the JIBS articles reviewed. According to Huber (1995, quoted by Denzin and Lincoln, 2000b), the positivist's understanding of the world presumes a stable, unchanging reality that can be studied with the empirical methods of objective social sciences. Proponents of positivist studies also claim that their work is done within a value-free framework (Denzin and Lincoln, 2000b). That is, positivist scientists claim that their skills in observation and reason enable them to step outside the vagaries of common opinion and political prejudice, to press beyond the frontiers of the unknown, and to obtain truth from the lands of mystery (Gergen, 1990). However, as Neilimo and Nasi (1980) state, positivism can be regarded merely as a loose framework without unique, unambiguous rules. They list some typical characteristics of positivism that include concepts like objectivity, closeness to the natural sciences, causality, explanation, verification, atomism, analytical thinking, operationalizing, the importance of empirical observations, neutrality of the researcher, the world outside the researcher, and the importance of sense perception. It is clear from the JIBS review that most IB research is positivist with respect to epistemology.

The examples found in the archival review of JIBS articles containing explicit mention of epistemology-related issues varied considerably. In particular, the review articles that ranked IB journals or IB literature (e.g., Morrison and Inkpen, 1991; Chandy and Williams, 1994; Inkpen and Beamish, 1994; Pierce and Garven, 1995; DuBois and Reeb, 2000) and state-of-art articles (e.g., Ricks, 1985; Wright and Ricks, 1994) touched upon epistemological issues. On the other hand, Brewer (1998: iv) was among the few in favor of an explicit discussion of the state of IB research that "…address issues of theory or method, or in some way consider issues of epistemology and the advancement of research on international business topics." Why, what, and how questions were preferred by Au (1999). Robinson (1981) also commented on the need for objectivity.

The normative tradition is also quite evident in the reviewed articles. For example, Caves (1998: 6) states, "… the business normative goal is to advise managers on the best choice for some business policy"; Adler (1983: 43) says, "…action research tends to emphasize what could be rather than what is…"; and Jacque (1981: 81) states that "…a normative view is taken."

One of the IB research areas, cross-cultural research has generated some discussion on epistemology since the 1980s. Adler (1983) presents six different approaches to researching cross-cultural management issues, and discusses their assumptions concerning the similarity and difference across cultures and the extent to which management phenomena are not universal. Negandhi (1983) discusses the three conceptual approaches used by comparative management theorists – namely the economic development orientation, the environmental approach, and the behavioral approach – and discusses their basic premises.

Elsewhere, Björkman (1999) ties FDI analysis to epistemological issues. He makes clear how the cognitive objective of the study, the research approach used, the type of knowledge gained, and the nature of the theoretical problems that occupy researchers are all interrelated. In other journals (e.g., Melin, 1992) and in doctoral dissertations (e.g., Luostarinen, 1979), holistic research is called for by Melin (1992) and Luostarinen (1979) as an eclectic approach in IB. In JIBS, Robinson (1981) called for the dynamics of change, as Luostarinen did in his dissertation.

Methodological issues

Methodological issues are guided by assumptions made regarding the nature of the social sciences (ontological, epistemological, and assumptions about human nature). The two extreme cases are the objectivist approach (positivism) and the subjectivist approach (social-constructionism). In the objectivist case, research focuses on the concepts, their measurement, and the identification of underlying themes. In the subjectivist case, the research focus is on an understanding of the way in which individuals and groups create, modify, and interpret the world (Burrell and Morgan, 1979/1994).

According to Neilimo and Nasi (1980) and Burrell and Morgan (1979/1994), the features of nomothetic research are as follows: (1) explains and answers why questions, often presenting law-like claims; (2) includes a conceptual phase in the study (either a framework at the beginning or a model at the end); (3) has an empirical phase (essential to the study);

(4) offers the framework and the empirical results for discussion; (5) makes the researcher a neutral outsider; (6) studies external behavior, but seldom the values or norms underpinning this behavior; and (7) has numerous regulations on how to acquire and treat data to insure objectivity.

Based on the analysis we claim IB research to be positivist and nomothetic and to favour quantitative studies. For example, the recommendations for research mainly concern methods (Neilimo and Nasi, seventh point above), especially quantitative ones. As an example of this, a search for "method*" in the JIBS archives found 774 references, whereas that for "qualitative method*" resulted in 112 references. It is apparent that methodology is understood to mean quantitative methods and their rigorous use, even if not discussed explicitly. When a greater depth of understanding is desired (e.g., Lyles and Salk, 1996), this means only a more sophisticated use of statistical methods. For example, Lyles and Salk (1996) proposed quantitative methods such as path analysis (see also Adler, 1983). It is no wonder that Brewer (1998) asked for a diversity of methodology.

At the same time, methodology is not a major issue raised in IB research reporting. For example, major IB conferences, like those of the Academy of International Business or of the European International Business Academy, have no methodology tracks. Even so, some scholars are aware of the lack of attention to methodological issues within IB research as Dymsza's remark suggests (1984: 11): "Since a new area of study, we insisted upon sound methodology, but preferred substance and advancement of knowledge over methodology."

According to Neilimo and Nasi (1980), this lack of attention to scientific assumptions is one of the characteristics of the nomothetic research tradition. Negandhi (1983) also shared this idea of IB as nomothetic research by calling for a shift from nomothetical to analytical research. Even though Hawkins (1984), among others, stated that IB research is a potpourri of methodologies, and mainstream IB research is clearly inside the tradition of nomothetic research (see also Sullivan, 1998), favouring quantitative survey methods. Daniels (1991) stated that methodologies have changed very little over time.

On the level of methods, the "right" type of IB research is, based on the analysis, conceptual, theory building, and integrative (Adler, 1983;

Table 1.4 Subjectivist and objectivist approaches to science

Subjectivist approach				Objectivist approach
Nominalism	◄ ---------	Ontology	--------- ►	Realism
Anti-Positivism	◄ --------	Epistemology	--------- ►	Positivism
Voluntarism	◄ --------	Human Nature	--------- ►	Determinism
Ideographic	◄ --------	Methodology	--------- ►	Nomothetic

Source: Burrell and Morgan (1979/1994).

Negandhi, 1983; Ricks, 1985; Wright and Ricks, 1994). For example, Wright and Ricks (1994: 698) look for conceptual and theory-building studies by arguing that "…research seems to lag behind in its approach to the multidimensional concept." Adler (1983: 45) shares this view when asserting that "…it is important not to limit to narrow conceptual tools nor to rigid methods but to take them in interaction."

Also, the preferred "right" type of research uses methodology rigorously, applies tests, operationalizes measurements, validates data and findings, checks correlations, uses sophisticated quantitative techniques, has a systematic and rigorous approach, and so on, as the majority of the articles reviewed called for (see, e.g., Boddewyn, 1981; Brewer, 1983; Hofstede, 1983; Sekaran, 1983; Dymsza, 1984; Daniels, 1991; Wright and Ricks, 1994; Mullen, 1995; Singh, 1995; Lenartowicz and Roth, 1999; Sivakumar and Nakata, 2001).

This can be seen very often when analyzing the articles starting from 2003 than previous ones. Only three articles were found to discuss methodological issues in 2003 (Ariño, 2003; Brock, 2003; Reynolds et al., 2003), but all the empirical articles presented their method quite in detail. A few theory-building ones have been published, but the great majority of published articles in JIBS had the structure "introduction–hypothesis development–data and methods–results–conclusion." Nevertheless, JIBS also published editorials, perspectives, award articles, comments, and book reviews in which the structure was not that strict.

The "right" type of research also includes longitudinal studies (Caves, 1998; Sullivan, 1998). Outside JIBS longitudinal studies were asked for already earlier, for example by Melin (1992) and Luostarinen (1979). Melin (1992) explained four types of longitudinal studies for the benefit of IB research. The longitudinal case method has also been called for and mainly used by European IB researchers (e.g., Stenberg, 1992; Marschan, 1996; Tahvanainen, 1998; Korhonen, 1999).

To sum up, the third discourse was about what is the "right" type of research. IB scholars have called for a strictly positivistic conceptualization, an integrative analysis, and the rigorous use of quantitative methods to further legitimize IB research. However, it might result in social reality not being studied with the best possible tools developed lately in the other social sciences.

Concluding discussion: A gap in conscious knowledge creation in international business

Unlike the inquiry into other business functional areas, IB inquiry has been unique as a field of study because of the near deafening absence of commentary and discussion on the paradigms and methodologies used. For example, marketing's inquiry has a rich history of debate regarding the development of its thought since many decades (e.g., Bartels, 1976), the domain of its inquiry (e.g., Kotler and Levy, 1969), and the paradigms, ontologies, epistemologies, and methodologies used (e.g., Hunt, 1983, 2003). Management also has its dialogues and the development of alternative paradigms and methodologies (see, e.g., Donaldson, 1985; Grant et al., 1998).

Nehrt et al. (1970) explicitly defined IB as narrowly concerned with firm-level activities that cross national boundaries. As opposed to this narrow view of IB, contradictory voices have been heard. The publishing policy of JIBS until 2003 alone does not explain why most IB scholars have restricted their studies to business entities "that cross national borders" (Nehrt et al., 1970), namely the international, multinational, global, or transnational enterprises. Maybe one reason is that in the 1960s and the 1970s the birth of MNEs was considered so fascinating that scholars just wanted to concentrate on that phenomenon. Also, it might be that it seemed too much to present two changes at a time – opening up with one new phenomenon was enough, and did not provide room to open up new ways to produce knowledge on IB at the same time. Essentially, from the early days, many IB scholars appear to believe that the ultimate purpose of IB inquiry is to persuade strictly "domestic" scholars of business to internationalize their functional inquiries. Once this has been accomplished, they can become conspicuous by their absence (e.g., Toyne and Nigh, 1997).

Since the change of editor-in-chief of JIBS in 2003, there seems to be an indication of a change in the air. For example, the AIB and the JIBS organized "Emerging Frontiers Conference" for the second time in 2004. The published IB research themes in JIBS seem to be extending – a development warmly welcomed by many. Nowadays there is a lot of international business outside production MNEs. For example, international service business is growing, internationalizing SMEs and Born Globals exist, international NGOs have a bigger role, and the public sector is internationalizing. Traditional IB research has lot to offer and learn from other fields of IB study. Who else would understand the complexity of internationalization than IB scholars?

Even after the identified change in the contents since 2002 and even when more Internet hits were found to mention the methodology or methods after 2002 than before, the methodological articles published since 2003 still discuss only the rigorous use of methods. They do not propose new methodologies for the field or discuss the knowledge creation in IB. Still, no articles discussed ontology or epistemology after 2003 either. And, even though JIBS policy (2006) states that JIBS is a methodologically pluralistic journal, only very few papers other than those involving mathematic modeling and empirical hypothesis-testing seem to be accepted. JIBS seems to be very theoretical in the theoretical–practical axis, and only objective in the subjective–objective axis, even though other valid methods have been developed nowadays (see, e.g., Denzin and Lincoln, 2000; Anttila, 2005).

The absence of dialogue among IB scholars may be the result of what Kuhn (1970) suggested is "normal science." That is, most IB scholars may view themselves merely as extensions of the business functional areas into the international arena (Toyne, 1997a). Consequently, they use what were the traditional paradigms, ontologies, epistemologies, and methodologies of their "domestic" function-focused colleagues. Essentially, they do not focus their attention on business, but rather on the various components of what is viewed as the activities undertaken by business firms. Moreover, they do not focus on building a "new" field, but merely on extending already established fields.

The IB scholars cannot ignore the increasing interest on the part of the social sciences in methodological, epistemological, and ontological questions. A social group's discourses and the assumptions, beliefs, ideas, norms, and values related to them construct, guide, and limit the choices available to the social group. When these limiting discourses are revealed, however, they can be openly discussed and it can contribute to some developments. Based on a review of articles in the JIBS archives, only very few IB scholars (e.g., Daniels, 1991; Toyne, 1989; Sullivan, 1998; Toyne and Nigh, 1998) have considered the importance of epistemological and ontological questions.

Another aspect of the near-deafening absence of commentary is the growing gap between the diversity of methodologies used by the "domestic" business functional areas and IB inquiry. For example, although Hawkins (1984) and several other IB scholars (e.g., Adler, 1983; Brewer, 1998; Sullivan, 1998b) have called for greater diversity of methodologies, very little has been done. On the contrary, our examination of JIBS indicates a general rejection of such appeals. In contrast, the business functional areas, particularly management and marketing, have been quite open to a discussion of, and the adoption of, alternative methodologies (Weick, 1979; Hunt, 2003). There is a growing community of business scholars who argue that alternate methodologies need to be explored. For example, Grant et al. (1998: 1) have argued as follows:

> The analysis of organizations, as they struggle to survive and expand within the context of globalizing market forces, present us with a bewildering diversity of managerial strategies, policies and practices. In order to make sense of progressively uncertain, inconsistent and fluctuating managerial behavior, commentators have increasingly turned to the identification and analysis of the language and symbolic media we employ to describe, represent, interpret and theorize to be the facticity of organizational life.

The relevance of such departures from IB's traditional approach to the study of international business is the assertion by Grant et al. (1998: 1) that their approach to organizational inquiry has enabled them to move to new levels of understanding. They further contend that this new understanding attests to the importance of, in their case, DA. As a consequence, " 'organizational discourse' is an emerging focus of interest in current management literature and thinking" (1998: 1).

Of course, the crux of the matter is whether IB scholars are essentially scholars who focus their inquiry on internationalized business functions using traditional methods of analysis (e.g., international strategy, international marketing, international human resource management), or scholars who focus their inquiry on IB and seek a diversity of methodologies to explain what they observe. Enormous progress has been made in the social sciences (see, e.g., Denzin and Lincoln, 2000a). Thus, as argued by Toyne and Nigh (1998) and Söderqvist (2002), IB research would benefit from the use of the knowledge and methodologies developed by these sciences since IB involves humans and their social processes. At the same time, however, the social sciences should consider IB's contributions, particularly as they contribute to a better understanding, for example, of the processes leading to globalization.

To sum up, the contributions of this chapter are threefold. First, this chapter makes explicit what preferences JIBS has had and has today. Having read about its knowledge production preferences, younger scholars find it easy to familiarize themselves with the field. Also, understanding the field precedes its renewal. It is typical for discourses to provoke change. In other words, change which has evidently begun is easier for the IB research community when implicit assumptions become explicit, and the community is able to find the new "big questions" (e.g., Buckley, 2002). The research has been highly concentrated on a few themes and on just one or two ways of finding the truth. However, it has been claimed (e.g., Suoranta, 1996) that in today's complicated world there is not just one truth, but many. IB exists also outside MNEs and calls for multiplicity in research topics.

Second, it was shown that a more interpretative approach, based on social constructionist thinking, would be beneficial in advancing the dialogue. That is, new types of questions would be engendered, and thus new methodologies and types of knowledge obtained. The role of humans is increasing, and more subjectivist-oriented ways of creating knowledge can capture the manifold social reality easily than a more objectivist approach. Now it is taken for granted that objective and theoretically oriented articles are automatically the best without even considering any alternatives, even though they do exist and are well developed.

Third, it was shown that although the IB field is still dominated by a positivist ontology, epistemology, and methodology, there does appear to be an undercurrent of discussion suggesting an alternative approach is needed if the field is to advance. Since 2003 the extended view of IB research contents is apparent in the themes of published articles.

It is quite apparent that further discussion is needed if this research field is to develop beyond being merely the internationalization of business functional areas.

References

Adler, Nancy J. (1983 Fall) A Typology of Management Studies Involving Culture, *Journal of International Business Studies*, 14: 29–47.

Albaum, Gerald and Peterson, Robert A. (1984) Empirical Research in International Marketing: 1976–1982, *Journal of International Business Studies*, 15(1): 161–173.

Anttila, Pirkko. (2005) *Tutkiva toiminta* [Researching Action]. Hamina: Akatiimi.

Ariño, Africa. (2003) Measures of Strategic Alliance Performance: An Analysis of Construct Validity, *Journal of International Business Studies*, 34(1): 66–79.

Au, Kevin. (1999) Intra-Cultural Variation: Evidence and Implications from International Business, *Journal of International Business Studies*, 30(4): 799–812.

Bartels, Robert. (1976) *History of Marketing Thought*. Santa Clarita: Grid Publishing.

Beamish, Paul W. and Calof, Jonathan L. (1989 Fall) International Business Education: A Corporate View *Journal of International Business Studies*, 20: 553–564

Behrman, Jack N. (1997) Discussion of "The Conceptual Domain of International Business." In Brian Toyne and Douglas Nigh (eds), *International Business: An Emerging Vision*. Columbia: University of South Carolina Press, 82–90.

Berelson, B. (1971) *Content Analysis in Communication Research*. New York: The Free Press.

Berger, Peter L. and Luckmann, Thomas. (1994/1966) *Todellisuuden sosiaalinen rakentuminen* [originally: The Social Construction of Reality]. Helsinki: Gaudeamus.

Björkman, Ingmar. (1999) On Economic and Decision Process Oriented Perspectives to Analyzing Foreign Direct Investment Decisions. In Uolevi Lehtinen and Hannu Seristö (eds), *Perspectives on Internationalization*. Helsinki: Helsinki School of Economics, 31–45.

Boddewyn, Jean J. (1981 Spring–Summer) Comparative Marketing: The First Twenty-Five Years, *Journal of International Business Studies*, 12: 61–79.

Boddewyn, Jean J. (1997) The Conceptual Domain of International Business: Territory, Boundaries, and Levels. In Brian Toyne and Douglas Nigh (eds), *International Business: An Emerging Vision*. Columbia: University of South Carolina Press.

Boddewyn, Jean J. (1999) The Domain of International Management, *Journal of International Management*, 5(1): 3–14.

Brewer, Thomas L. (1983 Spring/Summer) Political Sources of Risk in International Money Markets: Conceptual Methodological and Interpretive Elements, *Journal of International Business Studies*, 14: 161–164.

Brewer, Thomas L. (1998) Letter from the New Editor, *Journal of International Business Studies*, 29(1): iv–v.

Brock, Jürgen Kai-Uwe. (2003) The "Power" of International Business Research, *Journal of International Business Studies*, 34(1): 90–99.

Buckley, Peter J. (2002) Is the International Business Research Agenda Running Out of Steam? *Journal of International Business Studies*, 33(2): 365–373.

Buckley, Peter J. and Lessard, Donald R. (2005) Regaining the Edge for International Business Research, *Journal of International Business Studies*, 36(5): 595–599.

Van den Bulcke, Daniel. (2004) (reviewed) Havila Virpi, Forsgren Mats & Håkansson Håkan: Critical Perspectives on Internationalization, *Journal of International Business Studies*, 35(3): 251–254.

Burman, Erica and Parker, Ian (eds) (1993) *Discourse Analytic Research: Repertoires and Readings in Action*. London: Routledge.

Burrell, Gibson and Morgan, Gareth. (1979/1994) *Sociological Paradigms and Organisational Analysis: Elements of the Sociology of Corporate Life*. Gateshead: Athnaeum Press Ltd.

Casson, Mark. (1997) Economic Theories of International Business: A Research Agenda. In Brian Toyne and Douglas Nigh (eds), *International Business: An Emerging Vision*. Columbia: University of South Carolina Press, 181–193.

Caves, Richard E. (1998) Research on International Business: Problems and Prospects, *Journal of International Business Studies*, 29(1): 5–19.

Chandy, P.R. and Williams, Thomas G.E. (1994 Fourth Quarter) The Impact of Journals and Authors on International Business Research: A Citational Analysis of JIBS Articles, *Journal of International Business Studies*, 14: 715–727.

Chia, Robert. (2000) Discourse Analysis as Organizational Analysis, *Organization*, 7(3): 513–519.

Daniels, John D. (1991) Relevance in International Business Research: A Need for More Linkages, *Journal of International Business Studies*, 22(2): 177–186.

Denzin, Norman K. and Lincoln, Yvonna S. (eds) (2000a) *Handbook of Qualitative Research*, 2nd edn. Newbury Park: Sage Publications.

Denzin, Norman K. and Lincoln, Yvonna S. (eds) (2000b) The Discipline and Practice of Qualitative Research. In Denzin and Lincoln (eds), *Handbook of Qualitative Research*. Newbury Park: Sage Publications, 1–28.

Donaldson, Lex. (1985) *In Defense of Organizational Theory: A Reply to the Critics*. Cambridge: Cambridge University Press.

DuBois, Frank L. and Reeb, David M. (2000) Ranking the International Business Journals, *Journal of International Business Studies*, 31(4): 689–704.

DuBois, Frank L. and Reeb, David M. (2001) Ranking the International Business Journals: A Reply, *Journal of International Business Studies*, 31(4): 689–704.

Dunning, John H. (1989) The Study of International Business: A Plea for a More Interdisciplinary Approach, *Journal of International Business Studies*, 20(3): 411–436.

Dunning, John H. (1997) Micro and Macro Organizational Aspects of MNEs and MNE Activity. In Brian Toyne and Douglas Nigh (eds), *International Business: An Emerging Vision*. Columbia: University of South Carolina Press, 194–204.

Dymsza, William A. (1981) JIBS at Rutgers University, *Journal of International Business Studies*, 12(3): 11–12.

Dymsza, William A. (1984) Ten Years of JIBS at Rutgers Graduate School of Management, *Journal of International Business Studies*, 15(3): 9–12.

Eriksson, Päivi and Lehtimäki, Hanna (2001) Strategy Rhetoric in City Management. How Do the Presumptions of Classic Strategic Management Live On? *Scandinavian Journal of Management*, 17(2): 201–223.

Ervin, Marlene and Toyne, Brian (1987) The AIB Membership: Who We Are, and What We Are Interested In, *Journal of International Business Studies*, 18(2): 89–100

Eskola, Juha and Suoranta, Juha. (1998) *Johdatus laadulliseen tutkimukseen*, [Introduction to Qualitative Methods], 3rd edn. Tampere: Vastapaino.

Fairclough, Norman. (1997) *Miten media puhuu* [originally: Media Discourse]. Tampere: Vastapaino.

Fairclough, Norman. (1999/1995) *Critical Discourse Analysis: the Critical Study of Language*. Edinburgh: Longman.

Gergen, Kenneth J. (1990) Textual Considerations in the Scientific Construction of Human Character, *Style*, 24(3): 365–380.

Grant, David, Keenoy, Tom, and Oswick, Cliff (eds) (1998) *Discourse and Organization*. Thousand Oaks: Sage Publications.

Guba, Egon G (ed.) (1990) *The Paradigm Dialog*. Newbury Park: Sage Publications.

Hawkins, Robert G. (1984) International Business in Academia: The State of the Field, *Journal of International Business Studies*, 15(3): 13–18.

Hench, Thomas J. (1997) The Domain of International Business: Paradigms in Collision. In Brian Toyne and Douglas Nigh (eds), *International Business: An Emerging Vision*. Columbia: University of South Carolina Press, 90–100.

Hofstede, Geert. (1983) The Cultural Relativity of Organizational Practices and Theories, *Journal of International Business Studies*, 14 Fall: 75–89.

Holsti, O.R. (1968) Content Analysis. In G. Lindzey and E. Aronson (eds), *Handbook of Social Psychology vol.2*. Reading, Mass.: Addison-Wesley.

Hunt, Shelby, D. (1983) *Marketing Theory: The Philosophy of Marketing Science*. Homewood: Richard D. Irwin.

Hunt, Shelby, D. (2003) *Controversy in Marketing Theory: For Reason, Realism, Truth, and Objectivity*. Armonk: M.E. Sharpe.

Inkpen, Andrew. (2001) A Note on Ranking the International Business Journals, *Journal of International Business Studies*, 32(1): 193–196.

Inkpen, Andrew and Beamish, Paul W. (1994) An Analysis of Twenty-Five Years of Research in the Journal of International Business Studies, *Journal of International Business Studies*, 24(4): 703–713.

Jacque, Laurent L. (1981) Management of Foreign Exchange Risk: A Review Article, *Journal of International Business Studies*, 12(1): 81–101.

Jokinen, Arja, Juhila, Kirsi, and Suoninen, Eero. (1993) *Diskurssianalyysin aakkoset* [The ABC of Discourse Analysis]. Tampere: Vastapaino.

Jokinen, Arja, Juhila, Kirsi and Suoninen, Eero. (1999) *Diskurssianalyysi liikkeessä* [Discourse Analysis in Action]. Tampere: Vastapaino.

Keso, Heidi. (1999) *Suomalaisen lentokoneteollisuuden sankarit ja konkarit. Osaamisen diskursiivinen rakentuminen* [The Heroes and Veterans of the Finnish Aircraft Industry – Discursive Construction of Capabilities]. Doctoral Dissertations. Tampere: Tampereen yliopisto, http://acta.uta.fi.

Korhonen, Hell. (1999) *Inward-Outward Internationalization of Small and Medium Enterprises*. Doctoral Dissertations A-147. Helsinki: Helsinki School of Economics and Business Administration.

Kotler, Philip and Levy, Sidney J. (1969) Broadening the Concept of Marketing, *Journal of Marketing*, January: 10–15.

Kuhn, Thomas. (1970) *The Structure of Scientific Revolutions*, 2nd edn revised. Chicago: University of Chicago Press.

Lehtimäki, Hanna. (2000) *Strategiatarina kaupungista ja sen toimijoista* [Strategy Making Tells a Story of a City and Its Actors]. Doctoral Dissertations 746. Tampere: University of Tampere, http://acta.uta.fi.

Lehtonen, Mikko. (1996) *Merkitysten maailma, Kulttuurisen tekstintutkimuksen lahtokohtia* [The World of Meanings, Introduction to the Cultural Analysis of Texts]. Vastapaino: Tampere.

Lehtonen, Mikko. (2000) *The Cultural Analysis of Texts*. London: Sage.

Lenartowicz, Tomasz and Roth, Kendall. (1999) A Framework for Culture Assessment, *Journal of International Business Studies*, 30(4): 781–798.

Lincoln, Yvonna S. and Guba, Egon G. (1995) Emerging Criteria for Quality in Qualitative and Interpretive Research, *Qualitative Inquiry*, 1: 275–289.

Luostarinen, Reijo. (1979) *Internationalization of the Firm: An Empirical Study of the Internationalization of Firms with Small and Open Domestic Markets with Special Emphasis on Lateral Rigidity as a Behavioral Characteristic in Strategic Decision Making.* Helsinki: Helsinki School of Economics, Series A: 30.

Lyles, Marjorie A. and Salk, Jane E. (1996) Knowledge Acquisition from Foreign Parents in International Joint Ventures: An Empirical Examination in the Hungarian Context, *Journal of International Business Studies*, Special Issue, 27(5): 877–903.

Melin, Leif. (1992) Internationalization as a Strategy Process, *Strategic Management Journal*, 13: 99–118.

Marschan, Rebecca. (1996) New Structural Forms and Inter-Unit Communication in Multinationals: The Case of Kone Elevators. Doctoral Dissertations, A-110. Helsinki: Helsinki School of Economics.

Martinez, Zaida L. and Toyne, Brian. (2000) What is International Management, and What Is Its Domain? *Journal of International Management*, 6(1): 11–28.

Matikainen, Janne. (1999) Diskursiivisen organisaatiotutkimuksen lahtokohtia, [Discursive Aspects of Organizational Studies], *Hallinnon tutkimus*, 6(3): 221–231. (Text in Finnish, summary in English).

Moisander, Johanna. (2001) *Representation of Green Consumerism: A Constructionist Critique.* Doctoral Dissertations, A-185, Helsinki: Helsinki School of Economics and Business Administration.

Morgan, Gareth. (1984a) Exploring Choice: Reframing the Process of Evaluation. In: Gareth Morgan (ed.), *Beyond the Method: Strategies for Social Research.* Newbury Park: Sage Publications, 392–404.

Morgan, Gareth. (1984b) Research as Engagement. A Personal View. In Gareth Morgan (ed.), *Beyond the Method: Strategies for Social Research.* Newbury Park: Sage Publications, 11–18.

Morgan, Gareth and Smircich, Linda. (1980) The Case for Qualitative Research, *Academy of Management Review*, 5(4): 491–500.

Morrison, Allen J. and Inkpen, Andrew C. (1991) An Analysis of Significant Contributions to the International Business Literature, *Journal of International Business Studies*, 22(1): 143–153.

Mostyn, B. (1985) The Content Analysis of Qualitative Research Data: A Dynamic Approach. In M. Brenner, J. Brown, and D.Canter (eds), *The Research Interview: Uses and Approaches.* London: Academic Press.

Mullen, Michael R. (1995) Diagnosing Measurement Equivalence in Cross-National Research, *Journal of International Business*, 26 September: 573–596.

Negandhi, Anant R. (1983) Cross-Cultural Management Research: Trend and Future Directions, *Journal of International Business Studies*, 14(2): 17–28.

Nehrt, Lee, Truitt, Frederick, and Wright, Richard. (1970) *International Business: Past, Present, and Future.* Bloomington: Indiana University Graduate School of Business.

Neilimo, Kari and Nasi, Juha. (1980) *Nomoteettinen tutkimusote ja suomalainen yrityksen taloustiede, tutkimus positivismin soveltamisesta* [Nomothetic Approach and Finnish Business Studies, an Application of Positivism], Yrityksen taloustieteen ja yksityisoikeuden laitoksen julkaisuja, sarja A2: tutkielmia ja raportteja 12, Tampere: Tampereen yliopisto.

Neilimo, Kari and Nasi, Juha. (1994) A Field of Strangers in Search of a Discipline: Separatism of Public Management Research from Public Administration, Public Administration Review, 54(5): 486–488.

Nikander, Pirjo. (1998) Diskursiivinen kaanne sosiaalipsykologiassa [The Discursive Turn in (Social) Psychology], *Psykologia*, 32: 404–414.

Peng, Mike W. (2004) Identifying the Big Question in International Business Research, *Journal of International Business Studies*, 35(2): 99–108.

Phene, Anupama and Guisinger, Stephen (1998) The Stature of the Journal of International Business Studies, *Journal of International Business Studies*, 29(3): 621–632.

Pierce, Barbara and Garven, Garnet. (1995) Publishing International Business Research: A Survey of Leading Journals, *Journal of International Business Studies*, 26(1): 69–89.

Pietiläinen, Tarja. (2002) *Moninainen yrittäminen sukupuoli ja yrittäjänaisten toimintatila tietoteollisuudessa* [Female Entrepreneuring in ICT Industry]. Doctoral Dissertations A-207. Helsinki: Helsinki School of Economics.

Potter, Jonathan. (1996) *Representing Reality: Discourse, Rhetoric and Social Construction.* London: Sage Publications.

Potter, Jonathan and Wetherell, Margaret. (1987) *Discourse and Social Psychology, Beyond Attitudes and Behavior.* Newbury Park: Sage Publications.

Reynolds, Paul D. (1971) *A Primer in Theory Construction.* New York: The Bobbs-Merrill Company, Inc.

Reynolds N.L., Simintiras A.C., and Diamantopoulos A. (2003) Theoretical Justification of Sampling Choices in International Marketing Research: Key Issues and Guidelines for Researchers, *Journal of International Business Studies*, 34(1): 80–89.

Ricks, David A. (1985) International Business Research: Past, Present and Future, *Journal of International Business Studies*, 16(2): 1–4.

Ricks, David A., Toyne, Brian, and Martinez, Zaida. (1990) Recent Developments in International Management Research, *Journal of Management*, 16(2): 219–253.

Robinson, Richard D. (1981) Background Concepts and Philosophy of International Business from World War II to the Present, *Journal of International Business Studies*, 12(1): 13–21.

Safarian, Edward, A. (2003) Internationalization and the MNE: A Note on the Spread of Ideas, *Journal of International Business Studies*, 34(2): 116–124.

Schollhammer, Hans. (1997) Discussion of "The Conceptual Domain of International Business." In Brian Toyne and Douglas Nigh (eds), *International Business: An Emerging Vision.* Columbia: University of South Carolina Press, 76–82.

Sekaran, Uma. (1983) Methodological and Theoretical Issues and Advancements in Cross-Cultural Research, *Journal of International Business Studies*, 14 Fall: 61–73.

Shenkar, Oded. (2004) One more Time: International Business in a Global Economy, *Journal of International Business Studies*, 35(2): 161–171.

Singh, Jagdip. (1995) Measurement Issues in Cross-national Research, *Journal of International Business Studies*, 26(3): 597–619.

Sivakumar, K. and Nakata, Cheryl. (2001) The Stampede Toward Hofstede's Framework: Avoiding the Sample Design Pit in Cross-Cultural Research, *Journal of International Business Studies*, 32(3): 555–574.

Söderqvist, Minna. (2001a) Suomalaisen korkeakoulutuksen EPS-strategiat v.2000, CIMO reports (Ministry of Education/Center for International Mobility). Helsinki: Edita.

Söderqvist, Minna. (2001b) Internationalisation of Higher Education Institutions-Different Understandings of Internationalisation Influencing on Its Strategic Planning and an Analysis of European Policy Statements as Strategic Plans of Internationalisation, unpublished Licentiate Thesis. Helsinki: Helsinki School of Economics and Business Administration.

Söderqvist, Minna. (2001c) *The Internationalisation and Strategic Planning of Higher-Education Institutions-An Analysis of Finnish EPS Strategies.* Helsinki: Helsinki School of Economics and Business Administration, B-33, HeSe print.

Söderqvist, Minna. (2002) *Internationalisation and Its Management at Higher-Education Institutions-Applying Conceptual, Content and Discourse Analysis.* Doctoral Dissertations, A-206. Helsinki: Helsinki School of Economics.

Statement of Editorial Policy. (2005) *Journal of International Business Studies*, 36: 6.

Stenberg, Esa. (1992) *Steering of Foreign Subsidiaries, An Analysis of Steering System Development in Six Finnish Companies.* Doctoral Dissertations, A-82. Helsinki: Helsinki School of Economics.

Sullivan, Daniel. (1998a) The Ontology of International Business: A Comment on International Business: An Emerging Vision, *Journal of International Business Studies*, 29(4): 877–886.

Sullivan, Daniel. (1998b) Cognitive Tendencies in International Business Research: Implications of a "Narrow Vision," *Journal of International Business Studies*, 29(4): 837–862.

Suoranta, Juha. (1996) Kontekstualismi kasvatustieteen metodologiassa [Contextualism in Methodology of Education], *Kasvatus*, 27(5): 451–462.

Swedberg, Richard. 1990. *Economics and Sociology: Redefining Their Boundaries: Conversations with Economists and Sociologists.* Princeton: Princeton University Press.

Tahvanainen Marja. (1998) *Expatriate Performance Management, The Case of Nokia Telecommunications.* Doctoral Dissertations, A-134. Helsinki: Helsinki School of Economics.

Terpstra, Vern. (1973) The Future of the International Business Professor, Presidential Address, *Journal of International Business Studies*, 4(1): 67–78.

Toyne, Brian. (1989) International Exchange: A Foundation for Theory Building in International Business, *Journal of International Business Studies*, 20(1): 1–17.

Toyne, Brian. (1997a) Internationalizing Business Scholarship: The Essentials. In Tamer S. Cavusgil and Nancy E. Hom (eds), *Internationalizing Doctoral Education in Business.* East Lansing: Michigan State University Press, 61–96.

Toyne, Brian. (1997b) International Business Inquiry: Does it Warrant a Separate Domain? In Brian Toyne and Douglas Nigh (eds), *International Business: An Emerging Vision.* Columbia: University of South Carolina Press, 62–76.

Toyne, Brian and Nigh, Douglas (eds) (1997) *International Business: An Emerging Vision.* Columbia: University of South Carolina Press.

Toyne, Brian and Nigh, Douglas (eds) (1998) A More Expansive View of International Business, *Journal of International Business Studies*, 29(4): 863–876.

Tuusjärvi, Eiren. (2003) *Multifaceted Norms in Export Cooperation: A Discourse Analysis of Normative Expectations.* Doctoral Dissertations, A-226. Helsinki: Helsinki School of Economics.

Vaara, Eero. (1999) *Towards a Rediscovery of Organizational Politics: Essays on Organizational Integration Following Mergers and Acquisitions.* Doctoral Dissertations, A-149. Helsinki: Helsinki School of Economics and Business Administration.

Vargo, Stephen L. and Lusch, Robert F. (2004) Evolving to a New Dominant Logic for Marketing, *Journal of Marketing*, 68 January: 1–17.

Venaik, S., Midgley, David F. and Devinney, Timothy M. (2005) Dual Paths to Performance: The Impact of Global Pressures on MNC Subsidiary Conduct and Performance, *Journal of International Business Studies*, 34(6): 655–675

Verbeke, A. (2003) reviewed, Masaaki Kotabe, Aulakh Preet S. (eds): Emerging Issues in International Business Research, *Journal of International Business Studies*, 34(3): 312–313.

Watson, Tony J. (2000) Ethnographic Fiction Science: Making Sense of Managerial Work and Organizational Research Processes with Caroline and Terry. *Organization* 7(3): 489–510.

Weick, Karl E. (1979) *The Social Psychology of Organizing*. Reading: Addison-Wesley Publishing Company.

Wilkins, Mira.(1997) The Conceptual Domain of International Business. In Brian Toyne and Douglas Nigh (eds), *International Business: An Emerging Vision*. Columbia: University of South Carolina Press.

Willman, Arto. (2001) *Yhteistyön ristiriitaiset puhetavat, diskurssianalyyttinen näkökulma luokanopettajien tulkintoihin tiimityöstä*. Doctoral Dissertation. Oulu: University of Oulu.

Willman, Arto. (2002) Interview held by Minna Söderqvist Dr, Principal Lecturer with Arto Willman Dr, Principal Lecturer, Helsinki December 5th, 2002.

Wright, Richard W. (1970) Trends in International Business, *Journal of International Business Studies*, 1(1): 109–123.

Wright, Richard W. and Ricks, David A. (1994) Trends in International Business Research: Twenty-five Years Later, *Journal of International Business Studies*, 24(4): 687–701.

Xu, Qi. (2000) On the Way of Knowledge: Making a Discourse at Quality. *Organization* 7(3): 427–454.

Zhao, H., Yadong, L. and Taewon S. (2004) Transaction Cost Determinants and Ownership-Based Entry Mode Choice: A Meta-Analytical Review, *Journal of International Business Studies*, 35(6): 524–544.

2
Multinationality of the Firm: Conceptualization and Measurement

Ahmet H. Kirca

Internationalization has been a key construct that has attracted considerable attention in international business (IB) in the last four decades. A large body of research has focused on the internationalization of the firm because it potentially involves a central process that fundamentally affects the structure, functioning, strategy, and performance of the firm. In the extant literature, various conceptualizations have been employed to refer to the extent of firm internationalization (cf. Grant, 1987; Geringer et al., 1989; Sullivan and Bauerschmidt, 1990; Tallman and Li, 1996; Gomes and Ramaswamy, 1999, among others). Several terms, such as the degree of internationalization (Sullivan, 1994), multinationality (Grant, 1987), international geographic diversification (Vachani, 1991), geographic scale and scope of foreign operations (Qian and Li, 2002), have been used to refer to the extent to which firms are international (multinationality of the firm hereafter).[1]

To date, despite the widely acknowledged importance and extensive usage of the multinationality construct in theory development and testing, very limited attention has been devoted to developing scales to assess the extent of multinationality of the firm (see Sullivan [1994] for an exception). Researchers have often employed single indicators (e.g., ratio of foreign assets/sales/profits to total assets/sales/profits, number of foreign countries in which the firm has subsidiaries/operations) or a combination of a sub-sample of these indicators to operationalize firm multinationality (Sullivan, 1994). Although the use of such indicators readily available from secondary sources might be acceptable because of difficulties involved in data collection, several concerns have been raised concerning the use of single indicators in efforts to measure constructs. In particular, it has been suggested that single items have considerable measurement error and they represent only a limited portion of the domain and that measuring concepts with multiple items have higher reliability (Churchill, 1979; DeVellis, 1991). Furthermore, it has also been demonstrated that using single items for measurement tends to inflate the observed association between variables, thereby increasing the odds of finding significant relationships (Nunnally and Bernstein, 1994).

Given the centrality of the multinationality construct for IB discipline, there is obviously a need for further conceptual and empirical work delineating the nature of firm multinationality and identifying its dimensions and indicators. These efforts may increase the explanatory power of IB theories and decrease the risks associated with validity and reliability of generalizations obtained using single-item scales (cf. Churchill, 1979; DeVellis, 1991). For instance, several researchers have investigated the relationship between multinationality and organizational performance in the extant literature, but the empirical results were at best inconclusive (Contractor et al., 2003; Ruigrok and Wagner, 2003). It has been argued that contradictory findings regarding the effects of multinationality on performance might be explained by the diversity of measures employed in past research to assess firm multinationality (Sullivan, 1994). A recent meta-analysis by Ruigrok and Wagner (2004) confirms these observations by indicating that the conceptualization of multinationality affects the strength of the relationship between multinationality and organizational performance.

Thus, the purpose of the present research is to delineate the conceptual domain of the multinationality construct and propose a composite measure to assess the extent to which firms are international. As such, this chapter contributes to the extant IB literature by synthesizing the extant literature on multinationality and providing a comprehensive approach to operationalize the multinationality construct (cf. Sullivan, 1994; Ramaswamy et al., 1996). The chapter is structured as follows. First, drawing upon the Uppsala Model of internationalization of the firm, I distinguish between the state and process aspects of internationalization in an effort to propose a theory-based, working definition of firm multinationality. Next, I propose an alternative scale development procedure that involves the construction of an index to assess the extent of the firm's multinationality. Then, using a meta-analytic approach, I identify and categorize the variables used to measure the multinationality of the firm in the extant literature. Finally, the chapter concludes with a discussion of managerial and future research implications.

State and process aspects of internationalization of the firm

The extant literature in international business offers a number of theoretical frameworks to explain the internationalization process. One of the earliest attempts to theorize about the firm's internationalization relates to export development. The model is based on Rogers' (1962) stages of adoption process and focuses on the learning sequence in connection with adopting an innovation. From this perspective, the internationalization decision is considered an innovation for the firm within the context of export development process for small and medium size firms. Investigating the internationalization of the firm from a behavioral perspective, the export development model explains the internationalization process as a set of fixed stages that firms pass through as they increase their international involvement (Bilkey and Tesar, 1977; Cavusgil, 1980; Reid, 1981).

The Uppsala Model is another dominant theory in IB literature that investigates the internationalization of the firm. Based on the behavioral theory of the firm, the Uppsala Model conceptualizes internationalization of the firm as a learning process in which a firm gradually increases its international involvement (Johanson and Wiedersheim-Paul, 1975; Johanson and Vahlne, 1977). In this model, a distinction is also made between the state and process aspects of internationalization, such that the present state of internationalization is an important factor explaining the course of the following stages. According to the Uppsala Model, the state aspects relate to the knowledge about and resources committed to foreign markets and operations. The process aspects are decisions to commit resources and the performance of current business activities. Market knowledge and market commitment are assumed to affect both commitment decisions and the way current activities are performed and these, in turn, change market knowledge and commitment. According to the Uppsala Model, additional commitments can only be made gradually and firms tend to choose new markets with successively greater psychic distances (Johanson and Vahlne, 1977, 1990).

Consistent with the extant literature, the present chapter posits that a distinction should be made between the process aspect of internationalization and the state aspect of internationalization (i.e., multinationality of the firm) (cf. Johanson and Vahlne, 1977). As such, multinationality of the firm is one of its essential properties just like its size, age or ownership structure. It is an essential property because it is a property that the firm looses if it is transmuted into a firm of a different kind, that is, a multinational company is transmuted into a different kind – a domestic firm – should it loose its multinationality. On the other hand, internationalization is a process that requires knowledge about this particular property of the firm along with knowledge of other properties at different times (cf. Melin, 1992). The mechanism underlying the process of internationalization may be explained, first, by knowing the sequence of multinationality at consecutive times and, second, by observing the changes of this particular property as a result of interactions with its other properties (cf. Bunge, 1996). Stated differently, "internationalization is a development process through time, is a time-series of critical events, or states" (Melin, 1992: 101). Therefore, for a better understanding of the internationalization process, we need to focus on how to measure the state aspect of the internationalization (i.e., multinationality).

Multinationality of the firm: conceptual definition and dimensionality

Several definitions of internationalization have been proposed in the extant literature including internationalization as a sequential and orderly process of increasing involvement and associated changes in organizational forms (Bilkey and Tesar, 1977; Johanson and Vahlne, 1977; Reid, 1981), as the outward movement in a firm's international operations (Turnbull, 1987), as a process of increasing involvement in international operations (Welch and Luostarinen, 1988), as a process of adapting firms' operations to international environment (Calof and Beamish, 1995), or as a process of adapting exchange transaction modality to international markets (Anderson, 1997). Table 2.1 summarizes the various definitions of internationalization used in the literature.

Table 2.1   Existing definitions of internationalization

Author(s)	Definitions of Internationalization
Bilkey and Tesar (1977) Johanson and Vahlne (1977, 1990) Reid (1981)	A sequential and orderly process of increasing involvement and associated changes in organizational forms
Cavusgil (1980)	A process through which firms adopt IB activities
Turnbull (1987)	The outward movement in a firm's international operations
Johanson and Mattson (1988)	Establishment and development of positions in relation to counterparts in foreign networks through international extension, penetration, and international integration
Welch and Luostarinen (1988) Melin (1992) Young (1990) Chetty (1999)	The process of increasing involvement in international operations
Calof and Beamish (1995)	A process of adapting firms' operations (strategy, structure, resources, etc.) to international environment
Welch and Welch (1996)	A series of foreign market commitments that carry the company's international operations forward, or in some cases backward
Andersen (1997)	A process of adapting exchange transaction modality to international markets
Coviello and McAuley (1999)	A process by which firms increase their awareness of the influence of international activities on their future and establish and conduct transactions with firms of other countries
Eriksson et al. (1997)	A process of learning and knowledge accumulation

Although the definitions in Table 2.1 capture different aspects of the phenomenon, they share several common points: (a) they describe internationalization as a dynamic process that occurs at the organizational level of analysis; (b) they allude to its longitudinal character; and (c) they explain outward patterns of investment. The present study adopts the broad definition of internationalization proposed by Welch and Luostarinen (1988: 36) as "the process of increasing (or decreasing) involvement of a firm in international operations" because (1) it captures the essence of the construct as a dynamic process that results from the operations of the firm in international markets; (2) it is a clear definition that helps to operationalize the construct; and (3) it has been employed relatively more frequently in extant research (e.g., Young, 1990; Melin, 1992; Chetty, 1999). Accordingly, the multinationality of the firm is defined as a firm-level characteristic that refers to the level of involvement of the firm in markets outside its home country. As such, multinationality is a continuum with purely domestic firm on one end and a highly diversified MNC operating in multiple countries at the other end (cf. Cheng and Ramaswamy, 1989; Allen and Pantzalis, 1996).

As for the dimensionality of the multinationality construct, Thomas and Eden (2004) indicate that there are two broad dimensions of multinationality of the firm: (a) the *depth* of multinationality and (b) the breadth of multinationality (cf. Johanson and Vahlne, 1977; Welch and Luostarinen, 1988). According to Thomas and Eden (2004), while the depth dimension corresponds to foreign market penetration and/or production (i.e., the dependence of the firm on foreign markets), the breadth dimension refers to the scope of operations abroad. Thus, consistent with the extant literature, we conceptualize the depth of multinationality as the extent to which firms commit tangible and intangible resources to their international operations and generate returns from these resources. As such, multinationality includes firm-level attributes that measure the amount of tangible and intangible resources (e.g., assets, personnel, knowledge, time) dedicated to markets outside the home country and returns (e.g., sales, profits) obtained using these resources. The second dimension, breadth of multinationality refers to the spread of a firm's IB activity across different country environments, capturing the extent to which the firm has expanded the scope of its international operations across different cultural, political, and economic environments (cf. Kim, 1989; Tallman and Li, 1996). According to this dimension, a firm that operates in multiple markets with different cultural, political, and economic environments would score higher on multinationality than a firm that operates in only two markets with similar environments. Thus, unlike the depth dimension that focuses on the amount of involvement in foreign market operations, the breadth dimension of multinationality emphasizes the spread of involvement across various countries.

In the extant literature, the depth of involvement dimension has been investigated extensively. For example, Aharoni (1971) provides three sets of variables that define firm multinationality: structural criteria (e.g., ownership structure, national composition of top management), performance yardsticks (e.g., earnings, sales in foreign markets), and behavioral characteristics (e.g., corporate management orientation). Similarly, Sullivan's (1994) Degree of Internationalization (DOI) scale has three dimensions: structural, performance, and attitudinal dimensions. Several measures of DOI scale (i.e., foreign sales to total sales, foreign assets to total assets, foreign subsidiaries as a percentage of total number of subsidiaries, top managers' international experience) pertain to tangible and intangible firm resources or returns obtained using these resources in foreign markets.

Finally, Welch and Luostarinen (1988) identify six dimensions that describe the multinationality of the firm. While five of these dimensions relate to resources committed to international operations and returns obtained from these resources (i.e., depth of multinationality) (e.g., foreign operation methods, sales, organizational structure, personnel, and finance), the sixth dimension (target markets) captures the expansion of operations across countries with different political and cultural environments (i.e., breadth of multinationality). Thus, the extant literature in international business provides support for the contention that tangible and intangible resources committed to international operations reflect an important dimension of the firm's multinationality.

Past research also provides support for the use of breadth of multinationality as a separate dimension in assessing the extent to which firms are international. Sullivan (1994) employs psychic dispersion of international operations in the DOI scale to capture the breadth of multinationality. Although the measurement of this variable raises some concerns (Ramaswamy et al., 1996), Sullivan's approach captures the essence of the idea that multinationality of the firm is related not only to the magnitude of resources committed to foreign markets, but also to the diversity of markets in which the firm commits these resources. Moreover, researchers in international management and strategy often employ the concept of international diversification that essentially captures the breadth or scope of foreign operations (Geringer et al., 1989; Vachani, 1991).

In short, the extant research indicates that both the depth and breadth dimensions of firm multinationality are important factors in identifying the extent to which firms are international. However, much of the extant research employed indicators that represent either the depth or breadth dimensions of multinationality (Thomas and Eden, 2004). For instance, multinationality has often been measured using the foreign sales–total sales or foreign assets–total assets ratios (Sullivan, 1994), which only captures the one dimension of multinationality (i.e., depth of multinationality). As detailed subsequently, other common measures of multinationality include the number of foreign countries in which the firm has subsidiaries, which essentially captures the breadth dimension of multinationality. Therefore, further research is warranted integrating these two dimensions to provide a more complete picture of firm multinationality. A complete theoretical and psychometric analysis of the multinationality construct potentially provides researchers with a reliable and valid scale of multinationality that should address the shortcomings of some of the multinationality-performance studies (Thomas and Eden, 2004; Ruigrok and Wagner, 2004). The following sections propose an alternative scale development procedure for the construction of multinationality index that captures both the depth and breadth of multinationality.

Development of the multinationality index

Existing guidelines in research methodology focus almost exclusively on scale development, whereby items (i.e., observed variables) composing a scale are perceived as reflective indicators of an underlying construct (i.e., latent variable) (e.g., Churchill, 1979; DeVellis, 1991; Spector, 1992). This perspective is largely based on the domain sampling model developed to measure latent theoretical psychological constructs with multiple items (Nunnally and Bernstein, 1994). In some cases, however, it might be more appropriate to employ formative (causal) indicators, which involves the creation of an index rather than a scale by identifying observed variables that are assumed to cause a latent variable (Diamantopoulos and Winklhofer, 2001). Formative measurement is frequently used in literature to deal with organizational and social constructs when a latent variable is defined as a linear sum of a set of measures (Bagozzi, 1994). Typical examples of indexes constructed with formative indicators include socioeconomic status (Hauser, 1971), the human development index (UN Development Program, 1990), and the index of economic freedom (O'Driscoll et al., 2002).

In this chapter, I suggest that multinationality of the firm should be measured with formative indicators by constructing an index because it is not a theoretical psychological construct, but rather a latent variable caused by a set of indicators (cf. Bagozzi, 1994; Diamantopoulos and Winklhofer, 2001). Thus, I assume that firms are international because, for example, majority of their assets are located outside their home market or because they have a high number of foreign subsidiaries. In other words, the multinationality of the firm is determined by a linear combination of measures of independent variables (e.g., foreign assets to total assets ratio, number of foreign subsidiaries) and measures of multinationality produce the multinationality construct (cf. Diamantopoulos and Winklhofer, 2001). Therefore, the use of an index instead of a scale should more appropriate for the multinationality of the firm construct. Thus, unlike Sullivan (1994) who followed the traditional guidelines for the development of DOI scale, I adopt a measurement perspective that involves the construction of an index of multinationality with formative indicators (cf. Ramaswamy et al., 1996).

Index construction procedures

According to Diamantopoulos and Winklhofer (2001), four issues are critical for successful index construction: content specification, indicator specification, indicator collinearity, and external validity. This chapter concentrates on the first two steps of the index construction procedure and defers the last two steps to an empirical study that would refine the conceptualization proposed here with data from academic experts and multinational companies.

Content and indicator specification

The first step, content specification entails the specification of the scope of the latent variable, that is, the domain of content the index is intended to capture (Diamantopoulos and Winklhofer, 2001). Nunnally and Bernstein (1994: 484) state that breadth of the definition is extremely important in index development because failure to consider all facets of the construct will lead to an exclusion of relevant indicators. Preceding sections in this chapter specify the domain of the multinationality construct as a multidimensional firm-level characteristic consisted of depth and breadth of international involvement. According to the conceptualization presented in this chapter, while the depth of multinationality aspect refers to firm resources committed to international operations and returns obtained from these resources, the breadth of multinationality pertains to the dispersion of the firm's international activities across different economic, political, and cultural environments.

The next step involves the identification of potentially important variables for further investigation of multinationality index. Diamantopoulos and Winklhofer (2001) suggest that items employed as indicators must cover the entire scope of the construct domain as described under the content specification because failing to include at least one indicator for one of the dimensions or aspects of the construct would change the composition of the construct. Accordingly, for the multinationality index, selected indicators need to capture comprehensively the depth and breadth of multinationality of the firm.

In an effort to fully capture the domain of firm multinationality construct, the present study employs meta-analytic data collection procedures. More specifically, procedures similar to those recommended in the meta-analysis literature are followed to identify how multinationality of the firm has been measured in the extant literature (cf. Hedges and Olkin, 1985; Cooper and Hedges, 1994). Then, various indicators harvested from the literature have been categorized based on previously defined, theoretically relevant dimensions of multinationality of the firm in order to form the multinationality index. This approach is a way of extracting expert opinion that facilitates the comprehensive coverage of the entire scope of the latent variable as described under the content specification step previously (cf. Diamantopoulos and Winklhofer, 2001).

To begin, to ensure the representativeness and completeness of the database, ABI/INFORM and EBSCO computerized databases were searched for any studies published prior to November 2002, using keywords such as "multinationality," "internationalization," "degree of internationalization," and "internationality." Furthermore, I also searched citations found in the identified studies in this first step in an effort to ensure that most studies on the topic were included in the analysis. This procedure yielded a total of 347 studies to be examined.

In the evaluation process, the lists of articles obtained from the two databases were first cross-checked to eliminate redundancies and purely conceptual papers. Then, articles that are not related to the topic of interest were eliminated based on the information in the abstracts. In total, *sixty-six* studies that reported one or more measures of multinationality were identified when the research process was concluded.[2] These studies represented a total of 28 different journals, including *Journal of International Business Studies* (18 studies), *Management International Review* (9), *Academy of Management Journal* (7), and *Strategic Management Journal* (3). Across the sources, a total of 114 variables used to operationalize the multinationality construct were harvested. As a final step in the process, the variables obtained from the studies were classified into one of the previously defined dimensions of multinationality (i.e., depth and breadth dimensions). Table 2.2 below depicts the variables, categories, and frequency of each variable used to operationalize the multinationality of firm construct in the extant literature.

An obvious conclusion that can be drawn from Table 2.2 is that a wide variety of indicators have been employed to measure firm multinationality. Specifically, the literature review reveals that there have been 30 different measures of firm multinationality in the extant literature. The most frequent measures of multinationality have been the ratio of foreign sales to total sales (36), ratio of foreign assets to total assets (19), and number of countries in which the firm has subsidiaries (8). Other variables frequently used in the extant literature to operationalize the extent of the firm's involvement in international operations include ratio of foreign revenues to total revenues (5), Sullivan's (1994) psychic dispersion of international operations (5), and number of foreign subsidiaries (4). Moreover, although not reported in Table 2.2, the present analysis also provides evidence for the pervasive use of single-item scales to measure firm multinationality: while 50 studies (76%) used single items to assess the extent of multinationality, only 16 studies employed multiple item scales (24%), despite the recognition that using single-item indicators only provide a rough measure of multinationality (Geringer et al., 1989; Sullivan, 1994).

In summary, the present study builds upon the broad definition of multinationality of the firm as the extent to which a firm is involved in international

Table 2.2 Dimensions and indicators of multinationality

Dimension I: Depth of Multinationality				Dimension II: Breadth of Multinationality	
Resources Sub-dimension		**Returns Sub-dimension**			
Indicator	Freq.	Indicator	Freq.	Indicator	Freq.
Ratio of foreign assets to total assets	19	Ratio of foreign sales to total sales	36	Number of foreign countries in which the firm has subsidiaries	8
Number of foreign subsidiaries	4	Ratio of foreign revenues to total revenues	5	Psychic dispersion of international operations	5
Top managers' international experience	3	Ratio of exports to total sales	2	Number of countries in which the firm has business operations	5
Ratio of overseas subsidiaries to total subsidiaries	3	Ratio of foreign profit to total profit	2	Geographic proximity of international sales	2
Number of employees in foreign operations as percentage of total employees	2	Share of firm turnover sold abroad	1	Number of geographic segments in which the firm is present	2
Amount of foreign assets	1	Ratio of foreign earning to total earning	1	Geographic proximity of international production units	1

Breadth of nationalities in top management team	1	Ratio of foreign intrafirm trade to total sales	1	Ratio of the firm's subsidiaries in a region to its total global holdings	1
Number of international offices	1	Ratio of total sales to the firm value	1	Sales outside domestic market weighted by region	1
Percentage of the employees that spends over 50% of their time in international activities	1	Perceptions of expected performance in foreign operations	1	Ratio of a firm's number of subsidiaries in country i to the total number of foreign subsidiaries × weight given to each global market region	1
Ratio of the sum of the subsidiaries in the two countries with the largest number of the firm's subsidiaries as a fraction of the firm's total number of subsidiaries	1	Proportion of sales attributable to production abroad	1	Ratio of total number of countries in which a firm is involved to the total number of geographical areas in which the firm is active	1

operations and specifies *a priori* two distinct dimensions for a formative index, namely, the depth and breadth of multinationality. Table 2.2 presents the set of indicators that have been previously employed to measure each dimension in the extant literature, using a meta-analytic data collection procedure. The present chapter proposes that 31 indicators shown in Table 2.2 (20 indicators for depth and 11 indicators for breadth dimensions of multinationality) are sufficiently inclusive in order to fully capture the construct's domain of content (cf. Diamantopoulos and Winklhofer, 2001). However, this pool of items requires further refinement using empirical approaches, as in the classical scale development procedure. The index purification and validation stages of scale construction are described in more detail below.

Purification and validation of the multinationality index

According to index construction procedures recommended by Diamantopoulos and Winklhofer (2001), the third step of index development procedure involves index purification where empirical data are necessary to assess the collinearity of the indicators in the index. Indicator collinearity is an important issue because the formative measurement model is based on a multiple regression in which the strength of indicator coefficients is affected by the strength of the indicator intercorrelations and sample size (Diamantopoulos and Winklhofer, 2001). Because the objectives of this chapter are primarily to develop the conceptual domain of multinationality construct and to specify indicators used in the extant literature to measure it, empirical data have yet to be collected to identify the final set of indicators that will be included in the index of multinationality.

Finally, the last step in index construction concerns the assessment of external validity. Diamantopoulos and Winklhofer (2001) suggest that each indicator could be correlated to another variable (external to the index) to obtain an initial idea of the quality of individual indicators and only those indicators that are significantly correlated with the variable of interest would be retained. In order to assess the external validity of the firm multinationality index, the index might be correlated, for example, with costs of coordination and control in the organization because past research has shown that multinationality is positively related to such costs (Geringer et al., 1989; Gomes and Ramaswamy, 1999). Another approach to validation focuses on nomological aspects that involve linking the index to other constructs with which it would be expected to related (i.e., antecedents, and consequences). Thus, to establish the external validity of the multinationality index, data need to be collected for variables with which multinationality of the firm construct is theoretically related. Thus, collecting data on antecedents such as top management team demographic heterogeneity and the globalization of the industry in which the firm is embedded (Makhija et al., 1997) might be useful approaches in providing evidence for the validity of multinationality index.

Summary and Discussion

Theory development and testing have traditionally been more central concerns than measurement issues in the IB discipline (Sullivan, 1994). However, better conceptualization and measurement of constructs do not only increase the explanatory power of IB theories, but attention to such issues also minimizes the risks associated with the validity and reliability of generalizations that can be drawn from empirical research. This chapter attempts to clarify the conceptual domain of the multinationality of the firm in an effort to propose an index of multinationality that should assist researchers in their investigations.

In the first part of the study, the state and process aspects of internationalization have been discussed and various definitions of internationalization were drawn together from previous literature. In the second part, attention was given to the delineation and specification of the domain of internationalization and multinationality constructs. Then, two dimensions for the multinationality construct, depth and breadth of multinationality were derived from the extant literature. These dimensions provided a framework for the classification of indicators of a formative index that intends to measure the multinationality of the firm. Finally, steps to be followed to purify and validate the multinationality index were described for future research.

This chapter proposes a formal approach for the construction of multinationality index that consists of formative indicators. As opposed to classical scale development procedures that detail the process of measurement of abstract, latent psychological constructs (Churchill, 1979), this chapter argues that using a formative index might be more appropriate to measure firm multinationality (cf. Ramaswamy et al., 1996). In particular, the construction of a multi-dimensional, multiple-item index with theoretical support might be very useful in understanding some of the conflicting findings regarding the multinationality-performance relationship in the extant research (Gomes and Ramaswamy, 1999; Contractor et al., 2003). The present investigation suggests that methodological problems associated with single item measures to assess the multinationality of firms might have contributed to this problem. However, further empirical research seems to be warranted to assess the reliability and validity of the index of multinationality and investigate its effects on organizational performance.

In this chapter, the proposed index offers an opportunity to investigate a particular property of the firm at a certain time *t*. Since a process can be defined as a sequence of events, the data points from a longitudinal study of multinationality of the firm can be expected to form the trajectory of this particular property. This path of state changes can be compared with the paths of other properties of the firm to obtain empirical regularities, which will help reach mechanisms that underlie the internationalization processes. Various researchers suggested that the use of cross-sectional data has been a major methodological problem in international business (Welch and Luostarinen, 1988; Melin, 1992; Andersen, 1993; Calof and Beamish, 1995). By distinguishing the state and change aspects of internationalization, this also chapter emphasizes that temporal separation might be a useful framework to better understand how internationalization affects organizations (cf. Poole and Van de Ven, 1989).

In addition to the performance implications of the newly proposed multinationality index, researchers should also focus on the investigation of the effects of various moderators, such as industry characteristics (e.g., high tech vs low tech; B2B vs B2C; manufacturing vs services), country of origin, and organizational considerations (e.g., strategy type, organizational culture) on the multinationality-performance relationship. These models can be tested in an array of empirical settings, such as (1) a single-country, single-organization longitudinal study for studies investigating the effects of multinationality on organizational performance; (2) a single-country, cross-sectional data from multiple industries to assess the effects of industry context and organizational considerations on the multinationality-performance relationship; and (3) a multi-country, single-industry study to assess the moderating effects of country of origin on the multinationality-performance relationship.

Notes

1. For consistency, I will use the term "multinationality" to refer to the extent of firms' internationalization throughout this manuscript (cf. Grant, 1987).
2. A bibliography of the studies included in the meta-analysis is available from the authors.

References

Aharoni, Yair. 1971. On the Definition of a Multinational Corporation. *Quarterly Journal of Economics and Business*, 2 (3): 3–18.

Allen, Linda and Christos Pantzalis. 1996. Valuation of the Operating Flexibility of Multinational Corporations. *Journal of International Business Studies*, 27 (4): 633–653.

Andersen, Otto. 1993. On the Internationalization Process of Firms: A Critical Analysis. *Journal of International Business Studies*, 24 (2): 209–231.

Andersen, Otto. 1997. Internationalization and Market Entry Mode: A Review of Theories and Conceptual Frameworks. *Management International Review*, 32 (2): 27–37.

Bagozzi, Richard. 1994. *Principles of Marketing Research*. Oxford: Blackwell.

Bilkey, Warren and George Tesar. 1977. The Export Behavior of Smaller Wisconsin Manufacturing Firms. *Journal of International Business Studies*, 9 (2): 93–98.

Bunge, Mario. 1996. *Finding Philosophy in Social Science*. New Haven: Yale University Press.

Calof, Jonathan L. and Paul W. Beamish. 1995. Adapting to Foreign Markets: Explaining Internationalization. *International Business Review*, 4 (2): 115–131.

Coviello, Nicolle E. and McAuley, Andrew. 1999. Internationalisation and the Smaller Firm: A Review of Contemporary Empirical Research. *Management International Review*, 39(3); 223–256.

Cavusgil, Tamer S. 1980. On the Internationalization Process of the Firms. *European Research*, 8 (6): 273–281.

Cheng, Joseph L. and Kannan Ramaswamy. 1989. Towards a Systems Typology of Multinational Corporations: Some Conceptual and Research Implications. *Academy of Management Proceedings*, 106–110.

Chetty, Silvie. 1999. Dimensions of Internationalization of Manufacturing Firms in the Apparel Industry. *European Journal of Marketing*, 33 (1/2): 121–142.

Churchill, Gilbert A. 1979. A Paradigm for Developing Better Measures of Marketing Constructs. *Journal of Marketing Research*, 16 (1): 64–73.

Contractor, Farok J., Sumit K. Kundu, and Chin-Chun Hsu. 2003. A Three-Stage Theory of International Expension: The Link Between Multinationality and Performance in the Service Sector. *Journal of International Business Studies*, 34 (1): 5–18.

Cooper, Harris and Larry V. Hedges. 1994. *The Handbook of Research Synthesis*. New York, NY: Russell Sage Foundation.

DeVellis, Robert F. 1991. *Scale Development: Theory and Applications*. Newbury Park CA: Sage Publications.

Diamantopoulos, Adamantios and Heidi M. Winklhofer. 2001. Index Construction With Formative Indicators: An Alternative to Scale Development. *Journal of Marketing Research*, 38 (May): 269–277.

Eriksson, Kent, Jan Johanson, Anders Majkgard and Deo D. Sharma. 1997. Experiential Knowledge and Cost in Internationalization Process. *Journal of International Business Studies*, 28 (2): 337–360.

Geringer, J. Michael, Paul W. Beamish, and Richard C. DaCosta. 1989. Diversification Strategy and Internationalization: Implications for MNE Performance. *Strategic Management Journal*, 10: 109–120.

Gomes, Lenn and Kanna Ramaswamy. 1999. An Empirical Examination of the Form of the Relationship Between Multinationality and Performance. *Journal of International Business Studies*, 30 (1): 173–188.

Grant, Robert M. 1987. Multinationality and Performance among British Manufacturing Companies. *Journal of International Business Studies*, 18 (3): 79–89.

Hauser, Robert M. 1971. *Socio-economic Background and Educational Performance*. Rose Monograph Series. Washington DC: American Sociological Association.

Hedges, Larry V. and Ingram Olkin. 1985. *Statistical Methods for Meta-Analysis*. Orlando, FL: Academic Press.

Johanson, Jan and Lars-Gunnar Mattson. 1988. Internationalization in Industrial Systems – A Network Approach. In Hood N. and J. Vahlne (eds), *Strategies in Global Competition*. London: Croom Helm.

Johanson, Jan and Jan-Erik Vahlne. 1977. The Internationalization Process of the Firm: A Model of Knowledge Development and Increasing Foreign Market Commitments. *Journal of International Business Studies*, 8 (Spring/Summer): 23–32.

Johanson, Jan and Jan-Erik Vahlne. 1990. The Mechanism of Internationalization. *International Marketing Review*, 7: 11–24.

Johanson, Jan and Finn Wiedersheim-Paul. 1975. The Internationalization of the Firm-Four Swedish Cases. *Journal of International Business Studies*, 12 (3): 305–322.

Kim, Chan. 1989. Developing a Global Diversification Measure. Management. *Science*, 35: 376–383.

Makhija, V. Mona, Kwangsoo Kim, and Sandra D. Williamson. 1997. Measuring Globalization of Industries Using a National Industry Approach: Empirical Evidence

Across Five Countries and Over Time. *Journal of International Business Studies*, 28 (4): 679–710.

Melin, Leif. 1992. Internationalization as Strategy Process. *Strategic Management Journal*, 13: 99–118.

Nunnally, Jum C. and Ira H. Bernstein. 1994. *Psychometric Theory*. 3rd edition. New York: McGraw-Hill.

O'Driscoll, Gerald P., Kim R. Holmes, and Mary O'Grady. 2002. *Index. of Economic Freedom*. New York: The Wall Street Journal.

Qian, Gongming and Ji Li. 2002. Multinationality, Global Market Diversification and Profitability Among the Largest US Firms. *Journal of Business Research*, 55: 325–335.

Ramaswamy, Kannan, Galen K. Kroeck, and William Renforth. 1996. Measuring the Degree of Internationalization of a Firm: A Comment. *Journal of International Business Studies*, 27 (1): 167–177.

Reid, Stan D. 1981. The Decision-Maker and Export Entry and Expansion. *Journal of International Business Studies*, 12 (3): 101–112.

Rogers, Everett M. 1962. *Diffusion of Innovation*. New York: The Free Press.

Ruigrok, Winfried and Hardy Wagner. 2003. Internationalization and Performance: An Organisational Learning Perspective. *Management International Review*, 43 (1): 63–83.

Ruigrok, Winfred and Wagner, Hardy. 2004. Internationalization and Firm Performance: Metaanalytic Review and Future Research Directions, *Academy of International Business Proceedings*.

Spector, Paul E. 1992. *Summated Rating Scales Construction*. Newbury Park, CA: Sage Publication.

Sullivan, Daniel. 1994. Measuring the Degree of Internationalization of a Firm. *Journal of International Business Studies*, 25 (2): 325–342.

Sullivan, Daniel and Alan Bauerschmidt. 1990. Incremental Internationalization: A Test of Johanson and Vahlne's Thesis. *Management International Review*, 30 (1): 19–30.

Tallman, Steven and Jitiao Li. 1996. Effects of International Diversity and Product Diversity on the Performance of Multinational Firms. *Academy of Management Journal*, 39 (1): 179–196.

Thomas, Douglas and Lorraine Eden. 2004. What is the Shape of the Multinationality-Performance Relationship? *The Multinational Business Review*, 12 (1): 89–110.

Turnbull, Peter W. 1987. A Challenge to the Stages Theory of Internationalization Process. In P. J. Rosson and S. Reid (eds), *Managing Export Entry and Expansion*. New York: Praeger.

United Nations Development Program. 1990. *Human Development Index*. New York: United Nations Development Program and Oxford University Program.

Vachani, Sushil. 1991. Distinguishing Between Related and Unrelated International Geographic Diversification: A Comprehensive Measure of Global Diversification. *Journal of International Business Studies*, 22 (2): 307–322.

Andrew H. Van de Ven. 1989. Using Paradox to Build Management and Organization Theories. *Academy of Management Review*, 14 (4): 562–578.

Welch, Lawrance S. and Reijo Luostarinen. 1988. Internationalization: Evolution of a Concept. *Journal of General Management*, 14 (2): 34–55.

Welch, Denice E. and Lawrance S. Welch. 1996. The Internationalization Process and Networks: A Strategic Management Perspective. *Journal of International Marketing*, 4 (3): 11–28.

Young, Steven. 1990. Internationalization: Introduction and Overview. *International Marketing Review*, 7 (4): 5–10.

3
Mode Configuration Diversity: A New Perspective on Foreign Entry Mode Choice

Bent Petersen, Gabriel R.G. Benito, Lawrence S. Welch, and Christian Geisler Asmussen

There is a large body of literature on modes of entry in foreign markets, with a focus on make-or-buy decisions (Melin, 1992; Sarkar and Cavusgil, 1996; Datta et al., 2002; Malhotra et al., 2003). By using different theories and a large number of contextual variables, entry mode researchers have been quite successful in making predictions regarding such choices. They have had a dual aim of both testing theory and predicting firms' choice of foreign market operation method given a number of characteristics of firms, products, industries, and home/host markets. However, researchers' quest for theory testing and predictive vigor has, especially in an empirical context, led to simplifying the mode choices made by entrant firms. The success in theory testing and entry mode prediction comes at a cost: namely, the sacrifice of subtleties in how firms structure foreign activities – including the opportunities for using multiple and constantly changing mode packages in a foreign market (Benito and Welch, 1994; Petersen and Welch, 2002; Benito et al., 2005).

The current suation in entry mode research is to some extent similar to the development of marketing channel research 20 years ago: in the 1980s, marketing channel researchers were disinclined to engage in studies going beyond the make-or-buy choice and acknowledge the observed make-*and*-buy arrangements (later on denominated as "dual distribution") as a fact-of-life business phenomenon of its own right.[1] The prime motive of marketing channel research at that time was to test the predictive power of transaction cost theory on simple market–hierarchy binary variables. In the same way, one might see the entry mode as being very much embedded in internalization theory (Buckley and Casson, 1976) – devoted to the task of explaining the existence of FDIs and thereby MNCs – rather than as a research area of its own with an aim to identify and explain the diversity and dynamics of foreign market business arrangements. In this chapter, rather than seeking simplicity (as expressed in crude make-or-buy or degree-of-control measures) we attempt to present a general, yet realistic, framework describing how firms may configure value activities in foreign markets. In this framework, simple make-or-buy and degree-of-control measures are replaced by mode *configurations*, that is, multiple governance forms attached to a broad range of value activities.[2]

With this aim in mind we have organized the chapter in the following way: in the next section we look at the characteristics of entry mode studies and their explanatory ability. We demonstrate an imbalance and overt contrast between, on the one side, a large and sophisticated set of independent, explanatory variables (such as transaction cost factors) and, on the other side, a simplification of dependent variables that constitutes the range of modes among which firms are supposed to choose from. In the third section we account for a generic framework of foreign market mode configuration in which the decomposition of firms' value chains is crucial. Thus, we argue that in order to describe foreign business activities it is essential not only to consider the value chains of entrant firms to their full extent, but also at a disaggregated level. This is in contrast to the focus on one, or a few, broadly defined value activities. In addition to the value-added activities, our mode configuration framework comprises two other dimensions: the *governance form* and the *location* of value-added activities. These two dimensions are analyzed in the fourth section. In the fifth section we put together the three dimensions in a mode configuration framework. In matrix form, it is evident that even with relatively few value-added activities, governance forms, and locations to be considered, the number of potential foreign market mode configurations is immense and the optimization task of entrant firm decision-makers accordingly complex. Mode configuration diversity is considered as a strategic factor and a number of research propositions in relation to this concept are formulated in sixth section. The seventh section contains a conclusion and discussion of some managerial implications.

Strengths and weaknesses of previous entry mode research

Despite the considerable attention devoted by IB researchers to the entry mode topic, it is questionable to what extent this has led us to a genuine understanding of how firms organize their foreign market activities. International business (IB) researchers have developed comprehensive models to predict decision-makers' degree-of-control/make-or-buy choices in international business, for example the choice between licensing arrangements and production subsidiaries. Drawing on market imperfection explanations (i.e., transaction cost theory, information economics, agency theory), environmental factors, global strategy factors, and the resource-based perspective, such models have enriched our understanding and predictive ability of foreign operation mode choices (Hill et al., 1990; Madhok, 1997;

Dunning, 2001). Over the last three decades the entry mode studies of IB researchers have identified a large number of factors that potentially have an impact on such choices. Table 3.1 provides an overview of empirical studies since 1970.[3]

The steadily growing number of explanatory factors has resulted in today's multifaceted entry mode models. However, in striking contrast to this range of "independent variables," the range of "dependent variables" – capturing the degree of control in terms of the foreign operation arrangement – has

Table 3.1 Overview of independent variables in entry mode research: number of studies 1970–2004

Variable	Explanation	70–79	80–89	90–99	00–04	Total
Entrant firm diversification	M&A skills	1	7	4	3	15
Host market growth/potential	Expected scale	1	5	7	3	16
Entrant firm R&D intensity	Transfer of specific assets; dissemination risk; market imperfection	1	5	5	9	20
Host country political stability/risk	Cost of commitment	1	4	11	3	19
Cultural distance	Cost of foreignness	1	4	9	6	20
Entrant firm advertising intensity	Reputation; market imperfection	1	4	4	5	14
Host country/market size	Scale	1	4	4	1	10
Host country FDI/trade barriers	Direct constraints	1	3	6	1	11
Entrant firm size	Managerial, financial resources; scale	1	2	13	10	26
Foreign experience/inter-nationalization	Establishment chain		5	17	10	32
Relative subsidiary size	Managerial, financial resources		4	3	3	10
Host country R&D intensity	Input sourcing motive		4			4

Table 3.1 (Continued)

Variable	Explanation	70–79	80–89	90–99	00–04	Total
Host country advertising intensity	Entry barriers		4			4
Host market concentration	Entry barriers		3	3	1	7
Competition from home	Oligopoly behavior		2	1	1	4
Asset specificity	Transfer of specific assets; dissemination risk; market imperfection		1	3	3	7
Entrant firm global integration	Oligopoly behavior; activity specialization		1	2	4	7
Geographic proximity	Cost of foreignness, transportation		1	2		3
Home industry R&D intensity	Transfer of specific assets; Dissemination risk; market imperfection		1	1	2	4
Home industry Marketing intensity	Reputation; market imperfection		1	1	1	3
Home country uncertainty avoidance	Preference for risk			3		3
Home country power distance	Preference for control			3		3
Demand uncertainty	Cost of commitment			2	2	4
Entrant firm quality/differentiation	Transfer of specific assets; Dissemination risk; market imperfection			1	3	4
Host country income/pop	Market demand			1		1
Home market growth					2	2

been surprisingly constant and limited over a substantial period. Hence, in most studies the dependent (categorical) variables are limited to just a few, and rather broad, categories of foreign operation arrangements, for example sole ventures (i.e., sales or production subsidiaries), joint ventures, licensing, franchising, and exporting via local distributors: see Table 3.2.

This imbalance in terms of the variance of the independent variables vis-à-vis the dependent variables may be explained by the abovementioned fact that most entry mode survey studies have had *theory testing* as their prime research motive. Entry mode research has its offspring in the theory of foreign direct investment (FDI), the aim of which is to explain the existence and growth of multinational enterprises (Buckley and Casson, 1976; Hennart, 1982). Entry mode research basically emerged due to the FDI theorists' need for testing the make-or-buy choice in an international setting: When would the hierarchical solution (i.e., making an FDI) be preferred to a market or contractual solution? The latter governance form alternatives would include licensing, franchising, and certain types of joint ventures (Anderson and Gatignon, 1986). As an example, the licensing arrangement has been treated as an alternative to FDI in the form of a wholly owned production subsidiary, the independent distributor as an alternative to FDI in the form of a sales subsidiary, and franchised outlets as alternatives to company-owned outlets. In numerous studies the dependent variables have either been (a) dichotomous, that is make-or-buy choices, such as wholly owned production subsidiary versus licensing; (b) multiple categories, for example wholly owned production subsidiary versus partly owned production subsidiary (equity-JV) versus licensing; or (c) some measure of the focal actor's degree of ownership (<50–100%) in a foreign venture. Hence, the standard procedure in entry mode survey studies does not capture the subtleties of structural arrangements in foreign markets.

Table 3.2 Overview of dependent variable in entry mode research: number of studies 1970–2004

Operation Mode	70–79	80–89	90–99	00–04	Total
Wholly owned sub.	1	14	25	17	57
Equity joint venture.	2	7	24	9	32
Ownership %.		2	1	1	4
Contractual Form.			5	2	7
– Licensing.		1	5	3	9
– Franchising.		1	4		5
– Distributors.		1		1	2
– Mgt service.			1		1
Export			6	4	10
Localization.			2		2

A large proportion of entry mode studies use secondary data on equity control in foreign markets, and even studies based on primary survey data usually ask the respondents to indicate a primary mode among a few entry modes predefined by the researcher (Petersen and Welch, 2002). Whereas the typical research designs of large-scale entry mode survey studies by and large exclude entry mode subtleties, entry mode *case* studies should not be subject to these restrictions. By asking managers open questions about foreign market arrangements, a few in-depth case studies have been able to capture considerable diversity in entry modes. As an example, in their study of the entry modes used by the Canadian pharmaceutical MNC, Upjohn, Fina and Rugman (1996) registered ten different company-defined foreign operation modes. Case studies of companies operating in foreign markets via management service agreements found that combinations of different modes, for example management contracts and joint ventures, were not uncommon (Sharma, 1983; Welch and Pacifico, 1990). Contractor (1981) and Luostarinen and Welch (1990) also observed mode combinations in relation to licensing associated with equity arrangements.

To sum up, the entry mode research using quantitative methods (survey studies) has been less geared to capture subtleties of firms' foreign market arrangements, because the researchers' aim of theory testing has required simplicity as to what to measure. Furthermore, past and present entry mode research may be seen as an extension – if not a by-product – of FDI theory, rather than as an independent research area.

The value activity as unit of analysis

Because theory testing has been their prime motive, entry mode researchers have had a natural preference for focusing on one single value activity at a time. Entry mode research grew out of FDI theory with its prime aim to explain "international production" (Dunning, 2001). Hence, the attention of researchers was originally drawn to value activities labeled as "production," "manufacturing," or "operations." In addition, the multinational corporation was traditionally defined as a company undertaking manufacturing or production in several foreign countries (Buckley and Casson, 1976). Although the focus on manufacturing has been relaxed over the years thereby giving way to broader MNC definitions associated with the exercise of "value added activities" in foreign countries (Vernon, 1974; Rugman, 1988), researchers have generally been reluctant to appreciate the different characteristics of value activities in terms of scale, scope, resource requirements, asset specificity, and so on and the governance form implications of these differences. In other words, the narrow focus on "production" has allowed for one-dimensional control constructs – the need for control is chiefly measured in relation to manufacturing activities – thereby disregarding different control needs in relation to other value chain activities.

Even though value activities other than "production" have successively been introduced into the sphere of entry mode research, this has been done in a rather partial way.

Marketing scholars have contrasted sales subsidiaries with local distributors (Anderson and Coughlan, 1987) and franchised outlets with company-owned (Fladmoe-Lindquist and Jacque, 1995), but have disregarded other value chain activities. Similarly, international management scholars have contrasted in-house management with management service agreements (Contractor and Kundu, 1998), and supply chain management scholars have contrasted in-house logistics with local, independent suppliers (Levy, 1997). IB scholars have typically not looked at the value chain *to its full extent* in terms of the organization of foreign operations. This is strange given that the issues of outsourcing and the definition of core competencies have had prominent roles in the strategic management literature for several years (e.g., Prahalad and Hamel, 1990; Quinn and Hilmer, 1994). It is, therefore, appropriate to consider the complexity of firms' arrangement of their foreign market activities. Managers make control decisions for *all* value-added activities – not only for one or a few. This is obvious in relation to formulation of outsourcing strategies of firms (see, e.g., Reve, 1990; Quinn and Hilmer, 1994), but should be equally evident in relation to market entry strategies.

In a similar vein, we would expect managers to make decisions about *governance form* (including the appropriate degree of control) and *international location* in relation to each identifiable value activity of the firm. In other words, we take the individual value activity as the level of analysis in relation to firms' organization of their international activities. Thereby, we implicitly assume that at least some decision-makers are able to distinguish different value activities in terms of their optimal location and governance form. Although the individual value activity is taken as the unit of analysis, this does by no means imply that all decision-makers consider the same range or number of value activities in terms of optimal location and governance form. As we shall discuss later, the differentiation of value activities by location and governance form only makes economic sense if two preconditions are fulfilled: first, the individual value activity has to exceed a certain minimum economic scale in order to make it identifiable and independently amenable for benchmarking against market providers.[4] Hence, decision-makers of small firms may only know the economies of a few value activities whereas large MNC decision-makers may know many more. Second, the value activities should differ substantially in terms of optimal location and governance form, as per Porter's definition of value chain activities as business activities of significantly different economies (Porter, 1985).

Altogether, the different value activities constitute the value chain of the firm (Porter, 1985). Porter's value chain consists of nine business functions (five primary and four supporting business functions). According to Porter the categories of value activities are generic, that is valid across industries, but as pointed out by Stabell and Fjeldstad (1998), this may be a questionable claim. Porter's value chain fits a traditional manufacturing firm characterized by a long-linked (Thompson, 1967) or sequential, physical flow of raw materials, intermediary goods, and finished goods, but it is a poor description of non-manufacturing firms. For example, Varley and Rafiq (2004) modify Porter's value chain to apply to retailing firms. As significantly different alternatives to Porter's value chain, Stabell and Fjeldstad (1998) introduced two alternative value creation logics: the value *shop* and the value *network*. These value creation logics (or frameworks) were developed to describe the activities of service firms such as consulting firms and banks, respectively. In contrast to Porter's value chain, the primary activities of the value shop and the value network are non-sequential (e.g., cyclical or reciprocal). Still, the supporting activities are almost identical to those in the value chain.

Porter (1985: 35) makes a further distinction between business *functions* and business *activities*. "Marketing," as an example, is a business function that comprises various activities such as market analyses, sales calls, sales force training, after sales service, product modification, and so forth. These activities may differ substantially in terms of economics, resource requirements, strategic importance, asset specificity, and so on. The different economies and strategic characteristics translate into a need for different governance forms and locations. As pointed out earlier, whether or not this differentiation should be carried out depends on the economic scale of the activities. Conversely, even though the optimal governance form and location differ significantly among the value activities, the firm may be better off with only one, common governance form and location; either because the activities are inseparable in terms of factor inputs, and/or because the scales of the various activities are too small to justify the sunk costs of establishing separate governance forms and the costs of relocating activities.

To conclude, one should not expect to identify a generic, all-encompassing value creation logic that adequately applies to all entrant firms. Instead, one must define a value creation logic for the specific business sector (manufacturing, financial services, retailing, etc.) to which the focal entrant firms belong. Depending on the scale by which these activities are carried out by the individual entrant firm, the sector-specific value creation logic may yield more or less value activities, and for each of these the entrant firm has two basic choices: location and governance form. In the next section we analyze these two dimensions.

Location and governance forms

Location

The simplest basis for "location" is the distinction between home and host country (Hirsch, 1976). This is reflected in the export–localization dichotomy. When using this dichotomy we implicitly assume that third country value activities do not take place; in other words, only one focal, foreign country is considered in addition to the home country. This is an acceptable assumption to make when the underlying motive of the entry is market seeking, that is the generation of sales revenue in a particular market. The individual country may also be given when sourcing motives are involved – be it resource seeking, efficiency seeking, or strategic asset seeking (Dunning, 1993). In these cases, we assume that the localization advantages have been identified. However, in the special case of a strategy of a *concentrated* (Porter, 1986) or *global* (Yip, 1989) value chain configuration, the value chain of the MNC is geographically dispersed, but the *individual* value activity is carried out in one country only. As a consequence, the mode configuration takes place for individual value activities on the corporate level rather than the country level. We will come back to the distinction between local sales versus global sourcing motives and the implications thereof in the discussion of governance forms.

Governance form

As regards governance form (or, organizational form) the simplest framework is, like location, binary – namely, market versus hierarchy (Williamson, 1975; Buckley and Casson, 1976), or hybrid (contractual) versus market or hierarchy (Williamson, 1991). Occasionally, entry mode researchers have used market contracts and hierarchies as two opposite poles stretching a continuum of ownership control – where the proportion of equity held in the foreign market is the dependent variable. The more equity held by the entrant firm, the closer to the hierarchical form of maximum control (see, e.g., Gatignon and Anderson, 1988). Phrasing it in terms of scales of measurement this corresponds to the use of an interval or ordinal scale. However, in the following discussion we will associate modes of entry with points on a *nominal* scale, that is entry modes are defined as groups or classes. In other words, we define the various modes as categorical variables. By the same token, we do not attach a pre-specified degree of control to the various modes. What we do need for our configuration framework is a generic set of mode categories – "generic" in the sense that they apply across, and independently of, value activities and location. Hence, a "sales subsidiary" and a "franchise contract" are not value chain *generic* since they both relate to sales and marketing activities specifically. Moreover, the sales subsidiary relates to a specific location as well, namely, the host country. Similarly, "export" does not qualify as a generic governance form either, since it specifically relates to a home country location. In the same vein, the standard tripartite categorization – export entry modes *versus* contractual entry modes *versus* investment entry modes (Root, 1987) – is also a mix of location and governance form.

Our point of departure is to distinguish between the following four classes or categories of basic governance forms: (1) market or arm's length exchange, (2) equity sole venture, (3) equity joint venture, and (4) non-equity agreements (including non-equity strategic alliances).[5] The four generic governance forms have similarities, as well as dissimilarities, with conventional entry mode taxonomies: as an example, Hill (2007), in his widely used textbook, lists six entry modes that an entrant firm may choose among: (i) exporting, (ii) turnkey projects, (iii) licensing, (iv) franchising, (v) joint ventures with local partner(s), and (vi) wholly owned subsidiary. If we for a moment ignore the inherent implications of localization and specific value activities in the entry modes listed by Hill, the correspondence is quite evident: (i) and (vi) are equivalent to 2 (sole ventures), (v) is equivalent to 3, and (ii), (iii), and (iv) fall in the category of 4 (non-equity agreements). However, several well-known, non-equity contractual arrangements, such as management service agreements and outsourcing contracts, are not included in Hill's presentation.

Analyzing non-equity agreements

The numerous, different contractual forms that have been examined by entry mode researchers provoke a question of how reasonable it is to consider these as basically being one and the same governance form? Is it reasonable to consider a firm's international outsourcing contract, such as a manufacturing contract, as representing the same governance form as a management service agreement (i.e., an insourcing contract)? Or, does the governance form differ as to whether the entrant firm is sourcing or licensing out? In fact, it is reasonable to assume that these contracts are fundamentally different, so we will seek out a sub-categorization of non-equity agreements on the basis of the following two explicit requirements: (1) it should be relatively easy to fit in the various conventional, contractual investment modes mentioned above, and (2) the classification should consist of distinctly different sub-categories, and not only be different in terms of degree, as per our earlier definition of "modes" as categorical variables.

The literature offers a number of market contract classifications that are distinguished in terms of the *contract format*. Among others: contract length (see, e.g., Quinn and Hilmer, 1994), degree of contract formalization (e.g., Macauley, 1963), and degree of contract completeness and enforceability (Williamson, 1985). However, these contract classifications do not fulfill the latter requirement, since they differ in terms of degree and not qualitatively by distinct differences.

Another stream of literature is occupied with the different *property rights* of the contract parties. Hence, Grossman and Hart (1986) distinguish the contract parties as to their residual rights (or, control) and associated income of the assets governed by the contract.[6] The essential distinction is made between contract parties with pre-specified rights and parties with residual rights to the return of assets. However, we find it difficult to fit conventional, contractual investment modes in the residual claimant framework because in most cases assets of both parties are involved in the contract.

As an example, a franchising contract may involve property rights and management know-how assets of one party (the franchisor) and physical assets of the other (the franchisee). Hence, both parties will have specified as well as residual rights, and royalty payments – a standard ingredient in franchise contracts – reflect this residual return ambiguity quite well. The ambiguity in terms of establishing which of the contract parties is the residual claimant has been pointed out by Hart (1995): some contracts will be characterized by both parties being residual claimants.

Jensen and Meckling (1976) offer an alternative to the Grossman and Hart framework by distinguishing principals and agents as to which of the parties is choosing and designing the contract, and which is acting on behalf of the other – the principal and agent, respectively. We find this principal–agent distinction to be more suitable to distinguish the conventional, contractual investment modes. In most cases, it is unproblematic to establish if the focal entrant firm is the contractor or the contractee, that is whether or not the entrant firm appears as the principal, offering a contract to a local operator – an "agent" – to act on behalf of the entrant firm. This is obviously the case when the entrant firm outsources activities to a local, offshore operator and the entrant firm also appears as the principal in the case of an overseas licensing out operation. Following resource-based theory (Rumelt, 1984; Itami, 1987), we can consolidate the framework by specifying which types of assets the principal and agent possess. The principal possesses primarily brands, patents, and other ownership rights that altogether assign the principal the role as an "owner." In contrast, the agent possesses assets in the form of local networks, skills, knowledge, scale and scope, and access to low-cost production factors – assets that define the agent as being a "doer." As noted already, the relationship is governed by a contract, which is chosen and designed by the principal. Subsequently, the agent decides whether to accept the contract or not. Even though an international franchisor may provide some services to the franchisee that, strictly speaking, assigns the franchisor the role as an agent, it is usually easy to establish which one of the two contract parties that offered the contract in the first place and thereby appears as being the principal. A similar argument can be applied in relation to identifying which one of the contract parties is the "owner" and which one is the "doer." In general, franchisors own the assets that are crucial to the franchise – such as trademarks – but perform occasionally as agents in the relationship, for example as provider of stock replenishing computer services. Unless we are talking about special reciprocity contracts, such as cross-licensing, our contention is that it is relatively unproblematic in an entry mode context to identify which of the two contract parties is the principal/owner and which one the agent/doer.

In addition to the principal/owner *versus* agent/doer distinction it is useful to distinguish between contract investment modes on the basis of the *underlying motive* of the entrant firm. More specifically, we distinguish contractual investment modes as to whether the underlying motive of the entrant firm is – on the one hand – foreign market seeking ("selling") or – on the other hand – global sourcing. Market-seeking entrant firms want to generate sales in the foreign market and the optimal entry mode choice is the one that gets access to the local customers in the most cost-effective way. The sourcing motive of entrant firms may apply to different needs for assets; again, using Dunning's (1993) distinction, firms search for natural resources, efficiency, and strategic assets. Hence, firms' outsourcing of IT services is clearly driven by global sourcing motives (efficiency and strategic asset seeking), while it is sales generation that drives entrant firms to insource management services in a foreign market. Likewise, when firms license out production know-how to foreign operators the motive to do so is selling, whereas sourcing motives apply when firms become licensees in foreign markets.

The identification of the two discriminating factors – the underlying entry motive and the principal-*versus*-agent role – results in four, distinctively different sub-categories of contracts, as presented in Figure 3.1.

The principal/agent *cum* owner/doer distinction applies specifically, and exclusively, to contractual investment modes. Conversely, the entry motive distinction applies just as well to the other generic governance forms, say, sole ventures, joint ventures, and market exchanges. For example, it would hardly make sense to consider joint ventures motivated by sourcing as a governance form that is different from sales-oriented joint ventures. Nevertheless, we still see the entry motive distinction as vital for a genuine understanding of the mode choice of entrant firms. Therefore, it would make sense to present and exemplify mode configurations in two versions: one in the context of foreign market entry motivated by international sourcing, that

UNDERLYING MOTIVE of entrant firm ▶ *ASSET CHARACTERISTICS.& P/A role of entrant firm ▼*	**SOURCING** (Resource, efficiency, and strategic asset seeking)	**SELLING** (Market access/seeking)
"OWNER"/PRINCIPAL (Contracting out)	***Outsourcing*** e.g.: Outsourcing to a contract manufacturer or an IT operator in a foreign country	***Licensing out*** e.g.: Being licensor or franchisor of a foreign country operator
"DOER"/AGENT (Contracting in)	***Licensing in*** e.g.: Being licensee or franchisee in a foreign country	***Insourcing*** e.g.: Carrying out a turnkey project in a foreign country or being a management contractee

Figure 3.1   Sub-categorization of contractual investment modes

is *inward* internationalization, and one in the context of selling motives, that is *outward* internationalization (Welch and Luostarinen, 1988; Beamish et al., 2003). However, due to limited space we will not do so in this chapter, but only give one example of mode configuration that mixes the two motives (see the next section).

The conclusion of our discussion of sub-categorization of contractual investment modes is that we consider it imperative to distinguish between at least two forms of contractual governance forms depending on whether the entrant firm appears as owner/principal or doer/agent. The obvious terms for the two different contractual modes are *contracting out* and *contracting in*, respectively.[7]

To sum up, we have identified the following five governance forms: (1) market or arm's length exchange, (2) equity sole venture, (3) equity joint venture, (4) contracting out, and (5) contracting in.[8] Together with the localization and value chain dimensions these governance forms constitute the components of our mode configuration framework. In the next section we will outline the mode configuration framework based on the previous discussion of value activities, location, and governance forms and discuss its implications to management decision.

Formalization of the mode configuration framework

Formally, the foreign operation mode configuration of a given firm at any point in time can be captured by the matrix $\mathbf{M} = [m_{ij}]$, where $i = 1 \ldots I$ indexes the I countries in which the firm operates and $j = 1 \ldots J$ indexes J activities in the value chain. Each cell or element in the matrix is a categorical variable describing whether, and by which governance form, the given value activity is performed in the given country. An example of a foreign operation mode configuration is presented in Figure 3.2.

The hypothetical company in Figure 3.2 has four activities in its value chain and operates in six countries, of which Denmark is assumed to be the home country. The Danish parent company conducts R&D and exports the results of this R&D, in the form of blueprints and product designs, to Poland. The Polish subsidiary, established due to sourcing advantages such as the access to qualified and inexpensive labor, is an off-shoring operation that manufactures the product and exports it back to Denmark and to some of the other countries. Hence, there are no downstream activities in the Polish market.

The Swedish wholly owned sales subsidiary imports R&D and manufacturing activities, encapsulated in physical products, handles sales itself, and contracts out services to a particularly effective local service provider. There are no owned operations in the United Kingdom, but the firm exports to independent distributors there. The United States is too distant a market to be supplied by Polish production, which is why the entire value chain except

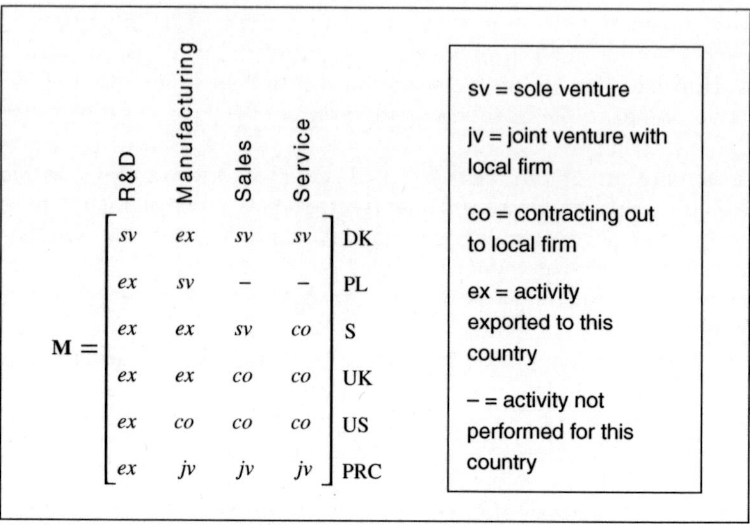

Figure 3.2   An example of foreign operation mode configuration

R&D is replicated there and handled by an independent contractee. Finally, to gain access to the Chinese market the company is required to form a joint venture with a local firm.

The configuration matrix shows that we can discuss the organization of foreign operation modes on different levels of aggregation. This important point should be kept in mind as it has implications for our unit of analysis.

- *Activity level*: On the most detailed level, configuration is about how a specific value activity is performed in a specific country, as measured by each individual element in the matrix, m_{ij}. For instance, the decision to contract out service activities in Sweden is an activity-level decision. However, this is the level to which the preceding governance/location discussion refers.
- *Country level*: The country-level configuration of activities is closest to the operation mode concept used in the extant IB literature. In our model, however, a country-level operation mode is not one, but a *vector* $m_i = (m_{i1}, m_{i2}, \ldots, m_{ij})$ of activity-level decisions. The decision to contract out everything but R&D in the US market is an example of a country-level decision. Internationalization driven by market-seeking motives often consists of a series of country-level decisions.
- *Corporate level*: On the highest level, the foreign operation mode configuration of the firm is the entire matrix **M**. Designing this matrix encompasses all activity-level and country-level decisions. Internationalization driven by sourcing motives (i.e., inward internationalization) typically requires the firm to work with this level. For instance, the

Polish offshoring operation presumably replaces manufacturing in other countries (most likely Denmark) and so the operation mode chosen here has an impact on the entire mode configuration matrix.

The mode configuration matrix is reminiscent of Porter's (1986) global activity configuration grid. However, where Porter's grid describes only the localization of value activities, this matrix goes one step further to include the governance form of each value activity as well.

Compared to the entry mode literature, the main contribution of the matrix is the fact that it explicitly incorporates a value chain distinction into traditional entry mode taxonomies. Most studies in the empirical literature either do not make this distinction – effectively averaging the operation mode over the entire value chain – or implicitly target only a part of the value chain, such as manufacturing or sales. Besides making it difficult to compare the findings, as different studies measure different operational constructs, traditional taxonomies result in a very coarse-grained classification. Thus, most empirical studies have only between two and six operation modes, while even the crude example in Figure 3.2 can potentially distinguish between $5^4 = 625$ different operation mode vectors in each country (assuming six options for each activity, including the option to import the activity); and this numerical example refers to a unified company with only one product group. Customer segmentation and product diversity may multiply the number of potential operation mode vectors.

To find the optimal mode configuration among the almost countless possibilities is a daunting managerial challenge in which the importance of bounded rationality and cognitive limitations become clear. Even with restrictive assumptions (few value activities, few control/governance forms, and few location alternatives) the calculation of an optimal mode *location* configuration has been demonstrated to be quite complicated (Buckley and Hashai, 2004). Since the potential mode combinations are close to endless, corporate managers should approach international strategy with an open mind rather than confine themselves to the generic textbook internationalization modes. In our example, with 625 options in each country and six countries we get a total of $625^6 = 60$ million billion (!) different ways in which that particular firm could configure its international operations.[9] Of course, we should expect corporate managers to narrow these options down considerably as many of them will be redundant, use various rules of thumb, and/or delegate decisions to divisional units (see, e.g., Larimo, 1995).

The example also illuminates the numerous options entrant firm managers have of introducing different governance forms not only on a global scale, but also on a country level. As such, the mode configuration *diversity* of entrant firms may be a potentially important strategic factor. In the next section, we will elaborate on this diversity aspect and derive a number of research propositions.

Research propositions

As our mode configuration approach points out, optimal locations and governance forms may differ considerably among the value activities of a firm. Presumably, the number of separable value activities that decision-makers can assess as to their contractual arrangement feasibility – and thus benchmark against the market – is to large extent contingent on the scale of the individual value activities. As an echo of Adam Smith's theorem that "the division of labour is limited by the extent of the market," we would expect the number of different governance forms used by (entrant) firms to be limited by the scale of the individual value activities. If a decision-maker is unable to differentiate the value activities in terms of scale and scope economies, asset specificity, and other economic characteristics – perhaps because the value activities are exercised by shared, indivisible production inputs – there is no real basis for introducing different governance forms and locations. Furthermore, the introduction of separate governance forms and locations has to be economically justified by the cost savings or revenue gains of the value activities that result from allotting them special locations and/or governance forms of their own. Again, scale matters. We will consider the size of the entrant firm as well as the size of the entered foreign market to be reasonable proxies for the scale of value activities. Accordingly, we would expect mode configuration *diversity* of international firms to be relatively low for small firms operating in small, foreign markets, and vice versa. The lowest degree of mode configuration diversity would be one and the same location and governance form for all value activities. As an example, all the activities of a small, Danish dot.com firm, serving customers in Luxembourg, may be exercised as in-house activities (sole ventures) from its home country. Conversely, a high degree of mode configuration diversity may be observed in a large Swedish multinational company serving its US customers through sole ventures in the United States and Sweden as well as via local joint ventures and contracting out operations.

Accordingly, on the level of analysis of the individual foreign country we can formulate the following two propositions relating to mode configuration diversity:

P1: *The mode configuration diversity in relation to a specific, foreign market increases with the size of the entrant firm.*
P2: *The mode configuration diversity in relation to a specific, foreign market increases with the size of the foreign market.*

Mode configuration diversity may also relate to the corporate level, that is mode configuration diversity of an MNC for foreign countries as a whole. On this level of analysis we expect mode configuration diversity to differ among international firms depending on their international strategy, that is, whether the firms are pursuing global or multi-domestic strategies (see, e.g., Bartlett and Ghoshal, 1989). A global strategy implication is the integration and standardization of business activities – including governance structures of various value activities – across country borders in order to achieve global scale economies and synergies. In contrast, a multi-domestic strategy permits greater autonomy to the local affiliates and one may expect a larger variety throughout the corporation as to how business activities are conducted – including the choice of governance structures of different value activities. On this background we formulate the following proposition:

P3: *All else being equal, mode configuration diversity of MNCs following a multi-domestic strategy is higher than among MNCs subscribing to a global strategy.*

Since we would expect some decision-makers of international firms to be hampered by path dependence (Nelson and Winter, 1982) or administrative heritage (Bartlett and Ghoshal, 1989), these firms forsake cost savings and income opportunities associated with a diversified foreign market mode configuration. As an example, some firms will stick to in-house, home-based operations and forsake potential cost savings associated with offshore outsourcing. On the other hand, mode configuration diversity can also be exaggerated; for example, the scale of the value activities may not justify the transaction costs associated with outsourcing an operation to an operator in a foreign country. In other words, the firm would be better off, in terms of profitability, by sticking to in-house/sole venture operations in the foreign country. Hence,

P4: *Above a certain minimum scale of value activities higher mode configuration diversity yields better foreign market performance.*

Conclusion and managerial implications

Mode choice can be an extremely complex managerial decision in international business. The entry mode literature has demonstrated with increasing theoretical and empirical sophistication that a large number of factors influence firms' entry mode choices. In contrast, the presentation of modes of entry among which managers choose tends to be oversimplified. Hence, only a handful of entry modes are considered and often the mode choice is presented as a make-*or*-buy choice disregarding possibilities of make-*and*-buy arrangements, that is the occurrence of more than one governance form in a foreign market. Because theory testing, and in particular testing of FDI theory, has been the general concern of entry mode research, simplicity at the expense of subtlety, and – to some extent – reality, has ruled. An advancement of entry mode research from positive to normative theory requires developing frameworks that are able to capture the many nuances and subtleties of mode choices. The difference between competitive advantage and disadvantage of an international firm may well lie in the ability of decision-makers to identify optimal governance forms and locations for *all* value activities, and not only for one major activity, such as manufacturing. In that respect, the extant entry mode research can hardly claim to have provided much guidance to managers of international firms.

The mode configuration framework outlined in this chapter holds the potential of capturing – in a systematic way – the mode choice opportunities of firms *to their full extent*. Although the number of potential mode configurations may be incredibly high, the three dimensions making up the mode configuration framework – value activity, location, and governance form – are themselves relatively simple and, to some extent, generic. In international business, as well as in other economic disciplines, it is easy to point out the complexity of the real world, including how complicated the environments of managers are, in contrast to the simplicity of researchers' empirical models. Our intention in this chapter has been to go beyond just pointing out the complexity of mode choices: the presented mode configuration framework should be seen as a practical instrument for analyzing this complexity in a manageable way.

Since firm size and market size tend to change over a period of time, the scale of the individual value activities will change accordingly. As a consequence, firms' mode configurations need to be adjusted from time to time. Multinational firms conducting large operations in foreign markets may adjust their mode configuration almost on a daily basis. The various value activities have to be trimmed in terms of governance forms and locations. Previous mode research has indicated that mode change is a common phenomenon in international business (Calof and Beamish, 1995; Clark et al., 1997; Pedersen et al., 2002; Benito et al., 2005). Our mode configuration framework makes it evident that there exists a pressing need for a dynamic approach to firms' mode choice. As such, mode *re*-configuration constitutes a challenging field for entry mode researchers.

Notes

1. According to informal information given by the marketing scholar, George John, the first dual distribution study (Dutta et al., 1995) was made several years after the first observations of dual distribution practices. However, the distribution channel studies in the late 1970s and early 1980s were designed with the aim of testing make-or-buy hypotheses derived from the – at that time – newly introduced transaction cost theory. The many observations of make-*and*-buy arrangements reported by respondents (US manufacturing firms in, e.g., the electronics equipment industry) were basically ignored inasmuch as they were classified as misconceived, and therefore unusable, replies.

2. The term "configuration" refers to the structural arrangement or assembly of parts of a system. The term has been widely used in astronomy (the relative positions of planets and stars), chemistry (the spatial arrangement of atoms in a molecule), and computer science (the several items of hardware making up a computing system). In the business/management literature, the term has in particular been used within contingency theory: to designate different combinations of contingency and response variables. Irrespective of the science or discipline in which the term "configuration" is used, it is related to relatively complex structural arrangements.

3. The table uses the references from Datta et al. (2002). Since their extensive review is delimited to foreign market entry either *from* or *into* the United States, a search on typical keywords was made in various article databases in order to further identify non-US studies. Also, the references of these studies were reviewed. The procedure resulted in 18 empirical studies with non-US data, which was added to the references from Datta et al. (2002) for a total resulting sample of 59 studies. A list of independent and dependent variables was then compiled for each study, and these variables were sorted according to the number of studies in which they were included.

4. In this discussion we focus on scale exclusively and ignore other factors that potentially determine whether or not the value activities of a company are separable. Porter (1985), as an example, argues that the existence of "linkages" between value chain activities is central to a genuine understanding of how companies organize their value chains. Also, Simon (1969) claims "interdependencies" to be pertinent to any division of labor within organizations, and as an elaboration of Simon, Mintzberg (1983) highlights interdependencies in terms of work-flow, process, and social relationships as criteria (other than economies of scale) for delegating tasks to independent units within an organization or a business network.

5. It is interesting to note that these four basic governance forms are mutually exclusive – with one important exception: a non-equity agreement (= contractual entry mode) may very well go along with an equity joint venture. As mentioned earlier there is ample empirical evidence of international contracts being combined with (minority) equity investments (Contractor, 1981; Sharma, 1983; Luostarinen and Welch, 1990; Welch and Pacifico, 1990; Clark et al., 1997). This means that multiple governance forms in one and the same foreign market are feasible even for distinct value activities at distinct foreign locations. Hence, multiple governance forms also appear as a result of entrant firms introducing different governance forms to separate value chain activities.

6. As pointed out by Hart (1988), decision rights and income rights may sometimes be held by *separate* parties. However, this separation is not essential for our argumentation and therefore not elaborated on.

7. The "in/out" terminology has for several years been part of entry mode researchers' vocabulary – thus, the terms outsourcing and licensing out and the inverse terms, insourcing and licensing in.

8. In order to present *mutually exclusive* governance forms that qualify as categorical variables we should actually add two more governance forms: (6) contracting out in combination with equity joint venture, and (7) contracting in combined with an equity joint venture.

9. This numerical example is referring to a unified company with only one product group defining the value chain (Porter, 1985). However, one could relax this simplification and consider a company characterized by multiple product groups (Petersen and Welch, 2002), multiple customer segments (Valla, 1986), as well as

different types of partners (Beamish et al., 2003). This would add three other dimensions to the configuration. Needless to say, if differentiation along product groups, customer segments, and partner types are added as choice variables the number of possible configurations increases significantly.

References

Anderson, E. and Coughlan, A.T. (1987). International Market Entry and Expansion via Independent or Integrated Channels of Distribution. *Journal of Marketing, 51*(1): 71–82.

Anderson, E. and Gatignon, H.A. (1986). Modes of Foreign Entry: A Transaction Cost Analysis and Propositions. *Journal of International Business Studies, 17*(3): 1–26.

Bartlett, C.A. and Ghoshal, S. (1989). *Transnational Management: Text, Cases and Readings in Cross-Border Management.* Boston: Irwin McGraw-Hill.

Beamish, P.W., Morrison, A.J., Inkpen, A.C., and Rosenzweig, P.M. (2003). *International Management* (5th edn). Boston, MA: McGraw-Hill.

Benito, G.R.G., Pedersen, T., and Petersen, B. (2005). Export Channel Dynamics: An Empirical Analysis. *Managerial and Decision Economics, 26*: 159–173.

Benito, G.R.G. and Welch, L.S. (1994). Foreign Market Servicing: Beyond Choice of Entry Mode. *Journal of International Marketing, 2*(2): 7–27.

Buckley, P.J. and Casson, M.C. (1976). *The Future of the Multinational Enterprise.* London: Macmillan.

Buckley, P.J. and Hashai, N. (2004). A Global System View of Firm Boundaries. *Journal of International Business Studies, 35*(1): 33–45.

Calof, J.L. and Beamish, P.W. (1995). Adapting to Foreign Markets: Explaining Internationalization. *International Business Review, 4*(2): 115–131.

Clark, T., Pugh, D.S., and Mallory, G. (1997). The Process of Internationalisation in the Operating Firm. *International Business Review, 6*(6): 605–623.

Contractor, F.J. (1981). The Role of Licensing in International Strategy. *Columbia Journal of World Business, 16*(Winter): 73–83.

Contractor, F.J. and Kundu, S.K. (1998). Modal Choice in a World of Alliances: Analyzing Organizational Forms in the International Hotel Sector. *Journal of International Business Studies, 29*(2): 325–357.

Datta, D.K., Herrmann, P., and Rasheed, A.A. (2002). Choice of Foreign Market Entry Modes: Critical Review and Future Directions. *Advances in International Management, 14*: 85–153.

Dunning, J.H. (1993). *Multinational Enterprises and the Global Economy.* Wokingham, England and Reading, Mass.: Addison Wesley.

Dunning, J.H. (2001). The Key Literature on IB activities: 1960–2000. In A.M. Rugman and A. Verbeke (eds), *The Oxford Handbook of International Business.* Oxford: Oxford University Press, pp. 36–68.

Dutta, S., Bergen, M., Heide, J.B., and John, G. (1995). Understanding Dual Distribution: The Case of Reps and House Accounts. *The Journal of Law, Economics & Organization, 11*(1): 189–204.

Fina, E. and Rugman, A.M. (1996). A Test of Internalization Theory and Internationalization Theory: The Upjohn Company. *Management International Review, 36*(3): 199–213.

Fladmoe-Lindquist, K. and Jacque, L.L. (1995). Control Modes in International Service Operations: The Propensity to Franchise. *Management Science, 41*(7): 1238–1249.

Gatignon, H. and Anderson, E. (1988). The Multinational Corporation's Degree of Control Over Foreign Subsidiaries: An Empirical Test of a Transaction Cost Explanation, *Journal of Law, Economics and Organization, 4*(2): 305–336.

Grossman, S.J. and Hart, O.D. (1986). The Costs and Benefits of Ownership: A Theory of Vertical and Lateral Integration. *Journal of Political Economy, 94*(4): 691–719.

Hart, O. (1988). Incomplete Contracts and the Theory of the Firm. *Journal of Law, Economics and Organization, 4*: 119–139.

Hart, O. (1995). *Firms, Contracts, and Financial Structure.* Oxford, UK: Oxford University Press.

Hennart, J.-F. (1982). *A Theory of Multinational Enterprise.* Ann Arbor, MI: The University of Michigan Press.

Hill, C.W.L. (2007). *International Business: Competing in the Global Marketplace* (6th edn). Boston: Irwin McGraw-Hill.

Hill, C.W.L., Hwang, P., and Kim, W.C. (1990). An Eclectic Theory of the Choice of International Entry Mode. *Strategic Management Journal, 11*: 117–128.

Hirsch, S. (1976). An International Trade and Investment Theory of the Firm. *Oxford Economic Papers, 28*: 258–270.

Itami, H. (1987). *Mobilizing Invisible Assets.* Cambridge: Harvard University Press.

Jensen, M.C. and Meckling, W.H. (1976). Theory of the Firm: Managerial Behaviour, Agency Costs and Ownership Structure. *Journal of Financial Economics, 3*: 305–360.

Larimo, J. (1995). The Foreign Direct Investment Decision Process: Case Studies of Different Types of Decision Processes in Finnish Firms. *Journal of Business Research, 33*(1): 25–55.

Levy, D.L. (1997). Lean Production in an International Supply Chain. *Sloan Management Review, 38*(2): 94–102.

Luostarinen, R. and Welch, L.S. (1990). *International Business Operations.* Helsinki, Finland: Helsinki School of Economics.

Macauley, S. (1963). Non-Contractual Relations in Business: A Preliminary Review. *American Sociology Review, 28*: 55–67.

Madhok, A. (1997). Cost, Value and Foreign Market Entry Mode: The Transaction and the Firm. *Strategic Management Journal, 18*(1): 39–61.

Malhotra, N.K., Agarwal, J., and Ulgado, F.M. (2003). Internationalization and Entry Modes: A Multitheoretical Framework and Research Propositions. *Journal of International Marketing, 11*(4): 1–31.

Melin, L. (1992). Internationalization as a Strategy Process. *Strategic Management Journal, 13*: 99–118.

Mintzberg, H. (1983). *Structures in Five – Designing Effective Organizations.* Englewood Cliffs, NJ: Prentice-Hall.

Nelson, R.R. and Winter, S.G. (1982). *An Evolutionary Theory of Economic Change.* Cambridge, Mass.: Belknap Press of Harvard University Press.

Pedersen, T., Benito, G.R.G., and Petersen, B. (2002). Foreign Operation Method Change: Impetus and Switching Costs. *International Business Review, 11*(3): 325–345.

Petersen, B. and Welch, L.S. (2002). Foreign Operation Mode Combinations and Internationalization. *Journal of Business Research, 55*(2): 157–162.

Porter, M.E. (1985). *Competitive Advantage.* New York, NY: Free Press.

Porter, M.E. (1986). Competition in Global Industries: A Conceptual Framework. In Michael, E. Porter (ed.), *Competition in Global Industries.* Harvard Business School Press.

Prahalad, C.K. and Hamel, G. (1990). The Core Competence of the Corporation. *Harvard Business Review, 68*(3): 79–91.

Quinn, J.B. and Hilmer, F.G. (1994). Strategic Outsourcing. *Sloan Management Review*, *35*(4): 43–55.

Reve, T. (1990). The Firm as a Nexus of Internal and External Contracts. In M. Aoki, B. Gustafsson, and O.E. Williamson (eds), *The Firm as a Nexus of Treaties*. London: Sage Publications.

Root, F.R. (1987). *Entry Strategies for International Markets*. Lexington, MA: Lexington Books.

Rugman, A.M. (1988). The Multinational Enterprise. In I. Walter and T. Murray (eds), *Handbook of International Management*. NY: Wiley, pp. 93–115.

Rumelt, R.P. (1984). Towards a Strategic Theory of the Firm. In B. Lamb (ed.), *Competitive Strategic Management*. Englewood Cliffs, NJ: Prentice-Hall, pp. 556–570.

Sarkar, M. and Cavusgil, S.T. (1996). Trends in International Business Thought and Literature: A Review of International Market Entry Mode Research: Integration and Synthesis. *The International Executive*, *38*(6): 825–847.

Sharma, D.D. (1983). Management Contracts and Internationalization: An Interaction Perspective. In L. Engwall and J. Johanson (eds), *Some Aspects of Control in International Business*. Stockholm: Almqvist and Wiksell, pp. 73–82.

Simon, H.A. (1969). *Science of the Artificial*. Cambridge, Mass.: The M.I.T. Press.

Stabell, C.B. and Fjeldstad, Ø.D. (1998). Configuring Value for Competitive Advantage: on Chains, Shops, and Networks. *Strategic Management Journal*, *19*: 413–437.

Thompson, J.D. (1967). *Organizations in Action*. New York: McGraw-Hill.

Valla, J.-P. (1986). The French Approach to Europe. In P.W. Turnbull and J.P. Valla (eds), *Strategies for International Industrial Marketing*. London: Crom Helm, pp. 11–41.

Varley, R. and Rafiq, M. (2004). *Principles of Retail Management*. New York: Palgrave Macmillan.

Vernon, R. (1974). Multinational Enterprises: Performance and Accountability. In J. Backman and E. Bloch (eds), *Multinational Corporations, Trade and the Dollar*. New York: New York University Press, pp. 65–86.

Welch, L.S. and Luostarinen, R. (1988). Internationalization: Evolution of a Concept. *Journal of General Management*, *14*(2): 34–57.

Welch, L.S. and Pacifico, A. (1990). Management Contracts: A Role in Internationalization. *International Marketing Review*, *7*(4): 64–74.

Williamson, O.E. (1975). *Markets and Hierarchies. Analysis and Antitrust Implications*. New York: Free Press.

Williamson, O.E. (1985). *The Economic Institutions of Capitalism. Firms, Markets, Relational Contracting*. New York: Free Press.

Williamson, O.E. (1991). Comparative Economic Organization: The Analysis of Discrete Structural Alternatives. *Administrative Science Quarterly*, *36*(2): 269–296.

Yip, G.S. (1989). Global Strategy . . . in a World of Nations? *Sloan Management Review*, *31*(1): 29–41.

4

Value Creation in International Electronic Markets: A Conceptual Framework

Saeed Samiee, Peter G.P. Walters, and Leslie Yip

The emergence of electronic markets in the 1970s fostered the development of numerous processes in business-to-business (B2B) markets that, in turn, led to greater efficiencies in distribution channels. Although the Internet has further fueled the growth of electronic markets during the 1990s, the primary objectives of firms in deploying electronic forms of exchange essentially remain unchanged. These goals include becoming more competitive by virtue of enhancing customer value and service, increasing market scope, and improving efficiency. Such objectives are consistent with the marketing philosophy, particularly the notion of creating greater customer value which has been the cornerstone of marketing theory and practice since the 1950s (Drucker, 1954; Day, 1990, 1994; Mizik and Jacobson, 2003). Given the potential benefits of leveraging off electronic media as a means of developing more efficient supply chain (SC) systems, and the high costs associated with logistics and supply chain management (SCM), the value creation potential of electronic media, such as the Internet, is an important topic for investigation.

It is widely acknowledged that marketing remains an expensive activity within firms and, in particular, expenses associated with logistics remain high. Thus, a greater emphasis on electronic markets and the Internet as partial means of developing more efficient SC systems is both necessary and understandable. Furthermore, as businesses have globalized, their SC systems are increasingly international and there is greater urgency to collaborate and coordinate activities through exchange of data, ideas, and knowledge (Normann and Ramirez, 1993; Morgan and Hunt, 1994; Overby and Min, 2001). Successful planning and implementation of SC strategies necessitate the cooperation of two or more channel members. One party may take a leadership position and envision and develop a more efficient SC system which is then implemented by other channel members who agree to cooperate with the initiator. The ways in which incremental value can be created and captured in the SC system have not been adequately addressed in the literature (Mizik and Jacobson, 2003), particularly in the context of the role of electronic communication systems as a facilitator of relational exchange and learning in international SCs. Since no one firm in the SC is normally in full control of activities that span the distribution network, benefits will likely have to be shared rather than accruing to any single organization in the system. Thus, value creation in a SC context implies that the value differential created through electronic exchanges is "captured" by several parties in the channel, although not necessarily on a proportionally equal basis, depending on the prevailing environmental conditions and channel and industry circumstances.

Electronic commerce is substantially or wholly dependent on the exchange of information and the acquisition of knowledge (Johnson and Whang, 2002), and learning activity commonly plays a central role in value creation in electronic markets. It should be noted that although the terms information and knowledge are not systematically distinguished in this chapter, they are different.[1] Huber (1991), for example, interprets information as essentially codifiable data whereas knowledge is more tacit, complex, and difficult to transfer. As such, virtually all business processes are knowledge based which, in turn, make their transfer difficult. In contrast, databases and accounting information are easily codifiable and can be readily transferred. Despite these differences, a central proposition in this study is that both are critical resources that can be shared in an electronic environment to achieve greater efficiency and to create incremental value.

Dyer and Singh (1998) identify four main sources of potential advantage arising from collaboration in terms of investment in relation-specific assets, the combination of complementary resources, lower transaction costs, and knowledge exchange. In this chapter the intent is to discuss the latter basis for advantage in the particular context of international electronic markets. The goal is to evaluate factors affecting knowledge exchange and learning and the impact of these activities as a basis for developing and enhancing competitive advantage in international markets. Apart from developing a conceptual model of knowledge exchange and joint learning in electronic supply chain (eSC) systems, the goal is to delineate the value created and captured through distribution network collaborative activities. Additionally, as a measure of the overall impact of knowledge and value creation, knowledge-based performance is considered. The firm's efforts in creating greater efficiency in its SC should necessarily lead to a better relational and financial performance, even if the value created is normally also captured by other members in the channel. In this context the following issues are explored and evaluated: (a) the nature of joint learning as a path to establishing competitive advantage in the management of the global SC; (b) the potential contribution of electronic media, notably the Internet, to the joint-learning process; and (c) ways in which joint learning in an eSC context can contribute to value creation for channel members.

Rationale and context for the study

A myriad of academic and practitioner-oriented publications have reported the critical importance of streamlining the firm's distribution network and achieving efficiency in the SC. Although significant accomplishments by some firms have been reported in the business press, the advances achieved at the Limited Brands in the late 1970s and Wal-Mart's well-publicized cross-docking process are noteworthy as they remain current SCM leaders in their respective industries. Inasmuch as their accomplishments would not have been possible without electronic communications (i.e., eCommerce), these firms were pioneers in electronic SCM (eSCM). Importantly, their SC activities are international in scope as they rely heavily on supplies from dozens of international locations. The purchasing arm of Limited Brands, for example, has manufacturing contracts with suppliers in nearly 40 countries and eSCM is crucial when managing the firm's global import operations. Consider, for example, that timing is of the essence in fashion markets and such firms as Limited Brands source identical products from multiple suppliers spread across the globe. Thus, Limited Brands has to monitor and coordinate production, quality, design, and delivery of their desired merchandise such that supplies are concurrently available across thousands of outlets it manages.

Achieving greater efficiency in the SC system demands direct and indirect investment with long-term anticipated incremental return to the system. Since such systems depend on participation by two or more members, the initiator's investment will often be complemented by investment by other SC members and the value created will normally be spread across all members of the SC. However, the eSCM initiator, in the role of system innovator, may create and appropriate much of the incremental value generated in the system (cf., Mizik and Jacobson, 2003). In the case of the Limited Brands, for example, value creation in the SC became a reality when the firm acquired its main supply link, Mast Industries, and invested in an automated warehousing system. Since the firm is vertically integrated, it has historically captured all the value it has created.

A field study of Sony Corporation of America (Samiee and deCamp, 2004), the US arm of the Japanese multinational corporation (MNC), is now briefly discussed since it highlights the importance of effective management of eSCM systems. Sony is dependent on supplies from over 75 Sony manufacturing plants around the world and also from many independent overseas suppliers. The company's "optimization sharing plan" requires channel members to share gains from SC innovation, particularly that arising from Sony's investment in new initiatives to enhance systems efficiency. This has helped Sony achieve an efficient SCM system, within and across its units, which also incorporates upstream suppliers and downstream distributors and retailers.

However, with so many manufacturing facilities spread around globe, computer and communications systems within Sony are not fully integrated and units use different software and have varying reporting requirements. Within these constraints, the firm has worked hard to increase parts and components commonality (currently at about 70%). Further, about half of Sony's output is shipped directly to its customers, thus minimizing logistics expenses, even though some orders are air-freighted. Process integration is more easily achieved in divisions where the firm has greater control. In the case of television sets, for example, the system is integrated from manufacturing to the retailer. This is possible because there are only five company-owned plants from which television sets are received and customer account requirements are very similar.

Sony has facilitated coordination across two critical divisions in the United States employing a process called "seihan," a Japanese term used for collaboration between marketing and manufacturing. This process covers production and forecasting for the coming week and up to one month ahead. Sony products are made to order and factories begin manufacturing when they receive a purchasing order from marketing, with the delivery objectives based on the ship-to-arrive date on the purchase order. The business process and information technology (IT) are thus well coordinated even though manufacturing and marketing use separate IT core systems.

Sony has established a separate research unit, Sony Nakamura Laboratory (SNL), which is focused on keeping the firm innovative in manufacturing and SCM (Portelligent, 2002). Further, Sony uses integrated IT in order to ensure up-to-the-minute communication with its partners and departments.[2] Importantly, Sony's extensive SC experience has taught it that trust is crucial and that the optimum exploitation of SCM opportunities requires the development of trusting relationships.

Sony's Consumer Electronics unit considers "optimization sharing from back to the front" (from the customer back to the factory) to be its key to success. Optimization sharing focuses on Sony's eSCM investments and efforts which have created or added value for customer accounts. The incremental value added through Sony's efforts ultimately enhances customer margins and performance. Sony also expects to capture significant value from greater efficiency and profitability. Sony manufacturing and marketing units are responsible for innovating and developing a more efficient SC system and, in turn, anticipate capturing a good deal of the gain which is shared among three main eSCM participants: customers, marketing, and manufacturing. Over the last five years, Sony has been able to ship approximately 50% of US sales direct from the factory to the customer, and the firm is focusing on the impact of eSCM innovations on the profitability of its customers as well as itself.

Customers typically place weekly orders with Sony and they normally receive their order very close to the scheduled delivery time since the company has achieved on-time weekly delivery rates of better than 95%. This allows retailers to maintain their in-store stock percentage in the high 90s. These arrangements have translated into lower channel inventories, fewer returns, higher in-store stocks, and less internal transfer of goods within the retailer's system. The system contributes an additional 4% margin to the channel. Sony captures added margins by requiring earlier payments, five days shorter credit time, or a price increase.

Although the SC accomplishments of Sony Corporation of America are significant, much of the value captured by Sony is from its domestic business. Inasmuch as SC relationships are more difficult to plan and manage internationally, developing and appropriating value across and within international markets are considerably more complicated. This is particularly the case for manufacturing where it is often necessary to integrate multiple, complex SCs. The situation in the electronics industry is further exacerbated because products tend to be short-lived, due to rapid innovation, coupled with rapidly declining prices for components and final products. Thus, high inventory turnover becomes critical to the success of firms such as Sony, Dell, and IBM where inbound inventory is measured in hours rather than days. The critical importance of an effective and efficient SC system in such firms is thus self-evident.

The Sony case highlights a more efficient coordination and management of SC functions such as forecasting and inventory management. However, value can be created in many different ways. With respect to service provision, for example, it is feasible for manufacturers to utilize electronic data retrieval systems that allow for customer sales and performance data to be evaluated and for feedback to be given to clients. Dawar and Vandenbosch (2004) report a case where a frozen food manufacturer is able to advise customers on appropriate promotional policy in light of data gathered from its customers around the world; another case concerns a firm which analyzes client performance data that is then aggregated and can be used by customers for benchmarking purposes. In these cases, the payback arises primarily in terms of generating increased value for customers via the introduction of new ideas, information, and services, with a beneficial impact on customer satisfaction and loyalty.

It is thus apparent that eSCM strategies can and do create value in many ways and that such initiatives are able to play an essential role in enhancing firm performance. It is also evident that, given the involvement of multiple "partners" in the chain, the benefits from the greater efficiencies created by a well-planned and managed eSCM will normally have to be shared among all the parties involved if the necessary trust and commitment are to evolve. In the next sections, the conceptual underpinning for the proposed model is introduced and related hypotheses are forwarded and discussed.

Conceptual framework

According to the resource-based view (RBV), firms are best conceptualized as a "bundle" of resources (Wernerfelt, 1984) with variations in enterprise performance viewed as fundamentally due to resource differences (Rumelt, 1984;

Barney, 1991). Scarce, valuable resources, and capabilities that are difficult to acquire and imitate provide the foundation for competitive advantages that lead to a superior and sustainable performance (Dierickx and Cool, 1989; Barney, 1991; Collis and Montgomery, 1995). The traditional RBV focus is on the individual enterprise, where idiosyncratic resources that are tacit, hard to transfer and replicate, and take time to develop are perceived as a particularly valuable source of competitive advantage (Dierickx and Cool, 1989; Szulanski, 1996).

Day (2001) has discussed the importance of information and market-based learning as a core organizational competence, with advantages accruing to firms able to interpret and anticipate the consequences of rapidly changing market forces. The perspective that information and know-how are resources that can provide a powerful platform for achieving competitive advantage has been endorsed in a number of studies. Grant (1996) and Eisenhardt and Santos (2002), for example, have discussed the development of "knowledge-based theory" where know-how is viewed as a key strategic resource. There is also evidence that superior learning improves performance. Li and Calantone (1998) differentiate between learning about customers and competitors, and find that such activity facilitates product development. Kohli and Jaworski (1990) define "market orientation" in terms of information generation and processing activity and demonstrate that such an orientation is associated with better performance. Similarly, Moorman and Miner (1997) have discussed the positive impact of organizational memory on creativity and financial performance.

Although RBV theorists traditionally emphasize firm-specific resources, it has been noted that enterprises are located in a network of relationships (Anderson et al., 1994), most obviously with customers and suppliers and that key resources "may span firm boundaries and may be embedded in inter-firm routines and processes" (Dyer and Singh, 1998: 661). Other marketing strategy scholars have also explored the value created and competitive position derived from collaboration (Srivastava et al., 1998; Anderson and Narus, 2003; Frels et al., 2003).

In a globalized, network-oriented, and knowledge-based economy competitive advantage can be facilitated by collaborative initiatives that cross organizational boundaries. For example, the profitable integration of the global SC requires firms to simultaneously manage both internal and external relationships of a dyadic and network nature (Nohira and Ghoshal, 1994). The potential for creating valuable inter-organizational capabilities and resources, which are often dependent on the nurturing of close relationships, is particularly great with respect to the management of the SC where collaboration is essential for effective performance. Asanuma (1989) demonstrated that skills developed as a result of relational exchange in the SC resulted in competitive advantages. Similarly, Saxenian (1994) has found that partnership between firms and physically contiguous suppliers is advantageous.

The value of developing an organizational learning orientation has been extensively discussed in recent years (e.g., Sinkula, 1994; Hurley and Hult, 1998) with a growing recognition that a primary direction for creating beneficial boundary spanning, resource-based advantages involves knowledge exchange (Dyer and Singh, 1998; Selnes and Sallis, 2003; Dawar and Vandenbosch, 2004). For example, in international buyer–seller relationships shared information can facilitate product innovation and enhance the efficiency of the SC, thereby generating added value for both vendors and customers (Helper and Sako, 1995).

However, knowledge sharing is but one dimension of learning. According to Bruner (1990: 89) an organization "learns if, through its processing of information, the range of its potential behaviors is changed" and this activity involves knowledge acquisition, information distribution, information interpretation, and organization memory. Learning competency provides a strong resource-based platform for differential advantage and there are obvious motivations for both customers and suppliers to develop this capability within the context of "relationship learning." This has been defined as sharing and jointly interpreting knowledge and information which is integrated into a common memory domain with a view to affecting current and future behavior (Selnes and Sallis, 2003).

Many learning skills are complex and not easily codified and copied and are, therefore, well-suited to provide a foundation for sustainable competitive advantage and value creation (Nelson and Winter, 1982; Szulanski, 1996). Of the four dimensions of learning, the acquisition and distribution of information and knowledge is likely to be more straightforward, particularly in an international context, than the processes of interpretation and establishing organizational memory. Interpretation involves giving meaning to information (Daft and Weick, 1984), requiring the development of shared understanding and is thus strongly affected by cognitive frameworks and the way in which information is labeled (Dutton and Jackson, 1987). Organizational memory is threatened by personnel turnover, the difficulty of deciding what information to store, and problems in making known and readily available the information and know-how that an organization possesses (Bruner, 1991).

The absorptive capacity of the parties involved is of critical importance in joint learning and, consequently, efficient management of the SC system. Absorptive capacity depends upon the development of effective routines for sharing information, know-how, and the establishment of common repositories of knowledge (Mowery et al., 1996). This requires sustained inter-firm relational exchange which is most likely when there are relatively few suitable partners, thereby limiting other options, and a willingness to commit resources which cross firm boundaries (Dyer and Singh, 1998). The development of mutual trust is viewed as important for sustaining relational exchange (Dwyer et al., 1987; Morgan and Hunt, 1994), particularly in the context of collaborative learning (Jap, 1999).

Bloom and Krathwohl (1956) have developed a taxonomy in which six categories of learning, ranging from simple recall of information to higher level activities such as evaluation, are proposed. Generally, greater value accrues from moving beyond simple recall and comprehension of information to deeper learning activity which involves substantial massaging of the data through analysis, synthesis, and the exercise of judgment. These later activities require far more than sharing information since active appraisal, manipulation, and assessment of the "meaning" of this data is necessary.

Joint learning based simply on sharing data will favor lower level learning goals. Deeper learning is likely in a joint process where the partners bring to bear differences in their affective domains arising from variance in their values, interests, and attitudes. Thus, the range of potential implications and outcomes envisaged in light of a given data set should increase as a result of the interplay of more varied analytical, creative, and judgmental frameworks. Huber (1991: 90) notes that "more organizational learning occurs when more and more varied interpretations are developed, because such a development changes the range of potential behaviors." But, as noted above, learning networks characterized by diversity in cultural and related factors are more likely to be turbulent and the development of strong ties and trust, which are central to smooth functioning of the SC, becomes problematic. Although joint learning in "culturally" homogeneous settings may be less turbulent and divisive, there is a price to pay in terms of the diversity of interpretations.

Joint learning and value creation in an electronic media context

Electronic media, such as the Internet, play a key role as an important facilitator of joint learning in a context of relational exchange in global SCs. Saloner and Spence (2002: 18) characterize the Internet as "a medium of unprecedented scope, depth, ubiquity and reach" and provide a detailed analysis of the advantages arising from its flexibility, ease of use, interactivity, personalization possibilities, and its asynchronous, encyclopedic nature. In terms of potential for creating incremental value in international SCs, the Internet can facilitate matching customers and suppliers, price comparison, inventory management, and greater command and control of the distribution and purchasing process. These attributes reduce transaction costs as well the expense of production and distribution. Additionally, market and sourcing uncertainties are reduced and service quality can be improved.

Electronic media, using sophisticated communication, indexing, and data retrieval systems, assist in promoting relational-based learning. Such systems allow for more real-time data to be collected and stored and facilitate rapid information exchange between multiple users and sources. Thus potential advantages of using the Internet as a communication channel in international markets include cost savings, enhanced business relationships, marketing benefits, and increasing opportunities for smaller firms to internationalize (Quelch and Klein, 1996; Hamill and Gregory, 1997; Samiee, 1998). Despite the undoubted promise of the Internet as a tool for generating competitive advantage, much remains to be learned about its successful implementation in an international SC context. Clearly, as firms learn to deploy electronic media to facilitate marketing and related SC functions, gaining a competitive edge via eSC will become increasingly difficult.

From the sellers' perspective, the Internet offers great promise as a medium for learning more about customer transactions and for capturing information about their needs, opinions, and consumption experience (Peterson et al., 1997; Porter, 2001). This can be accomplished by point of sales data collection, pre- and post-sales interaction with customers, and market research undertaken using the World Wide Web. Buyers are also empowered and able to derive information benefits from usage of the Internet (Porter, 2001). At a basic level, visiting the sites of potential suppliers may yield valuable information on a vendor and its products and services. If further feedback is needed, the Internet can serve as a convenient and inexpensive communications means for entering into a dialogue with potential suppliers on prices, conditions of sale, and other transaction-specific data.

A critical advantage of the Internet, within the context of eSCM, is that it is a relatively low cost (vis-à-vis other media for electronic exchange, e.g., private networks or virtual private networks) means for reaching SC members. However, given the Internet's common use in business, a well-designed web site offers only limited competitive advantages (Samiee, 1998). Rather it is the eSCM system and procedures instituted by the firm that can initiate and sustain competitive advantage. To realize optimum joint learning and communication, IT systems need to be compatible and integrated with a consequent need for relation-specific investment in hardware, systems, and management time. Once eSCM has been instituted, the strength of relationships within the channel and the commitment to ongoing, joint learning are likely to be key factors for success.

A variety of communications modes are feasible for operationalizing eSCM. The first-movers in adopting an eSCM system established or leased their own networks (e.g., private networks, virtual private networks, dedicated telephone lines). Private networks have a major security advantage that the Internet cannot match and, inasmuch as first-movers invested heavily in these systems, many have opted to remain them. However, the Internet has a major advantage: it is "ubiquitous, cheap, and available nearly all over the world, and to small as well as large companies" (Terpstra and Sarathy, 2000). In recent years, high speed Internet communication, using broadband connections, has further improved the efficiency of Internet connectivity. Information management can be further expedited by linking the external Internet with internal corporate electronic systems, such as the intranet, so that seamless communication is facilitated both within and outside the organization.

In addition to the Internet's convenience and interactive potential, electronic communication via the Internet allows for the targeting of specific customer or supplier groups (Blattberg and Deighton, 1991). Although practical Internet-based segmentation methods are yet to emerge, such a step will be extremely beneficial as it permits products and services to be customized to meet the specific needs of customer groups, customer and supplier relationships can be optimally managed, and valuable data for forecasting demand can be gathered. The Internet also offers the opportunity to reduce search costs, better ensure that customers' needs in terms of quality, price, and delivery are communicated, and facilitates tracking of order fulfillment.

Apart from the advantages offered with respect to collecting and distributing data, the Internet also creates opportunities for furthering joint learning between business partners. Although the value added from such activity will vary between the supplier and buyer, this is not problematic so long as the learning partners perceive that the division of benefit is equitable. In this regard, it has been argued that "sellers find it easier to anticipate the value of knowledge exchange than buyers" (Davenport and Jarvenpaa, 2001). Thus it is apparent that customer information has immediate utility in areas such as understanding customer needs, product development and innovation, pricing, service provision, promotion, and manufacturing activity. Hence, sellers place greater value on customer-related information.

Although buyers may need to be made more aware of the benefits of information exchange, proactive action by suppliers can increase the value of joint learning for customers. One approach is to offer incentives for valuable information by, for example, adding value to the data provided and then sharing the knowledge developed. When weak ties exist between buyers and sellers, a need for economic incentives is likely to be paramount. On the other hand, strong ties of a "family" nature should facilitate information exchange and interactive learning. Thus, an important dimension of the learning strategy adopted should be not only to demonstrate the value added for all parties, but also to stimulate trusting relationships and movement toward a "community" model (Kannan et al., 1998).

The transfer and absorption of know-how presents special challenges which may need the deployment of "rich" communication channels allowing for personal interaction. Sharing information and a willingness to enter into joint analysis will be also problematic unless there is a belief that confidentiality will be respected and that incremental costs and value will be shared fairly. This is unlikely unless trusting relationships are established (Davenport and Jarvenpaa, 2001). These potential problems are particularly relevant in global SCs where cultural and institutional distance are complicating factors.

The development of strong learning relationships is more difficult when the participants in the information exchange and learning process do not share common cultural characteristics (Riesenberger, 1998). However, cultural values are developed at the national, group, and organizational levels, and productive interaction can lead to the development of common behavioral norms, irrespective of ethnic background.

Additional factors that affect the nature of relational ties in a learning network include "group" access criteria and reputation (Uzzi, 1996), as well as sanctions for behaviors that violate community norms (Jones et al., 1997). The development of shared behavioral norms, close attention to reputational signals and the evolution of collective sanctions should facilitate both the development of the confidence and trust that characterizes strong ties and more interactive learning using electronic media.

The concept of a learning community is helpful in understanding the importance of relational exchange as a facilitator of information exchange and learning. If trust can be established between buyers and sellers, information exchange is more likely. Strong ties may have their foundation in cultural similarity and congruence of learning objectives. Unfortunately, electronic media are not efficient channels for developing deep relational ties. The fact that some governments exert control over the public's use of the Internet, coupled with its occasional use for questionable or fraudulent motives, has raised concerns for individuals and firms. More importantly, the Internet is an impersonal channel which does not enjoy the "richness" of face-to-face contact. Although the Internet has the potential to accommodate video-conferencing and one-on-one communications, eSCM strategies tend to be process based, partially or wholly automated, and impersonal. This implies that electronic media may need to be supplemented by richer modes of interaction, particularly when transferring tacit know-how, for example, through personal contact in cross-national teams (Subramaniam and Venkatarman, 2001).

However, information flows through the Internet can be managed efficiently and rapidly, and this reduces the likelihood of misunderstanding and conflict because of insufficient knowledge about current transactions and the operating context. In short, the Internet offers a powerful communication tool which increases transactional transparency and the real-time monitoring of ongoing business arrangements. On the foundation of the common understanding so generated, joint learning designed to promote higher learning goals becomes more likely, as does the development of mutual trust and commitment (Helper and Sako, 1995).

The sharing of experience is likely to be most relevant for suppliers who wish to persuade customers to enter into collaborative learning relationships. Essentially the notion is to initiate a virtuous circle where value is added to the data supplied by customers and the "enhanced" information is then fed back. In this way, customers are provided with an economic return from their willingness to share information. Carefully managed, this strategy can promote the development of stronger ties and build a commitment to the supplier. For example, favored suppliers can be given access to information on demand in the end-user market, thereby facilitating production planning.

A key objective should be to establish organizational systems that permit the SC to "function as a network rather than as a collection of unrelated nodes" (Dawar and Vandenbosch, 2004). The Internet can play a crucial role in operationalizing such transnational organizational links. For example, by relaying experiential information from one customer to another, by allowing for data aggregation which provides performance benchmarks for customers, and by facilitating the analysis and diffusion of the conclusions reached following evaluation of the data gathered. In this way it is possible to derive outputs that are of direct assistance to customers when undertaking activities such as policy formulation and forecasting.

Facilitating benchmarking requires persuading customers and suppliers to provide confidential performance-related data. For this to occur, trusting relationships need to be established. In developing such relationships, the means of transmission deployed (e.g., the Internet) will have a subsidiary role. However, once confidence has been developed, the Internet is an excellent channel for the collection of data from customers and the diffusion of subsequent conclusions.

The development of electronic channels provides opportunities for both sellers and buyers to disenfranchise intermediaries and to capture the value added by these facilitators (Benjamin and Wigand, 1995). This process of "disintermediation" results in direct interaction as buyers use the Internet to identify, contact, and deal with potential suppliers in a convenient and rapid manner. Suppliers can also use electronic channels to identify and serve customers abroad, thereby circumventing intermediaries who formerly enjoyed this advantage because of their control over scarce information. However, by their nature, intermediaries tend to be agile and adaptive and, consequently, are among the first to deploy new technologies to validate and economically justify their presence in the SC. Thus, system goals should not center on streamlining the SC through the premature elimination of intermediaries who may continue to offer significant added value, often through their innovative use of electronic media.

Of course, the Internet is not an all-powerful source of information and communication. Certain critical information may be of a proprietary nature, which is not readily transferred and contextual knowledge may be required if the correct questions and conclusions are to be arrived at. Despite these concerns, the potential contribution of electronic media, such as the Internet, to global SC efficiency and value creation is significant and it has been argued that, under a collaborative electronic exchange model, a firm's resources are equal to the sum of all participants in the network (Tapscott et al., 2000). Information and knowledge acquired by access to data from a collaborative network, and joint learning, are valuable resources for competitive advantage and the creation of incremental value when managing a global SC network on a collaborative basis.

In this light, drawing on resource-based theory, the notion of knowledge as a critical resource for achieving competitive advantage, and the potential advantages of joint relational learning in a digital environment, a conceptual framework is proposed in Figure 4.1. In this framework, collaboration in IT integration, investment, and the operation of electronic SC systems, along with the development of strong working relationships are conceptualized as important forces promoting joint learning as a driver of value creation when managing global SCs. Emphasis is also placed on the importance of trust and cultural and organizational "distance" between channel members and the role of uncertainty as factors influencing both the propensity to work together in developing the infrastructure for integrated eSC systems and interaction based on relational exchange.

In the model, four key dimensions of learning activity are delineated. It can be noted that collaboration is viewed to be particularly important in the establishment of joint organizational memory and that "distance" variables are viewed as having a major impact on joint interpretation because "richer" communication is needed to supplement electronic-based channels when building common understanding. Principal propositions arising from the foregoing discussion are now offered and examined in order to provide a road map for future research in this important field of scholarship.

Propositions

Drivers of eSC activity

Three factors are expected to affect the propensity for collaboration, namely, the level of environmental uncertainty, the degree of trust, and cultural distance as between collaborating organizations. As discussed earlier, trust has been found to have an important impact on relational exchange, and cultural distance has been identified as a key variable affecting international collaboration, particularly with respect to knowledge management (Riesenberger, 1998). Environmental uncertainty is relevant because information and knowledge are essential to understanding the context for business and problem solving, and collaborative exchange is an important response to the risks posed by external environmental forces (Van de Ven, 1976).

P1: There is a positive relationship between:
    a. environmental uncertainty and collaboration.
    b. trust and collaboration.

P2: There is a negative relationship between cultural and organizational distance and collaboration.

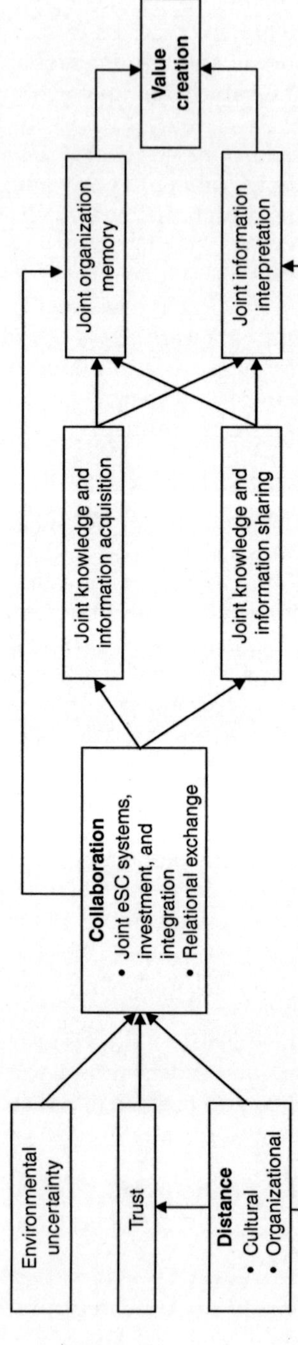

Figure 4.1 Joint learning and value creation in global supply chain systems: a conceptual model

Information acquisition

Information and knowledge acquisition is crucial to the learning process and is the starting point for strategy development and planning activity. Gathering information is a costly process which can be undertaken jointly or by a single initiating firm which bears the responsibility for accumulating, classifying, and distributing it in appropriate contexts. The latter approach is known as the "single point of contact" phenomenon (Overby and Min, 2001) and offers advantages in terms of coordination and control of the acquisition process.

Primary modes of knowledge acquisition identified by Huber (1991) include experiential learning, obtaining information second hand by monitoring the actions of competitors, hiring new "knowledge rich" staff, and by scanning relevant environmental fields. Joint approaches to information acquisition allow members of the SC to engage in a division of labor where they can take optimum advantage of their position in the chain to collect relevant information and know-how. This is cost efficient, facilitates the scope and depth of the information collection process, and ensures that the relevant information needed in their domain is captured.

The virtues of collaboration are particularly valuable in a global context where relevant information is geographically dispersed and a lack of experiential know-how has been identified as a fundamental problem for internationalizing firms targeting new markets (Johanson and Vahlne, 1977). Joint effort also offers the more mundane advantages noted of avoiding duplication of effort and promoting division of labor in line with a channel members' position in the international SC, resources, and experience.

Data acquisition is promoted by the usage of electronic channels, such as the Internet, where the benefits of rapid, personal, asynchronous contact will significantly increase the scope and efficiency of the process. Thus in a multinational context, where key individuals are separated by time, distance, culture, and organizational affiliation, electronic media that facilitate rapid communication and feedback are highly valuable. In particular they help overcome time and distance barriers and, at the same time, encourage engagement in learning by extending the scope of the processes of information acquisition and information sharing.

P3: Joint information acquisition activity enhances division of labor in the data collection process and increases the relevance of the information gathered.

P4: Electronic media are particularly valuable in international markets as they facilitate rapid and efficient data acquisition, transmission, and storage across national boundaries.

Knowledge sharing

Although knowledge can be transferred through external markets, where price is the benchmark of value, important problems impact the efficiency of the market for know-how. Much knowledge is tacit in nature and is thus hard to trade and price. Additionally, there is the danger that transferred knowledge may strengthen existing competitors (Buzzell and Ortmeyer, 1995) or help to establish new ones. Rather than sharing information through market or other channels it has thus been argued that firms should seek to protect their knowledge from appropriation by competitors (Liebeskind, 1996). Even if markets are efficient and there are no competitive threats of the type noted above, it has been maintained that internal knowledge transfer is most effective for tacit know-how because of absorption capacity problems, particularly in an international context (Kogut and Zander, 1993). "Internalization" of knowledge and other valuable resources within the firm is thus viewed as a powerful force which helps to explain foreign direct investment (Hymer, 1960; Buckley and Casson, 1976).

Knowledge sharing is an important factor contributing to competitive success (Levinson and Asahi, 1996; Spencer, 2003) and, despite the "public good" and tacit nature of much information, and significant potential agency problems, it has been suggested that knowledge sharing routines can be devised that facilitate inter-firm learning (Grant, 1996). Few organizations have a monopoly over relevant knowledge and, even when they do, alternative interpretations of the "meaning" and implications of the data available are desirable. In the case of innovation, for example, von Hippel (1988) argues that efficient knowledge sharing routines in the value chain enhances product development.

Productive inter-firm knowledge sharing and learning depend upon collaborators developing systems that allow for information sharing and absorption across organizational boundaries. Keys to success include the development of overlapping knowledge bases, routines for accessing and diffusing information to where it is needed, and interaction aimed at building confidence and facilitating trust development.

Confidence that opportunistic behavior in the SC will not prevail is also important. Devising appropriate incentive structures (Roth and O'Donnel, 1996) that encourage transparency and discourage "free riding" are important to deal with potential agency problems. Shared characteristics between partners, such as common core values and experience, reduce goal incongruence and facilitate communication (Nohira and Ghoshal, 1994; Rogers, 1995).

An important means to address these problems is provided by joint initiatives to develop common systems to codify and to manage information distribution within and across national and organizational boundaries. In the case of tacit knowledge, where direct and ongoing interaction is often necessary if valuable know-how is to be transferred (Polanyi, 1966), collaboration in facilitating absorption capacity in the SC system becomes crucial. In this context, electronic media can be expected to play a larger role in the transfer of information as compared to knowledge, which often requires the usage of "rich" communication channels which allow for the transmission of the comprehensive signals and cues needed to maximize understanding.

P5: Electronic systems will be more valuable for the international distribution of information, as compared to know-how, in the global SC.

P6: Joint, relational-based interaction is more important for sharing know-how, as compared to information, in the global SC.

Information interpretation

For learning to occur, information has to be interpreted such that it has meaning and it is argued that a more complete understanding of phenomena is promoted by widespread engagement in this process (Bruner, 1991). Speed of data transmission and convenience are important potential advantages insofar as the utility of electronic channels is concerned (Saloner and Spence, 2002). However, in a multinational context, organizations and individuals are separated not only by time and distance, but also by culture, both national and corporate. This means that there is often significant inertia that constrains the interpretation process, even when using sophisticated eSC systems (Attewell, 1992; Tiemessen et al., 1997; Simonin, 1999a).

Cultural differences arising from ethnicity and the corporate context will affect the cognitive framework of the information processor and, thus, have a crucial bearing on interpretation (Zajonic and Wolfe, 1966). The efficacy of electronic channels in overcoming cultural "distance" is doubtful, since they do not offer a "rich" medium in the sense of being good means for sending crucial cues to aid interpretation. Collaboration in the learning process, particularly that involving direct personal contact, will breed familiarity and thus a better appreciation of the respective "mind sets" of the persons and units involved, and this should support the development of common understanding.

P7: Joint learning will facilitate the development of a common understanding of the meaning of information and know-how.

P8: Electronic media need to be supplemented by personal contact for the development of shared comprehension of knowledge.

Organizational memory

Over time knowledge accumulates within enterprises as organizational memory which consists of the total information and know-how held by the organization as well as the systems for storing and retrieving them (Walsh and Ungson, 1991; Anand et al., 1998). Effective utilization of organizational memory is facilitated by the development of directories and locators for data management and retrieval. Very important knowledge, which is often tacit in nature, is generally located in the personal memory of group members along with personal directories on the existence and location of knowledge held by others (Wegner, 1986). Therefore, despite the automation benefits of eSCM, human resources play a critical role in the storage and retrieval of information that is essential to well-functioning SC systems.

Organizational memory plays a central role in learning activity because it delineates the cognitive frame of reference and systems for information acquisition and distribution in place. Without new learning, organizational memory will atrophy, and memory loss may occur when staff leave. Codifying and storing such know-how mitigates this problem. However, in the case of tacit information, this is often easier said than done. Another difficulty arises in knowing what information to discard to avoid information overload. Experience provides a good guide in this regard, but by nature it is hard to pass on.

Despite the challenge posed regarding storage of personal memory, electronic computer-based systems have much to offer in terms of the automatic capture, storage and retrieval of information. Thus, Huber (1991, p. 106) has noted that "computer resident organizational memories with certain properties, such as completeness and precision,.... are superior to the human components of organizational memories."

P9: Electronic media play a vital role in facilitating the storage and retrieval of information, but their utility is much less for storing know-how.

Cultural and organizational distance

In general, value creation in marketing results from developing a good understanding of conditions under which customers function. The deleterious effects of cultural distance on information acquisition and interpretation have already been noted and there is evidence that performance in global SCs improves when strategy is adapted to take account of the cultural context (Griffith and Myers, 2005). Research has demonstrated that cultural distance impacts eSCM collaboration (Lyles and Salk, 1996) and also the underlying processes of knowledge management (Tiemessen et al., 1997) and knowledge transfer (Mowery et al., 1996; Simonin, 1999b). Thus, at the very least, cultural distance will require managers to spend more time on communication (Olk, 1997) and can result in serious misunderstanding even when information is shared.

Simonin (1999b) highlights two aspects of cultural distance that are particularly detrimental to joint learning in a collaborative arrangement. First, cultural barriers impede joint learning by heightening barriers to understanding partners and the nature of their competitive advantages. Secondly, marketing opportunities might be missed because cultural distance makes market mechanisms and opportunities less transparent. Cultural distance is thus expected to have a particular impact on knowledge transfer between collaborating firms and on the process of information interpretation, and will thus negatively influence joint learning.

Firms entering into SC partnerships do not shed their original identities and are likely to maintain different mindsets which translate into divergent organizational cultures and goals. Organizational distance, conceptualized as the magnitude of difference between SC members' business practices and organizational culture (cf., Simonin, 1999a), exists in a domestic context. However, distance is potentially greater internationally due to differences in the institutional environment between markets which will influence behavior. In the context of joint learning and value creation, greater organizational distance between partners is expected to impede knowledge sharing and interpretation and, hence, impact negatively on learning.

P10: Organizational and cultural distance will negatively affect knowledge and information sharing and interpretation and are thus inversely related to joint learning.

eSCM investment

Investment is essential when developing effective SC systems. The most obvious commitment required is the time and resources needed to develop a SC strategy and corresponding processes to accommodate communication between channel participants with respect to data collection and distribution. Such investments typically involve hardware, software, and training, and software developers have been offering standardized, scalable software to accommodate SC activities for some time. Although the adoption of such software and related personnel training is often expensive, the relative uniformity of off-the-shelf software packages makes it difficult to achieve significant competitive advantage through their adoption. For this reason, some firms have opted for proprietary software that incorporates unique processes tailored to the firm's particular strategy.

Collaborating firms also should invest in an information-based infrastructure to enable them to handle massive amounts of information and, in particular, to establish a research group that develops, tests, and implements SC processes aimed at streamlining the international distribution activities of the firm. It is the collection of these proprietary processes which, combined with firm-specific software or off-the-shelf software that is uniquely configured, can lead to a strong competitive position for the entire SC.[3]

Another dimension of SC-related investment is relationship specific. A SC is made up of a number of players and participants (with special reference to the key eSC initiator) who must invest in cultivating, coordinating, and nurturing relationships. It is noteworthy that the initiating member of the SC assumes a leadership position and tends to make disproportionately larger initial investments which lead to control over relationship-specific assets which often correspond with the value that is eventually captured by the firm. SC relationships, however, are two-way streets and an unwillingness to share, and perceptions of inequities in relationship-specific investments and value appropriation throughout the SC, can negatively affect relationship longevity and prospects for joint learning.

P11: A willingness to invest in systems needed to facilitate productive eSC interaction and the time and effort to establish relational exchange are crucial for effective joint management of the global SC and joint learning.

Conclusions

The goal in the preceding discussion is to develop a model and to offer corresponding propositions relating to joint, eSC-based learning collaboration in the management of global SCs. The analysis is founded upon a review of the relevant literature, with the expectation that the model and propositions will be helpful in providing a platform for future research in this important area.

The foundation for the discussion rests upon a number of key ideas that are now briefly summarized. Knowledge is a powerful basis for resource-based sustainable competitive advantage, and joint learning between participants in global SCs facilitates the development of knowledge-based capabilities. Electronic media, such as the Internet, are seen to offer a powerful channel for acquiring and transmitting information across national boundaries, particularly "declarative" information of a factual nature. Within the context of eSCM, the primary value of the Internet lies in its relative low cost and ease of access for SC members around the world. However, instituting an electronic-based SC system in an international context of collaboration is much more complex than those planned and implemented strictly at the domestic level, primarily because of cultural and organizational "distance." It is also important to note that, in the case of tacit knowledge, contact mediated via the Internet normally needs to be complemented by "rich" communication media characterized by more direct contact potential. It is also the case that electronic media are not an ideal medium for promoting knowledge interpretation which involves the analysis and synthesis of information. However, computer-based eSCM systems can play a major role in establishing and developing organization memory capacity.

Joint information and knowledge capture, exchange, and interpretation are facilitated by the development of strong ties, trust, and commitment between members of an exchange network. Other requirements include a willingness to invest time and resources in the establishment of proprietary eSCM infrastructure and a desire to develop trusting relationships that facilitate joint learning.

Finally, it should be noted that value creation through international collaboration in an eSCM context and the maintenance of ongoing competitive advantage are at a constant state of flux and analogous moving targets. As more firms seek to develop better SC systems, they erode the competitive advantage of early entrants to the eSCM landscape. This means that the advantages arising from collaboration in eSCM cannot be taken for granted, and that continuing effort is needed to ensure that joint-learning opportunities are fully exploited so as to ensure that significant value continues to be generated in the global SC.

Notes

1. The literature makes a distinction between information and knowledge (e.g., Grant, 1996). The essence of the distinction is that the former is codifiable and factual in nature whereas the latter is characteristically tacit, complex, and often of a process form. A similar distinction is made by Paris, Lipson, and Wixson (1983) who talk about knowledge as being either "declarative," that is essentially factual, or "procedural" know-how. In this chapter these distinctions are not rigorously observed and the terms information and knowledge are used interchangeably. It is noteworthy, however, that transfer and absorption problems is greater for tacit knowledge (Polanyi, 1966; Szulanski, 1996) and an important issue concerns how the inter-organizational transfer of such information is to be achieved.
2. Sony currently uses three IT systems in its SC: Legacy, Oracle, and SAP. The Legacy system (deployed in the 1970s) is the order management platform for some of the consumer electronics divisions. The other systems were introduced as needs arose. For example, when the company started its PC business and another business in the late 1990s, which require made-to-order and configure-to-order functionality in their order management systems, the Oracle Management System and SAP were added because the Legacy system could not meet those requirements. Currently, four Sony units use Legacy, two other units and all factories use Oracle as their order management systems, and one division uses only SAP. Sony's IT systems are still somewhat fragmented but the company is currently undergoing a multi-million dollar integration of all IT systems into one. In addition to integrating the current systems, the company is converting into a SAP system on the marketing side for order management, Oracle in all factories across the globe, and Oracle Financials. The SAP package includes the demand planning tool and a supply netting front end.
3. In practice, SC members may be required to adopt the established system by the initiating firm, which typically requires direct investment in software, training, and appropriate communication modes. Additionally, SC members may have to rearrange their own internal operations to accommodate the SC processes being implemented. The extent to which suppliers and customers may be required to invest to join in the SC system is in part a function of the relative channel power of the initiator. Wal-Mart, for example, requires all its key suppliers to adopt special software and to comply with other requirements.

References

Anderson, J. and J. Narus. (2003), *Business Market Management: Understanding, Creating & Delivering Value*. Upper Saddle River, NJ: Prentice-Hall.

Anderson, J.C., H. Hakanson, and J. Johanson. (1994), "Dyadic business relationships within a business network context," *Journal of Marketing*, 58(October), 1–15.

Anand, V., C.C. Manz, and W.H. Glick. (1998), "An organizational memory approach to information management," *Academy of Management Review*, 23(4), 796–811.

Asanuma, B. (1989), "Manufacturer-supplier relationships in Japan and the concept of relation specific skill," *Journal of the Japanese and International Economies*, 1–30.

Attewell, P. (1992), "Technology diffusion and organizational learning: The case of business computing," *Organization Science*, 3(1), 1–19.

Barney, J.B. (1991), "Firm resources and sustained competitive advantage," *Journal of Management*, 17, 99–120.

Benjamin, R. and R. Wigand. (1995), "Electronic markets and virtual value chains on the information superhighway," *Sloan Management Review*, 36, 62–72.

Blattberg, R.C. and J. Deighton. (1991), "Interactive marketing: Exploiting the age of addressability," *Sloan Management Review*, fall, 33(1), 5–14.

Bloom, B.S. and D. Krathwohl. (1956), *Taxonomy of Educational Objectives: The Classification of Educational Goals, Handbook 1: Cognitive Domain*, New York: Longmans Green.

Bruner, J.S. (1990), *Acts of Meaning*, Cambridge, MA: Harvard University Press.

Bruner, J.S. (1991), *Critical Inquiry*, 18, 1–21.

Buckley, P.J. and M. Casson. (1976), *The Future of the Multinational Enterprise*, New York: Holmes and Meier.

Buzzell, R.D. and G. Ortmeyer. (1995), "Channel partnerships streamline distribution," *Sloan Management Review*, spring, 36(3), 85–96.

Collis, D.J. and C.A. Montgomery. (1995), "Competing on resources," *Harvard Business Review*, 73(4), 118–128.

Daft, R.L. and K.E. Weick. (1984), "Toward a model of organizations as interpretation systems," *Academy of Management Review*, 9(2), 284–295.

Davenport, T. and S.L. Jarvenpaa. (2001), "Digital marketing and the exchange of knowledge," in J. Wind and V.J. Mahajan (eds), *Digital Marketing: Global Strategies from the World's Leading Experts*, New York: John Wiley, pp. 130–160.

Dawar, N. and M. Vandenbosch. (2004), "The seller's hidden advantage," *Sloan Management Review*, winter, 45(2), 83–88.

Day, G.S. (1990), *Market-Driven Strategy: Processes for Creating Value*, New York: The Free Press.

Day, G.S. (1994), "The capabilities of market-driven organizations," *Journal of Marketing*, 58(October), 37–52.

Day, G.S. (2001), "Learning about markets," in R. Deshpande (ed.), *Using Market Knowledge*, Thousand Oaks, CA: Sage Publications, pp. 9–29.

Dierickx, I. and K. Cool. (1989), "Asset stock accumulation and sustainability of competitive advantage," *Management Science*, 35, 1504–1513.

Drucker, P.F. (1954), *The Practice of Management*, New York: Harper & Row.

Dyer, J.H. and H. Singh. (1998), "The relational view: Cooperative strategy and sources of interorganizational competitive advantage," *Academy of Management Review*, 23(4), 660–679.

Dutton, J.E. and S.E. Jackson. (1987), "The categorization of strategic issues by decision makers and its links to organizational actions," *Academy of Management Review*, 12 (January), 76–90.

Dwyer, F.R., P.H. Schurr, and S. Oh. (1987), "Developing buyer-seller relationships," *Journal of Marketing*, 51(April), 11–27.

Eisenhardt, K.M. and F.M. Santos. (2002), "Knowledge-based view: A new theory of strategy," in A. Pettigrew, T. Howard, and R. Whittington (eds), *Handbook of Strategy and Management*, London: Sage.

Frels, J.K., T. Shervani, and R.K. Srivastava. (2003), "The integrated networks model: Explaining resource allocations in network markets," *Journal of Marketing*, 67(1) (January), 29–45.

Grant, R.M. (1996), "Toward a knowledge based theory of the firm," *Strategic Management Journal*, 17(winter), 109–122.

Griffith, D.A. and M.B. Myers. (2005), "The performance implications of strategic fit of relational norm governance strategies in global supply chain relationships," *Journal of International Business Studies*, 36, 254–269.

Hamill, J. and K. Gregory. (1997), "Internet marketing in the internationalization of UK SMEs," *Journal of Marketing Management*, 13, 9–28.

Helper, S.R. and M. Sako. (1995), "Supplier relations in Japan and the United States: Are they converging," *Sloan Management Review*, spring, 36(3), 77–84.

von Hippel, E. (1994), "Sticky information and the locus of problem solving: Implications for innovation," *Management Science*, 44(May), 629–44.

Huber, G.P. (1991), "Organizational learning: The contributing processes and the literature," *Organizational Science*, 2(1), 88–114.

Hurley, R.F. and G.T.M. Hult. (1998), "Innovation, market orientation and organizational learning," *Journal of Marketing*, 62(July), 42–54.

Hymer, S.H. (1960), The International Operations of National Firms: A Study of Foreign Direct Investment, Ph.D. Dissertation, MIT.

Jap, S.D. (1999), "Pie-expansion efforts: Collaboration processes in buyer-seller relationships," *Journal of Marketing Research*, 36(November), 461–475.

Johanson, J. and J.E. Vahlne. (1977), "The internationalization process of the firm: A model of knowledge development and increasing foreign market commitment," *Journal of International Business Studies* (spring–summer), 23–32.

Johnson, M.E. and S. Whang. (2002), "e-business and supply chain management: An overview and framework," *Social Science Research Network Electronic Paper Collection*, 27(November), http://ssrn.com/abstract=385540.

Jones, C., W.S. Hesterly, and S.P. Borgatti. (1997), "A general theory of network governance: Exchange conditions and social mechanisms," *Academy of Management Review*, 22(4), 911–945.

Kannan, P.K., A. Chang, and A.B. Whinston. (1998), "Marketing information on the i-way," *Communications of the ACM*, March, 35–43.

Kogut, B. and U. Zander. (1993), "Knowledge of the firm and the evolutionary theory of the MNC," *Journal of International Business Studies*, 24(4), 625–645.

Kohli, A. and B. Jaworski. (1990), "Market orientation: The construct, research propositions, and managerial implications," *Journal of Marketing*, 54(2), 1–18.

Levinson, N.S. and M. Asahi. (1996), "Crossnational alliances and interorganizational learning," *Organizational Dynamics*, 24, 51–63.

Li, T. and Roger J. Calantone. (1998), "The impact of market knowledge competence on new product advantage: Conceptualization and empirical examination," *Journal of Marketing*, 62(4), 13–29.

Liebeskind, J.P. (1996), "Knowledge strategy and the theory of the firm," *Strategic Management Journal*, 17(winter), 93–107.

Lyles, M.A. and J.E. Salk. (1996), "Knowledge acquisition from foreign parents in international joint ventures: An empirical examination in the hungarian context," *Journal of International Business Studies*, 27(5), 877–903.

Mizik, N. and Robert Jacobson. (2003), "Trading off between value creation and value appropriation: The Financial Implications of Shifts in Strategic Emphasis," *Journal of Marketing*, 67(January), 63–76.

Moorman, C. and A.S. Miner. (1997), "The impact of organizational memory on new product performance and creativity," *Journal of Marketing Research*, 34(February), 91–106.

Morgan, M. and D. Hunt. (1994), "The commitment-trust theory of relationship marketing," *Journal of Marketing*, 58(3)(July), 20–38.

Mowery, D.C., H.E. Oxley, and B.S. Silverman. (1996), "Strategic alliances and interfirm knowledge transfer," *Strategic Management Journal*, 17, 77–91.

Nelson, R.R. and S.G. Winter. (1982), *An Evolutionary Theory of Economic Change*, Cambridge, MA: Belknap.

Nohira, N. and S. Ghoshal. (1994), "Differentiated fit and shared values: Alternatives for managing HQ-subsidiary relations," *Strategic Management Journal*, 15(6), 491–502.

Normann, R. and R. Ramirez. (1993), "From value chain to value constellation: Designing interactive strategy," *Harvard Business Review*, 71(July–August), 65–77.

Olk, P. (1997), "The effect of partner differences on the performance of R&D consortia," in P. Beamish and J. Killing (eds), *Cooperative Strategies, North American Perspectives*, San Francisco: New Lexington Press.

Overby, J.W. and S. Min. (2001), "International supply chain management in an internet environment: A network-oriented approach to internationalization," *International Marketing Review*, 18(4), 392–419.

Paris, S.G., M.Y. Lipson, and K.K. Wixson. (1983), "Becoming a strategic reader," *Contemporary Educational Psychology*, 8, 293–316.

Peterson, R.A., S. Balasubramanian, and B.J. Bronnenberg. (1997), "Exploring the implications of the internet for consumer marketing," *Journal of the Academy of Marketing Science*, 25(fall), 329–346.

Polanyi, M. (1966), *The Tacit Dimension*, London: Routledge & Kegan Paul, Ltd.

Portelligent. (2002), "Sony establishes research firm to study manufacturing innovations," *Portelligent Competitive TechAlert Service*, http://portelligent.com/tas/subscribers/archive/comp alert archive/2002 accessed August 28.

Porter, M.E. (2001), "Strategy and the internet," *Harvard Business Review*, March, 79(3), 62–78.

Quelch, J.A. and L.R. Klein. (1996), "The internet and international marketing," *Sloan Management Review*, 37(spring), 60–75.

Riesenberger, J.R. (1998), "Knowledge – the source of sustainable competitive advantage," *Journal of International Marketing*, 6(3), 94–107.

Rogers, E.M. (1995), *Diffusion of Innovations*, New York: Free Press.

Roth, K. and S. O'Donnel. (1996). "Foreign subsidiary compensation strategy: An agency theory perspective," *Academy of Management Journal*, 39(3), 678–703.

Rumelt, R.P. (1984), "Towards a strategic theory of the firm," in R.B. Lamb (ed.), *Competitive Strategic Management*, Englewood Cliffs, NJ: Prentice-Hall, pp. 556–571.

Saloner, G. and A.M. Spence. (2002), *Creating and Capturing Value: Perspectives and Cases on Electronic Commerce*, New York: Wiley & Sons.

Samiee, S. (1998), "Exporting and the internet: A conceptual perspective," *International Marketing Review*, 15(8), 413–426.

Samiee, S. and Catherine deCamp. (2004), "Supply chain management: The case of the U.S. subsidiaries of Japanese consumer electronics firms," paper presented at international symposium of supply chain management at Meiji University, Tokyo, fall.

Saxenian, A. (1994), *Regional Advantage*, Cambridge, MA: Harvard University Press.

Selnes, F. and J. Sallis. (2003), "Promoting relationship learning," *Journal of Marketing*, 67(July), 80–95.

Simonin, B.L. (1999a), "Ambiguity and the process of knowledge transfer in strategic alliances," *Strategic Management Journal*, 20, 595–623.

Simonin, B.L. (1999b), "Transfer of marketing know-how in international strategic alliances: An empirical investigation of the role and antecedents of knowledge ambiguity," *Journal of International Business Studies*, fall, 30(3), 463–490.

Sinkula, J.M. (1994), "Market information processing and organizational learning," *Journal of Marketing*, 58(January), 35–45.

Spencer, J.W. (2003), "Firm's knowledge-sharing strategies in the global innovation system: Empirical evidence from the flat panel display industry," *Strategic Management Journal*, 24, 217–233.

Srivastava, R.K., T. Shervani, and L. Fahey. (1998), "Market-based assets and shareholder value: A framework for analysis," *Journal of Marketing*, 62(January), 1–14.

Subramaniam, M. and V. Venkatarman. (2001), "Determinants of transnational new product development capability: Testing the influence of transferring and deploying tacit overseas knowledge," *Strategic Management Journal*, 22(4), 359–378.

Szulanski, G. (1996), "Exploring internal stickiness: Impediments to the transfer of best practice within the firm," *Strategic Management Journal*, 17, 27–43.

Tapscott, D., D. Ticoll, and A. Lowy. (2000), *Digital Capital: Harnessing the Power of Business Webs*, Boston: Harvard Business School Press.

Terpstra, V. and R. Sarathy. (2000), *International Marketing*, NY: Harcourt Dryden.

Tiemessen I., H.W. Lane, M.M. Crossan, and A.C. Inkpen. (1997), "Knowledge management in international joint ventures," in P. Beamish and J. Killings (eds), *Cooperative Strategies, North American Perspectives*, San Francisco: New Lexington Press, pp. 370–399.

Uzzi, B. (1996), "Causes and consequences of embeddedness for the economic performance of organizations: The network effect," *American Sociological Review*, 61, 674–698.

Ven, A.H. (1976), "On the nature, formation and maintenance of relations among organizations," *Academy of Management Review*, 1(October), 24–36.

Walsh, J.P. and G.R. Ungson. (1991), "Organizational memory," *Academy of Management Review*, 16(1), 57–91.

Wegner, D.M. (1986), "Transactive memory: A contemporary analysis of the group mind," in B. Mullen and G.R. Goethals (eds), *Theories of Group Behavior*, New York: Springer, pp. 185–208.

Wernerfelt, B. (1984), "A resource based view of the firm," *Strategic Management Journal*, 5(2), 171–180.

Zajonic, R. and D. Wolfe. (1966), "Cognitive consequences of a person's position in a formal organization," *Human Relations*, 19(139–150).

5

Decision Factors Influencing MNEs' Regional Headquarters Location Selection Strategies

John Holt, William R. Purcell, Sidney J. Gray, and Torben Pedersen

ECCO, a leading Danish manufacturer and retailer of footwear decided in 2004 to establish their Asia-Pacific headquarters (HQ) in Hong Kong for retail, sales, sourcing, distribution and general management functions. The German company, Atotech, has established RHQs in Rock Hill, South Carolina, USA, and Yokohama, Japan. Corning from the United States has a RHQ and its shared centre for financial transactions in Shanghai and there are a number of other examples of establishment and relocation of RHQs. A report from UNCTAD (2003) suggested a "world market for corporate headquarter operations" is emerging and provided many recent examples of relocations of HQ operations. In fact, UNCTAD (2003) counted 829 establishments or relocations of HQ operations worldwide between January 2002 and March 2003, which clearly indicate that the relocation of HQ operations is on the rise, and as such it merits careful academic consideration.

UNCTAD (2003) speaks of a new trend where increasing sophistication of ICT and transportation technology enables firms to slice up their HQ value chain of activities and optimize each individual value-adding activity's geographic location, for example, by relocating activities to RHQs. But, while there is a well-established literature on location of business activities like manufacturing, sales, R&D and so on, little is concerned with location of HQ operations and RHQs (Birkinshaw et al., 2006).

The issue of RHQs is a new area in international business (IB) research (Aoki and Tachiki, 1992; Morrison and Roth, 1992; Sullivan, 1992; Lehrer and Asakawa, 1995, 1999; Lasserre, 1996; Schutte, 1997; Lasserre and Schutte, 1999). The role of regionalism in MNE strategy is, however, not a new concept. Heenan and Perlmutter (1979) recognized regio-centrism as a further option in structuring the operations of the MNE by adding the regional category to their earlier observed ethnocentric, geocentric and polycentric typology more than 20 years ago. Throughout the 1980s, however, research remained firmly focused on the design and implementation of global strategies (Kogut, 1985; Ghoshal, 1986; Porter 1986) and with resolving the bipolar tensions of global integration and local responsiveness. Away from academe, however, local subsidiary managers continued to champion national responsiveness while HQ executives remained firmly convinced of the need for integration (Pralahad and Doz, 1981). Ohmae (1990) first observed a change in US MNE practice away from markets in Asia being handled by the MNEs' international divisions towards a new configuration centred on RHQs. He also observed the decentralization of responsibility for strategy and operations by Japanese MNEs to each of the triad markets.

Following Ohmae, researchers also began to theorize on the advantages of more regionally oriented strategies (Morrison et al., 1991). Among the reasons suggested for the growing preference of regional to global organization are economic (limits to economies of scale), geopolitical (regionalization of EU, NAFTA, APEC), strategic (regional differences in markets and employees) as well as organizational (the need to protect special subsidiary competencies and initiatives from a narrow HQ mentality) factors (Lehrer and Asakawa, 1995).

At a theoretical level the RHQ fitted neatly into the Bartlett and Ghoshal I-R framework with its mission to mediate the tension between HQ's call for global efficiency and local subsidiaries' push for national effectiveness. Executing this mandate, however, required the regional executive to maintain a matrix of sensitivities alert to the imperative of pooling resources, gaining synergies, promoting standardization and managing product life cycles, while simultaneously safeguarding the benefits of subsidiaries' responsiveness to local employees, competitors, markets and governments (Sullivan, 1992). Lehrer and Asakawa (1995, 1999), however, point to significant national differences in the organizational responses of multinational enterprises to regional management issues. The differences have been attributed to the level of "hands on management", attachment to the status quo, administrative heritage and structural preferences.

While the approach of most MNEs has been to formalize a triadic approach to the regionalization of their global operations, setting up RHQs in North America, Europe and Asia (Aoki and Tachiki, 1992; Lasserre, 1996), the issues surrounding specific location attractiveness within regions remain complex. Locations within regions vary in their attractiveness due to factors that include geography, population, infrastructure and government policies.

Variables associated with location attraction

While there has been no systematic attempt to exhaustively identify the variables associated with location attractiveness, studies of RHQs cite a number of possible variables associated with making RHQ location decisions. Most recently, a report by the Economist Intelligence Unit (2002) referring to a research study on RHQs in the Asia-Pacific region by Michael Enright and

Edith Scott, pointed to the significance of industry-type density as being a significant factor in location choice: partly explaining the dominant position of Hong Kong as the major RHQ centre for service sector firms because of its dense professional network of financial and service firms; Singapore as the dominant RHQ centre for manufacturing firms because of its leading role as a regional location for manufacturing industries and Sydney as the dominant centre for IT-based RHQs because of its vibrant IT market. Among individual key decision-making criteria, Enright and Scott cite "political stability", "proximity to potential customers", "telecommunications infrastructure", "proximity to existing customers" and "stable economic policy" as being the most significant, followed by "transport infrastructure", "legal transparency", "absence of corruption", "proximity to other regional markets", "access to the national markets" and "availability of skilled managers". Lasserre and Schutte (1999) suggest that the main criteria to influence the decision of where to locate an RHQ include "regional centrality", "convenience and cost factors" and "proximity to business". Aoki and Tachiki (1992), on the other hand, identified two first-order concerns that they observed were an influence on site attractiveness and hence the decision to locate RHQs. The first of these concerns referred to the importance of locating RHQs in a country or city where the MNE already manufactures or has a substantial market share. The second focused around minimizing the "cultural and economic distance", including the cost and time of transportation, communications and local operating expenses. Aoki and Tachiki (1992) described the second order concerns influencing location choice as superior infrastructure (seaports, container and warehouse facilities, airports and international communications systems), business climate (deregulation), a well-trained workforce (especially at managerial and professional levels) and favourable government policies (especially taxation) as being important.

In addition to these sources, the professional literature tends to suggest that the decisions determining the location of RHQs are more inclined to be complex, multidimensional and sometimes idiosyncratic. Tully (1998) writing on RHQs in Europe cited the quality of life, central location and infrastructure quality as the most important determinants of the ranking of Amsterdam and Brussels as the first and second ranked cities in Europe for RHQs. Yoost and Fisher (1996) listed excellent infrastructure and tax incentives as being the main determinants of Hong Kong and Singapore's comparative advantage in attracting RHQs within the Asian region. Forster (1996) cited Sydney's skilled multilingual workforce and its quality supply of real estate as being central to the decision of Bankers Trust and Amex to locate their Asian RHQs in Australia. In contrast, Kellogg established its RHQ for the Asia-Pacific in Australia because of its belief that Australia had the best raw materials, labour and R&D development in the region. Political stability, local skills and operational costs were cited by IBM as the key variables in the firm's location of its Regional Computing Services Center planned for Asia in Sydney (Jarrett,

1994). However, Hoechst's decision to shift its RHQ from Hong Kong to mainland China seems principally motivated by the company's desire to signal to the Chinese authorities its long-term commitment to China (Murdoch, 1997).

A significant criticism that can be raised against these studies is that they have not followed a standardized approach to identifying and measuring those variables closely associated with location attractiveness. This limitation not only prevents the comparison of attractiveness variables and their use across organizations, but also limits the generalizability of these studies by preventing the ability to meaningfully determine the variability in strategic importance that organizations attach to particular variables.

Explaining and investigating location choice

The literature suggests that there are many location selection factors that feature in different ways in individual firms' location decision processes. However, no study has yet systematically examined the complex of location issues surrounding RHQ investments. While these studies do articulate variables associated with making location decisions, there is no specifically articulated theory of RHQ location choice that helps us to understand the nature of the decision-making process and how it is related to RHQ location choice. Anecdotal evidence suggests that there is a broad spectrum of factors that are related to and influence location choice in some way, even though the variables that make up this spectrum is not fully known. While we accept that firms attach different levels of importance to these decision variables, we do not understand the mechanism that determines which variables firms find most attractive when making location choices. For example, no one has investigated how the contextual nature of firms, such as strategic orientation and the nationality of company origin, is related to the decision criteria they use. Consequently, the extent to which such organizational characteristics explain the patterns of decision criteria that MNEs use is not known. The issue of what factors determine the best location for an RHQ, and how these factors link with the firms' contextual characteristics, remains largely uninvestigated (Aoki and Tachiki, 1992; Morrison and Roth, 1992; Sullivan 1992; Lehrer and Asakawa, 1995).

Understanding the nature of this linkage, across a cross-section of organizations, will not only provide the basis for better explaining location choice, but also contribute to theory development. Furthermore, better understanding of the complex pattern of location variable interaction in the RHQ location decision has important implications for firms, state policy makers and researchers. From a firm perspective, MNEs can benefit from understanding the complex fit between the operational and business context of international firms and the type of location selection strategies such firms use when making RHQ location decisions. For government policy makers, knowledge of whether or not firm nationality, strategic purpose, technological capacity and RHQ function influence the efficacy of incentive regimes may be crucial to attracting RHQ investment. The purpose of this study is to specifically investigate (1) the nature of the decision-making processes underlying MNEs' RHQ location selection strategies and (2) the interface with a firm's contextual characteristics. To achieve this objective, two discrete research tasks present themselves.

Identifying the spectrum of location decision variables

Before any investigation can be conducted into the way MNEs use location selection criteria differently, there is a need to identify and understand what is the full spectrum of decision variables that are used in association with location choice. In the absence of any previous studies that do this, our first task is to map the range of decision variables that MNEs generally associate with making RHQ location choices. Only when the broad spectrum of location selection factors are identified, can the way organizations use these factors be examined. The problem is that no instrumentation consisting of a large spectrum of variable items, related to the task of making RHQ location choice, presently exists. The first research objective of this study thus becomes one of developing a standardized procedure (instrument) that profiles the importance organizations attach to specific variables when making location selection decisions.

Identifying classification categories and defining hypotheses

Having the means to profile organizations' decision criteria, a method of classifying organizations into different contextual categories needs to be determined, before the patterns of criteria usage can be compared. The research question that interests us here is: to what extent do MNEs, when grouped according to some distinctive contextual characteristic, use discernibly different decision criteria when making location selection decisions? To investigate this question it becomes necessary to determine which classification method is to be used for the purposes of examining the potentially different decision priorities that operate in different organizations.

A review of the international business and strategy literature suggests a number of possible classification categories that represent different operational and strategic mindsets spanning from the early EPG-framework of Perlmutter (1969), over Hofstede's work on the significance of national culture to more recent contributions on transnational strategies (Bartlett and Ghoshal, 1989). When it comes to making decisions about locating RHQs, three categories that come to the fore are (1) the strategic purpose for which RHQs are to be used; (2) the nationality of firms' origin; and (3) the industry sector to which they belong. Below we describe each type of classification category, together with a statement about how we hypothesize the relationship between organizations' strategic context and their decision criteria profile.

Strategic purpose of RHQ

Confronted with tension between needs for global integration and needs for national responsiveness multinational enterprises can behave in several ways. Some integrate their operations across borders, others let their subsidiaries in various companies behave almost as if they are national companies (Prahalad and Doz, 1981; Bartlett and Ghoshal, 1989; Doz and Ghoshal, 1994; Lehrer and Asakawa, 1995). MNE integration and local responsiveness constitute accepted generic choices, which represent polar strategic priorities, integration or responsiveness. One strategy usually remains preferred to the other and patterns of strategic decisions reflect patterns over time. Some MNEs, however, try to avoid developing a clear pattern of preference for national responsiveness or global integration, but attempt to combine elements of both. The strategies of such companies can be labelled as multifocal. Consistent with this extensive body of literature on MNE strategic choice and based on the global integration/ local responsiveness framework (Prahalad and Doz, 1981; Doz, 1986; Bartlett and Ghoshal, 1989; Lasserre and Schutte, 1999), it is hypothesized (H1): *that location decision priorities will differ in relative importance across strategic purpose categories.*

Nationality of company origin

There is a substantial international business and cross-cultural management literature that argues the importance of country-of-origin effects. Numerous studies have shown that the behaviour of MNEs is strongly influenced by a firm's nationality and that the decision criteria firms use are likely to differ consistently with the national priorities and preferences of the parent company's origin (e.g., Hofstede, 1994; Hodgetts and Luthans, 1999). Johanson and Vahlne (1977) first suggested a country-of-origin effect between psychic distance and location strategy. Kogut and Singh (1988) further explored the implications for entry mode behaviour of the psychic distances between countries. They found strong support for the effect of national culture on entry choice. Hennart and Larimo (1998) also found national origin affected the entry strategies of European and Japanese multinational enterprises entering the United States. In a different context researchers have pointed to the differential costs arising out of national differences associated with cross-border acquisitions and joint ventures (Morosini and Singh, 1994; Barkeema and Vermeulen, 1997). Given this research on the impact of national origin on entry strategy, we expect to see evidence of different criteria depending on the nationality of the parent company driving RHQ location selection strategies. It is hypothesized (**H2**): *that location decision priorities will differ in relative importance across the nationality of company origin categories.*

Industry sector

In this chapter we also control for industry sector. Many studies have shown that the relative importance of host country factors vary according to the particular investing industry. For example, different industries will require different kinds of customized location assets, such as labour skills, technical knowledge, management expertise, public infrastructure and technological capacity. Guisinger (1985) found that the impact of incentive regimes varied significantly across industries. Infrastructural requirements have also been shown to vary in importance depending on the special requirements of different industries (Loree and Guisinger, 1995).

There is also the suggestion that different location advantages favour different industry RHQs (EIU, 2002). Hong Kong is regarded as the RHQ centre for service sector firms because of its closeness to markets, quality management and its dense network of service and financial firms. Singapore's dominant position as a centre for manufacturing RHQs is often ascribed to government polices and excellent infrastructure, while Sydney's vibrant IT market, excellent telecommunications, multi-skilled workforce and lifestyle advantages make it an attractive RHQ location in industries where recent technological developments have arguably diminished the intra-regional importance of geography. The final hypothesis (**H3**) states: *that location decision priorities will differ in relative importance across the three industry sector categories of services, manufacturing and technology.*

Method

Sample

Our sample was drawn from a cross-section of the largest non-European MNEs with RHQs in Europe and non-Asia-Pacific MNEs with Asia-Pacific RHQs (located specifically in Australia). The sampling frame was limited to these RHQ locations on the grounds of the local knowledge of the researchers and accessibility. As a result, the findings of this study must be viewed as exploratory and subject to further research. The chief executives of these regional offices were used as the primary informants in the study. The regional CEO was considered to be the individual most cognizant of the firm's thinking and rationale about which issues and factors are important when making RHQ location decisions for the firm. However, it is recognized that this provides only one perspective on the RHQ location decision. Clearly, senior executives at corporate HQ may have different perspectives and experiences.

The CEOs of major RHQs within the European region (N = 342) and Australia as an important RHQ location in the Asia-Pacific region (N = 225) were mailed a survey questionnaire. The majority of the questionnaires were completed by CEOs from the Asia-Pacific site of Sydney, Australia. The European sites returning questionnaires represented locations such as London (UK), Belgium (Brussels) and Frankfurt (Germany). It was particularly difficult to obtain responses from the European RHQs. Despite a number of follow-up requests, a total of only 57 completed questionnaires (39 Australian and 18 European RHQs) were returned, resulting in an overall response rate of 10%. While this is a very low response rate, perhaps owing to the sensitivity and complexity of RHQ location decisions, the sample is adequate for the purposes of conducting an exploratory statistical analysis. Table 5.1 shows that the 57 companies used in this study represent a broad range of industry types. These were categorized into three groups: Computer Software (35.1%), Manufacturing (21.1%) and Health/Pharmaceutical (6%) sectors.

Research measures/survey design

A two-part questionnaire was developed to collect the necessary data for this study. Part A of the survey gathered demographic information about participating organizations such as nationality of parent origin; core business activity; the purpose of establishing present RHQ; the number of staff operating at RHQ; and the number of years the RHQ was established. Part B gathered information about the importance companies placed on a range of variables considered influential in making RHQ location decisions *in general*.

Table 5.1 Frequency distribution of organizational sample across industry type

Industry type	Count	%
Computer software	20	35.1
Health/pharmaceuticals	6	10.5
Professional services	2	3.5
Manufacturing	12	21.1
Telecommunications	3	5.3
Construction	3	5.3
Financial services	4	7.0
Education	1	1.8
Transport	1	1.8
Chemical	2	3.5
Insurance	1	1.8
Wholesale	1	1.8
Food	1	1.8
Total:	57	100.0

This section did not refer to factors relevant to the specific location of the RHQ in question.

Identifying location decision variables

The variables influencing RHQ location decisions are described in this study as location decision variables (LDV). The LDV items were chosen for inclusion in the survey following detailed content analysis of the IB location literature dealing with matters related to making decisions about RHQ selection. The items identified from this broad range of sources were intended to be as specific as possible in order to form a comprehensive set of factors associated with influencing location selection decisions. A total of 39 individual items were identified (see Table 5.3) relating to workforce characteristics; competitive business inputs; technological/educational infrastructure factors; government incentives; company characteristics factors; social, political and legal factors; economic factors; compatibility factors; financial factors; and intra-regional accessibility.

This part of the survey was designed to obtain measures of the strategic importance organizations attributed to specific location decision variables when making the decision to locate a specific RHQ. Such measures could be used to map the decision criteria underpinning specific RHQ location choices. In making the decision to locate an RHQ, respondents were required to indicate, on a 5 point Likert scale (where 1 = low importance and 5 = high importance), the level of importance their organization would place on each individual item when making such a decision. The objective here was for respondents to show how much each individual item would influence the decision process.

Classifying contextual categories

The three contextual categories chosen in this study to examine the presence of contrasting location decision mindsets are, as we have already discussed, Strategic Purpose, Nationality of Company Origin, and Industry Sector. To obtain measures representing different *strategic purposes* underlying RHQ establishment, respondents were asked to indicate by ticking the appropriate box, whether their present RHQ was established to (a) co-ordinate and facilitate global operations, or (b) to serve and be responsive to regional markets. The measure used to indicate the national origin of respondents' parent company was based on respondents' describing the national origin of their company.

Table 5.2 displays the sample distribution across these classification categories. In the first instance, we see that across our sample a total of 34 RHQs were established to pursue Regional Market Responsiveness strategies, with a total of 23 RHQs being established to pursue Global Co-ordination and Facilitation strategies. Table 5.2 also reveals that 35 companies were of North American, 12 of European and 10 of Asian origin.

Table 5.2 Frequency distribution of sample across classification categories

Classification categories	N	%
Strategic purpose (of RHQ establishment):	34	59.6
Regional market responsiveness	23	40.4
Global co-ordination and facilitation		
Total:	57	100
Nationality of company origin:		
North America (sub-total)	35	61.4
USA	30	
Canada	5	
Europe (sub-total)	12	21.1
Belgium	1	
Britian	5	
Germany	2	
Ireland	2	
Holland	2	
Asia (sub-total)	10	17.5
Hong Kong	1	
Japan	7	
Australia	2	
Total:	57	100
Industry sector:		
Services	11	19.30
Manufacturing	23	40.35
Technology	23	40.35
Total:	57	100

Results

Location decision variables: Relative importance

Each of the 39 specific variables associated with influencing location decisions are ordered according to their overall mean measure of importance. The median measure across the sample was 3.37. Nineteen location decision variables exceed this measure. A number of variable clusters emerge across the attributed importance ratings. Table 5.3 reveals that across all respondents the highest ranked group of decision variables centre around *infrastructure-related variables* such as communications, educational and transport infrastructure concerns. "Reliable communications infrastructure" (4.42) was the most important variable associated with the RHQ location decision followed equally by the "availability of highly skilled" (4.26) and "English-speaking staff" (4.26). Linked to the supply of available English-speaking staff was an "English-speaking environment" (4.11). The fifth most

Table 5.3 Relative importance of location decision variables

Location Decision Variables	Rank	Mean	SD
Reliable communications infrastructure	1	4.42	0.84
Availability of high-skilled staff	2 =	4.26	0.99
English-speaking workforce	2 =	4.26	1.01
English-speaking environment	4	4.11	0.98
Frequent and efficient international flights	5	4.04	1.05
Economic stability	6	3.98	0.92
Accessible geographical location	7	3.88	0.98
Local market growth potential	8	3.86	1.14
Presence of key technology suppliers	9	3.79	1.22
Commercial compatibility with home-base	10	3.72	1.11
Availability of reliable suppliers	11	3.63	1.23
Strong cultural links with region	12 =	3.61	1.05
Access to regional financial centre	12 =	3.61	1.10
Attractive company taxation regulations	14	3.58	1.24
Stable exchange rates	15	3.53	1.15
Regional telecommunications hub	16	3.49	1.23
Low priced telecom circuitry	17	3.46	1.12
Cultural compatibility with home-base	18	3.40	1.07
Competitively priced telecommunications	19	3.39	1.18
Competitively priced rent	20 =	3.37	1.17
Low operating costs	20 =	3.37	1.17
Competitively priced labour	22	3.30	1.13
Moderate interest rate environment	23	3.25	1.06
Attractive dividend withholding taxes	24	3.21	1.15
Low inflation environment	25	3.18	1.04
High quality health services	26	3.12	1.12
Flexibility of employment contracts	27	3.02	1.19
Local government tax incentives	28	2.96	1.22
Attractive government regulatory environment	29	2.91	1.27
Local government financial incentives	30	2.81	1.38
Central government establishment incentives	31	2.79	1.39
Central government financial incentives	32	2.75	1.37
Low-cost workforce	33	2.74	1.25
Local government infrastructure inputs	34	2.70	1.24
Local government establishment incentive	35	2.68	1.30
Low levels of industrial disputes	36	2.61	1.31
Low cost of health insurance	37	2.58	1.12
Low cost of cars	38	2.56	1.15
Low cost of schools	39	2.51	1.10

Notes: 1. The mean is the average on a scale of 1 (="low importance") to 5 (="high importance"). 2. SD = standard deviation important variable and final factor measuring above four on our 5 point Likert scale was "frequent and efficient international flights" (4.04). The importance of communications infrastructure reflects the need to manage and co-ordinate dispersed activities over the region; the availability of English-speaking, highly skilled staff reflects the most important direct input into RHQ operations; while access to world-class air transportation infrastructure reflects the need for regional managers to undertake frequent travel around the region.

The second order of variables relate firmly to *market-related location variables* such as "economic stability" (3.98), "accessible geographic location" (3.88), "local market growth potential" (3.86), "presence of key technology suppliers" (3.79), "commercial compatibility with home base" (3.72) and "reliable suppliers" (3.63). Economic stability is ranked far more highly than low taxes and government incentives, which rank lowly on the scale. The third group of variables that centre around the median score of importance consists of six factors related to *cultural ties* – "strong cultural links with region" (3.61) and "cultural compatibility" (3.41); *finance* – "attractive company taxation regulations" (3.58) and "stable exchange rates" (3.53); and *telecommunications* – "regional telecommunications hub" (3.49) and "low priced telecommunication circuitry" (3.46).

The variables below median importance were dominated by three groups of variables: *input costs* – "competitively priced telecommunications" (3.39), "competitively priced rent" (3.37), "low operating costs" (3.37), "competitively priced labour" (3.30), "moderate interest rate environment" (3.25), "attractive dividend withholding taxes" (3.21), "low inflation environment" (3.18), "low cost workforce" (2.74) and "low levels of industrial disputes" (2.61); *government incentives* – "local government tax incentives" (2.96), "attractive regulatory environment" (2.91), "local government financial incentives" (2.81), "central government establishment incentives" (2.79), "central government financial incentives" (2.75) and "local government establishment incentives" (2.68); and *cost of living factors* – "low cost of health insurance" (2.58), "low cost of cars" (2.56) and "low cost of schools" (2.51). Below we use principal components analysis to further understand the role these items play in influencing RHQ location decisions.

Identifying the factor dimensions underlying location decision variables

The data were examined to determine factorability. Initial examination of the correlation matrix reveals a good distribution of large and small coefficients, suggesting the presence of homogeneous sets of variables. Furthermore, with an overall Kaiser-Meyer–Olkin measure of sampling adequacy of .73 and with the Bartlett Test of Sphericity highly significant ($p < .00000$), the correlation matrix is considered appropriate for factoring. Assuming that all location decision variables are common variables associated with location choice decisions, principal components analysis was used to identify the common dimensions underlying the 39 location decision variables. This extraction method using varimax rotation yielded 9 factor dimensions accounting for 78.9% of the total variance. The reproduced correlation matrix and residual correlations indicate that this 9 factor structure model is a good fit with the data. The factor loadings and corresponding questionnaire items together with the percentage of variance accounted for are reported in detail in Table 5.4. A total of nine interpretable location decision factors emerge from the pattern of loadings displayed in Table 5.4 and were labelled as: Favourable Government Incentives, Low Operating Costs, Low Living Costs, Favourable Financial Environment, Effective Regional Links, Compatibility with Home-Base, Supportive Business Environment, Economical IT Infrastructure and Favourable Employment Relations. The factor scores for all nine dimensions were calculated using the regression method, which saved scores standardized around a mean of zero (Norusis, 1993) for further analysis.

Comparing location decision priorities across contextual categories

To determine how the 9 location decision factor dimensions are used differently across organizational contextual categories, the mean standardized factor scores derived above were analysed using the Oneway ANOVA procedure. Table 5.5 reports the ANOVA results comparing each location decision factor score mean across each set of contextual category subgroups.

Standardized factor scores are particularly useful in this kind of comparative task. They not only permit the comparison of scores relative to a mean of zero (Norusis, 1993), but also reveal the relative weight a particular factor possesses in relation to all other factors (Mendenhall et al., 1977). Applied to Table 5.5, it means that location decision factors with scores equal or close to zero are, compared to others, given an *"average importance weighting"* when making decisions about RHQ location. However, when decision factors are given scores above zero, that is a "positive" (+) value, it indicates in relative terms that such factors are given an *"above average importance weighting"* when making location decisions. By contrast, scores with "negative" (−) values indicate in relative terms factors' *"below average importance weighting"* in location decisions.

Using standardized means in this way allows us to compare how individual location decision factors differ in importance between subgroups of interest. That is, when the full set of decision factors are viewed as a whole, individual decision factors are seen against a set of complex inter-relationships that characterize the nature of each subgroup's decision priority mindset. The importance weightings presented in Table 5.5 capture the unique way individual factor dimensions are inter-related within each contextual category subgroup. Examining the way the factor dimensions are configured or

Table 5.4 Factor loadings of location decision variables

Factor Dimension Labels LSF Items	Factor 1	Factor 2	Factor 3	Factor 4	Factor 5	Factor 6	Factor 7	Factor 8	Factor 9
Factor 1: Favourable Government Incentives									
Local government financial incentives	0.9430								
Central government establishment incentives	0.9347								
Local government establishment incentives	0.9045								
Central government financial incentives	0.8447								
Local government infrastructure inputs	0.8246								
Local government tax incentives	0.7480								
Attractive company tax regulations	0.6433								
Attractive government regulatory environment	0.5692								
Factor 2: Low Operating Costs									
Low operating costs		0.8530							
Competitively priced labour		0.8348							
Low-cost workforce		0.8028							
Competitively priced rent		0.6996							
Factor 3: Low Living Costs									
Low cost of health insurance			0.8793						
Low costs of schools			0.8498						

Table 5.4   (Continued)

Factor Dimension Labels LSF Items	Factor 1	Factor 2	Factor 3	Factor 4	Factor 5	Factor 6	Factor 7	Factor 8	Factor 9
Low cost of cars			0.8236						
High quality health services			0.6331						
Factor 4: Favourable Financial Environment									
Moderate interest rate environment				0.7303					
Low inflation environment				0.7138					
Access to regional financial centres				0.6792					
Attractive dividend withholding taxes				0.6512					
Economic stability				0.5754					
Stable exchange rates				0.5255					
Factor 5: Effective Regional Links									
Frequent and efficient international flights					0.7800				
Accessible geographical location					0.7703				
Strong cultural links within region					0.6862				
Availability of highly skilled staff					0.5990				
Factor 6: Compatibility with Home-Base									
English speaking workforce						0.7836			
Commercial compatibility with home-base						0.7288			
English-speaking environment						0.6643			
Cultural compatibility with home-base						0.6529			

Factor 7: Supportive Business Environment									
Availability of reliable suppliers									0.7065
Presence of key technology suppliers									0.6202
Local market growth potential									0.6148
Regional telecommunications hub									0.6025
Factor 8: Economical IT Infrastructure									
Competitively priced telecommunications costs									0.6904
Low priced telecommunications circuitry									0.6784
Reliable communications infrastructure									0.5836
Factor 9: Favourable Employment Relations									
Flexibility of employment contracts									0.7660
Low level of industrial disputes									0.6722
Percentage of Variance Explained (Total = 78.9%)	38.5	9.9	6.3	5.6	4.8	4.1	3.7	3.1	2.8
Eigenvalue	15.02	3.86	2.47	2.17	1.86	1.61	1.43	1.22	1.09

Notes: 1. K-M-0 Measure of Sampling Adequacy = .7309
2. Bartlett Test of Sphericity = 2022.4533; *p* = .0000

Table 5.5   Factor score means and Mann–Whitney statistics compared across contextual categories

Factor Dimensions	Strategic Purpose of RHQ Establishment			Nationality of Company Origin				Industry Sector			
	RMR N=34 M(SD)	GCF N=23 SM(SD)	F-value	North America N=35 SM(SD)	Europe N=12 SM(SD)	Asia N=10 SM(SD)	F-value	Service N=11 SM(SD)	Manuf'ing N=23 SM(SD)	Technol'gy N=23 SM(SD)	F-value
Favorable government incentives	−.01 (1.03)	.01 (0.96)	0.00	.09 (0.94)	−.42 (1.22)	.20 (0.85)	1.43	−.66 (0.82)	.12 (1.07)	.19 (0.89)	3.19*
Low operating costs	.01 (1.11)	−.02 (0.82)	0.02	−.04 (1.03)	.30 (1.06)	−.22 (0.79)	0.82	−.01 (0.64)	.07 (1.13)	−.07 (1.13)	0.11
Low living costs	−.16 (0.96)	.24 (1.02)	2.33	.05 (0.96)	−.11 (1.27)	−.04 (0.81)	0.12	−.31 (0.85)	.22 (1.15)	−.07 (0.88)	1.14
Favorable financial environment	−.14 (0.95)	.21 (1.04)	1.65	−.01 (0.90)	.33 (1.29)	−.34 (0.89)	1.25	.24 (1.22)	.17 (1.01)	−.28 (0.83)	1.60
Effective regional links	−.08 (1.19)	.12 (0.60)	0.55	.11 (0.97)	.03 (1.11)	−.43 (0.92)	1.19	−.73 (1.34)	.30 (0.89)	.04 (0.74)	4.48**
Compatibility with home-base	.01 (1.05)	−.02 (0.93)	0.02	.17 (0.94)	−.06 (1.03)	−.51 (1.06)	1.85	.22 (1.22)	−.23 (0.91)	.12 (0.96)	1.05
Supportive business environment	−.13 (1.13)	.19 (0.74)	1.42	−.04 (0.92)	.15 (1.10)	−.03 (1.20)	0.17	−.26 (0.59)	−.15 (1.2)	.27 (083)	1.49
Economical IT infrastructure	.04 (1.10)	−.06 (0.84)	0.11	.13 (0.83)	−.17 (1.23)	−.25 (1.24)	0.78	−.16 (0.90)	.02 (0.92)	.05 (1.13)	0.17
Favorable employment relations	−.34 (0.86)	.51 (0.97)	11.86**	−.04 (1.00)	.15 (1.32)	−.05 (0.49)	0.18	−.06 (0.96)	.06 (0.79)	−.03 (1.20)	0.07
Mann–whitney statistic	**Mean rank** = 6.56 *cf* 12.44 *U* = 14.07 Z Score = −2.34 2-Tailed *p* = .01 (cft)			USA cf Europe	**Mean rank** = 9.78 *cf* 9.22 *U* = 38.0 Z Score = −.22 2-Tailed *p* = .82 (cft)			Manuf cf Tech	**Mean rank** = 10.39 *cf* 8.61 *U* = 32.5 Z Score = −.70 2-Tailed *p* = .47 (cft)		
				Europe cf Asia	**Mean rank** = 11.56 *cf* 7.44 *U* = 22.0 Z Score = −1.63 2-Tailed *p* = .10 (cft)			Service cf Manuf	**Mean rank** = 7.28 *cf* 11.72 *U* = 20.5 Z Score = −1.76 2-Tailed *p* = .07 (cft)		
				USA cf Asia	**Mean rank** = 12.61 *cf* 6.39 *U* = 12.5 Z Score = −2.47 2-Tailed *p* = .01 (cft)			Service cf Tech	**Mean rank** = 7.78 *cf* 11.22 *U* = 25.0 Z Score = −1.36 2-Tailed *p* = .17 (cft)		

Notes: 1. **RMR** – Regional market responsiveness; **GCF** – Global coordination and facilitation.
2. * $p < .05$; ** $p < .01$; cft – Corrected for ties.

structured for each subgroup provides insight into the mindset that each subgroup brings to the task of making RHQ location decisions.

Table 5.5 also presents the Mann–Whitney Statistics. The Mann–Whitney procedure is an assumption free test used to determine whether two independent samples come from populations that have the same distribution of importance weightings (Howell, 1982; Meddis, 1984). This procedure examines the distribution of difference between samples by examining the way groups *distribute their ranks* and by comparing the *relative magnitude of the weightings* each group attributes to the same items. As a measure of relative standing, the *z* score depicts the standard deviation between the range of values associated with each of the location decision items and the mean of those values. The importance of this procedure for this study is that it enables us to determine the extent to which contextual category subgroups reveal significant dissimilarities in the distribution of location decision priorities, thus demonstrating the presence of distinctive and contrasting location decision mindsets.

Figure 5.1 compares the decision priority schema across the subgroups of each classification category. By displaying the mean importance values (standardized factor score means) relative to a centre point, Figure 5.1 enables differences in the distribution of location decision priorities to be examined and compared.

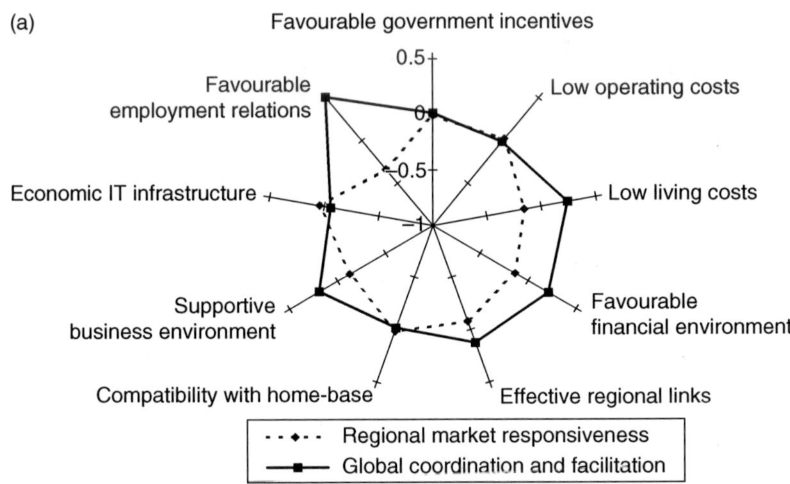

Figure 5.1 Location decision priority structures compared across contextual categories. (a) Strategic purpose of RHQ (b) Nationality of company (c) Industry sector.

(b)

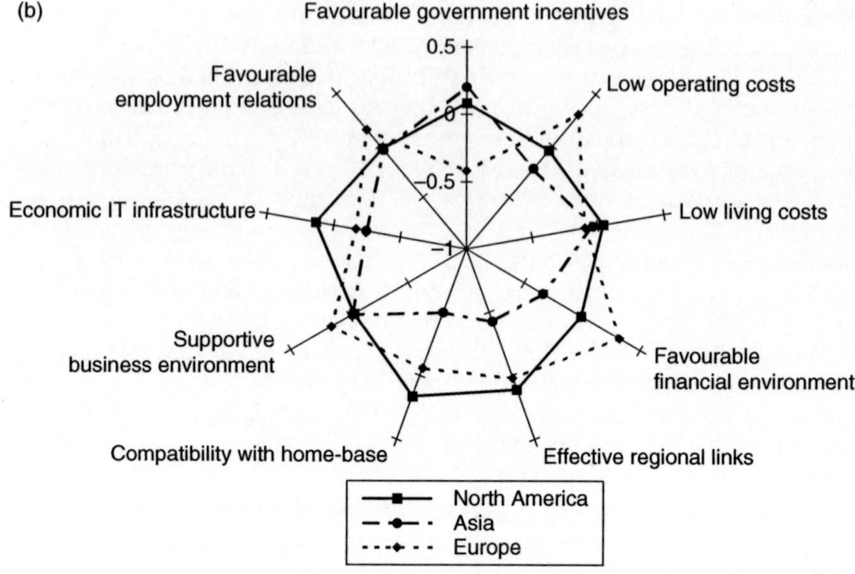

(c)

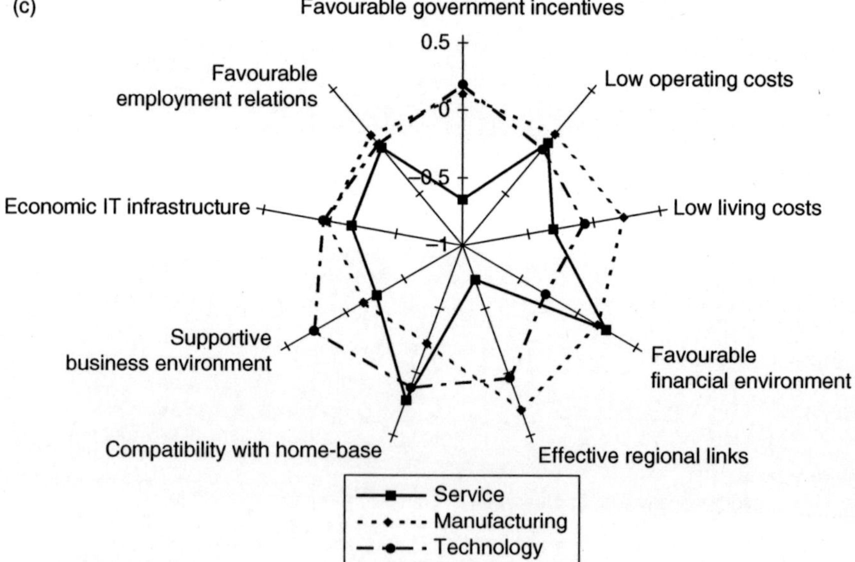

Figure 5.1 (Continued)

Examining hypothesis one

The first hypothesis is concerned with testing whether the location decision priority structures differ significantly according to the strategic purpose for which RHQs will be used. To investigate whether we see any support for this hypothesis, we must examine how the pattern of decision priority structures compare across the strategic purpose subgroups of this study – Regional Market Responsiveness and Global Co-ordination. In the first instance, Table 5.5 reveals that only one location decision factor, "Favourable Employment Relations" ($F = 11.86$, $p < .01$), was found to differ significantly between subgroups. However, Table 5.5 tells us more about the decision priorities of these groups by revealing a complex set of inter-relationships that reflect the nature and character of each groups' location decision mindset. Below we describe the way groups' contrasting location decision priorities are structured.

Location decision priorities for RHQs pursuing regional responsiveness strategies

Examining Table 5.5 we find that the strategic mindset of firms whose RHQ is to pursue a regional responsiveness strategy is characterized by the following decision priority structure. In this strategic mindset, the location decision factor of "Economical IT Infrastructure" ($SM = 0.04$) dominates this group's decision priority structure (i.e., given *above average importance weightings*). Factors such as "Compatibility with Home-Base" ($SM = 0.01$), "Low Operating Costs" ($SM = 0.01$), and "Favourable Government Incentives" ($SM = -0.01$) are given *average importance weightings* (i.e., factor scores close to zero). Factors receiving *below average importance weightings* are "Favourable Employment Relations" ($SM = -0.34$), "Low Living Costs" ($SM = -0.16$), "Favourable Financial Environment" ($SM - 0.14$), "Supportive Business Environment" ($SM = -0.13$) and "Effective Regional Links" ($SM = -0.08$).

What we learn from this decision priority structure is that the primary goal of this type of RHQ is to get as close as it can to its market. That being the case, it means that for these organizations the basis of choice is in fact very limited. A decision priority structure does exist, as we can see, but given the primary goal the basis of choice is in practical terms limited. If it has a choice, then the first factor to be taken into consideration in locating an RHQ is having access to an economical IT infrastructure. This is followed by consideration being given to a location that offers some compatibility with the firm's prior experience, low operating costs and favourable government incentives. Location decisions for this group are based around the pragmatic concerns of operational costs.

Location decision priorities for RHQs pursuing global co-ordination strategies

In a similar way, we observe that for RHQs pursuing a global co-ordination strategy the factors that feature highly in the decision priority structure (i.e., factors given *above average importance ratings*) of these firms, include

"Favourable Employment Relations" ($SM = 0.51$), "Low Living Costs" ($SM = .24$), "Favourable Financial Environment" ($SM = 0.21$), "Supportive Business Environment" ($SM = 0.19$) and "Effective Regional Links" ($SM = 0.12$). Location decision factors lower down the priority structure (i.e., given *average importance ratings*) include: "Favourable Government Incentives" ($SM = 0.01$), "Low Operating Costs" ($SM = -0.02$), and "Compatibility with Home-Base" ($SM = -.02$). At the bottom of this group's decision priority structure (i.e., given *below average importance weightings*) is the factor "Economical IT Infrastructure" ($SM = -0.06$).

We observe from this decision priority structure that RHQs pursuing a global co-ordination strategy, compared to those pursuing a regional responsiveness strategy, have the luxury of being able to base their location decisions on a broader range of decision criteria. A global co-ordination strategy does not necessarily require the RHQ to be close to its market or regional operations. The nature of a co-ordination role means that such an RHQ can base its location criteria on a range of very different issues. We learn from this priority data that for these firms the primary concern in making location choices is with such things as the type of employment relations the environment presents, the presence of a supportive business environment, the cost of living in general, the presence of a favourable financial environment and efficient access to regional links. This type of RHQ does not need to be particularly close to its market per se. How quickly it can get to any part of the region, and beyond, is what is strategically important to these firms. Not only does this group have more choices, but its decision criteria centre around more intangible concerns, rather than concerns of pragmatic operational costs.

Figure 5.1(a) schematically maps the decision priority structures of the two groups just described. The Mann–Whitney procedure concludes that the location decision priority structures representing each strategic purpose subgroup differs significantly ($U = 14.0$, 2 Tailed $p = .01$) due to two contributing factors. First, the difference in mindset is due to a difference in the way subgroups *distribute their ranks*. For example, compared to the regional responsiveness group, results reveal that with a mean rank of 12.44 the global co-ordination group had the largest number of location decision factors that were given "above average" weightings. The second factor contributing to mindset differences is the way groups *vary in the magnitude of the weightings* they attribute to each of the location decision factors, as represented by the Mann–Whitney computed z score. As a measure of relative standing, the z score depicts the standard deviation between the range of values associated with each of the location decision items and the mean of those values. A z score of -2.34 represents a significant level of value dispersion. An overall Mann–Whitney Statistic (U) of 14.0 also confirms that this level of dispersion is associated with more systematic than random differences in the distribution of priorities.

The evidence described here illustrates the point that the location decision priorities associated with each group represents different and contrasting location decision strategies that match groups' strategic purpose. Such evidence supports our first hypothesis that the intended role of the RHQ determines the particular decision priority structure on which the location decision is based.

Examining hypothesis two

Our second hypothesis is concerned about testing the proposition that location decision priority structures differ according to firms' nationality of company origin. We test this proposition by examining the importance weightings that firms from North America, Europe and Asia gave to each of the location decision factors, as presented in Table 5.4. Given the small sample size associated with two of the nationality of country origin groups (Europe = 12 and Asia = 10), no significant F values were generated. However, Figure 5.1(b) reveals that when the standardized means for each factor dimension are plotted across all country-of-origin groups the North American, European and Asian decision priority structures are seen to be uniquely structured. Below we describe the nature of each group's location decision priority structures.

Location decision priorities of North American-based firms

The location selection priorities of North American firms were found to be structured in the following way. The location selection factors at the top of the priority structure (i.e., attracting *above average importance weightings*) are "Compatibility with Home-Base" ($SM=0.17$), "Economical IT Infrastructure" ($SM=0.13$), "Effective Regional Links" ($SM=0.9$), "Favourable Government Incentives" ($SM=0.9$) and "Low Living Costs" ($SM=0.05$). Given *average importance weighting* is the factor – "Favourable Financial Environment" ($SM=0.01$). Further down the priority structure again are the factors receiving *below average importance* ratings, such as: "Low Living Costs" ($SM=-0.04$), "Favourable Employment Relations" ($SM=-0.04$) and "Supportive Business Environment" ($SM=-0.04$). What we learn from this decision priority structure is that the RHQ location decision of North American firms is driven primarily by a mix of business efficiency and incentive concerns. That is, the choice of location appears to be predicated upon efficiencies derived from compatibilities with home-base, established infrastructure and incentives.

Location decision priorities of European-based firms

The location decision priorities used by our sample of European firms reveal a priority structure that attributes *average or above importance weightings* to "Favourable Financial Environment" ($SM=0.33$), "Low Operating Costs" ($SM=0.30$), "Supportive Business Environment" ($SM=0.15$),

"Favourable Employment Relations" ($SM=0.15$) and "Effective Regional Links" ($SM=0.03$). Those items given *below average importance weightings* were "Favourable Government Incentives" ($SM=-0.42$), "Economical IT Infrastructure" ($SM=-0.17$), "Low Living Costs" ($SM=-0.11$) and "Compatibility with Home-Base" ($SM=-0.06$). This priority structure appears to be driven by a unique mix of strategic intangibles (nature of operational environment) and bottom-line cost concerns.

Location decision priorities of Asian-based firms

Our results reveal that the location decision priority schemas associated with Asian firms are structured very differently to those of North American and European firms. Asian firms' decision priority structure was found to attribute *average or above importance weightings* to "Favourable Government Incentives" ($SM=0.20$), "Supportive Business Environment" ($SM=-0.03$), "Low Living Costs" ($SM=-0.04$) and "Favourable Employment Relations" ($SM=-0.05$). The rest of the decision priority structure, arranged in descending order of importance is "Compatibility with Home-Base" ($SM=-0.51$), "Effective Regional Links" ($SM=-0.43$), "Favourable Financial Environment" ($SM=-0.34$), "Economic IT Infrastructure" ($SM=-0.25$) and "Low Operating Costs" ($SM=-0.22$). The driving force behind this priority structure is almost solely one that is driven by government incentives, and to a lesser extent, cost concerns.

Despite the elements of difference in North American and European decision priority schemas described above, the Mann–Whitney procedure reveals that the difference between these schemas was not significant ($U=38.0$, 2 Tailed $p=.82$). Figure 5.1(b) reveals that while there is some indication of difference in the prioritization of location decision factors on all measures of relative standing, these differences are small with a relatively similar mean rank. On the other hand, while the differences between European and Asian firms' location decision priorities are not statistically significant, the lower Mann–Whitney statistic ($U=22.0$) suggests that the distribution of priorities are due more to the nationality of company origin than to chance. As for comparing the North American with Asian decision priority schemas, our results show that with a mean rank of 12.61 (North American) and 6.39 (Asian) and a Mann–Whitney (U) of 12.5, the differences between North American and Asian decision priority schemas are highly significant ($p < .01$). Overall, the location decision priority differences observed across the nationality of company origin categories are in support of our second hypothesis. In so doing, we witness both the influence of cultural distance (explaining closeness of American and European priorities and the difference with Asian priorities), as well as the effects of intra-regional dynamics shaping decision schema structure.

Examining hypothesis three

The third hypothesis sets out to explore the proposition that the relative importance of location decision priorities will vary across industry sector. Table 5.5 presents the mean importance weightings that service, manufacturing and technology firms placed on each of the location decision factors. An examination of these means reveal that two location decision factors, "Favourable Government Incentives" ($F = 3.19$, $p < .05$) and "Effective Regional Links" ($F = 4.48$, $p < .01$), differ significantly across the three industry sector subgroups. Comparing standardized means across subgroups, we learn that technology firms in particular place the factor of "Favourable Government Incentives" near to the top of their decision priority structure ($SM = 0.19$), while service firms place the same decision factor near to the bottom of their decision priority structure ($SM = -0.66$). We also learn that manufacturing firms place the location factor "Effective Regional Links" at the top of their priority structure ($SM = 0.30$) when making RHQ location selection decisions, while the same location factor appears at the bottom of service firms decision priority structure ($SM = -0.73$). Furthermore, a closer examination of the mean scores in Table 5.5 reveals how each group's location decision priorities are structured very differently. Below we briefly describe the nature and character of these differences.

Location decision priorities of service sector firms

Table 5.5 reveals that for service sector firms their decision priority structure is dominated (i.e., given above average importance weightings) by factors such as "Favourable Financial Environment" ($SM = 0.22$) and "Compatibility with Home-Base" ($SM = 0.24$). Average importance weightings (i.e., factor scores close to zero) are given to factors such as "Low Operating Costs" ($SM = -0.01$) and "Favourable Employment Relations" ($SM = -0.06$). Factors placed at the bottom of the decision priority structure are found to include "Effective Regional Links" ($SM = -0.73$), "Favourable Government Incentives" ($SM = -0.66$) and "Low Living Costs" ($SM = -0.26$). Here we see that the decision process is convenience driven, that is, driven by a favourable financial environment and a familiar operational environment.

Location decision priorities of manufacturing sector firms

The sample of manufacturing firms used in this study exhibit decision priorities that are characterized in the following way. For this group of firms, the location decision factors that were placed at the top of their priority structure are "Effective Regional Links" ($SM = 0.30$), "Low Living Costs" ($SM = 0.22$), "Favourable Financial Environment" ($SM = 0.17$), "Favourable Government Incentives" ($SM = 0.12$), "Low Operating Costs" ($SM = .07$) and "Favourable Employment Relations" ($SM = 0.06$). The factor given average importance when making location decisions is "Economical IT Infrastructure" ($SM = 0.02$). On the other hand, factors of least importance in making location decisions are "Compatibility with Home-Base" ($SM = -0.23$) and "Supportive Business Environment" ($SM = -0.15$). What we learn from the priorities structure of these manufacturing firms is that RHQ location decisions are driven primarily by cost effectiveness.

Location decision priorities of technology sector firms

The distribution of mean scores reveal here that for technology firms the location decision factors that carry the highest weighting when making location decisions are factors such as "Supportive Business Environment" ($SM = 0.27$), "Favourable Government Incentives" ($SM = 0.19$), "Compatibility with Home-Base" ($SM = 0.12$) and "Economical IT Infrastructure" ($SM = 0.05$). Factors receiving average importance weightings are "Effective Regional Links" ($SM = 0.04$) and "Favourable Employment Relations" ($SM = -0.03$). By contrast, the lowest priority factors are "Favourable Financial Environment" ($SM = 0.28$), "Low Operating Costs" ($SM = -0.07$) and "Low Living Costs" ($SM = -0.07$). Compared to other sectors, the decision priorities of technology firms appear here to be driven by broad concerns for a supportive environment, spread across business and government and a familiar operational culture.

The Mann–Whitney test was used to determine the structural similarity or difference between groups' decision priorities. This test reveals that while there was no statistically significant difference between the mean rank of any industry subgroup's decision priorities, the difference between the priority structure of service firms (7.28) and the mean rank of manufacturing firms (11.72) was approaching significance ($U = 20.5$, 2 Tailed $p = .07$). The evidence described here, that is, the differences in decision factor scores (Table 5.5), the low U of 20.5 and the schematic contrasts between the prioritization patterns illustrated in Figure 5.1(c), when viewed together provide general support for our third hypothesis.

Discussion

The lowering of trade and investment barriers in combination with the increasing sophistication of ICT and transportation technologies enable firms to slice up HQ activities and relocate them at the regional level in RHQs. This increase in the mobility of HQ activities takes place against the background of the current wave of offshoring and outsourcing of service-related activities.

In terms of the broader implications of the research, the most important point is that the drivers of RHQ location are very different from the location drivers of other business activities like manufacturing, sales, R&D and so on. The evidence that emerges from this study provides general support for our research propositions on the factors determining the location decision for RHQs. In doing so, this evidence lays a foundation for better understanding of how MNEs' contextual characteristics are related to their RHQ location selection strategies. Below we discuss the contribution this exploratory research makes to understanding RHQ location decision processes.

Dimensionality of location decision factors

The principal components analysis results described here are significant because they provide for the first time an empirically derived set of dimensions that underlie MNEs' RHQ location selection strategies. All nine factors identified are generally reflective of the types of factors alluded to throughout the prescriptive and professional IB literature (Aoki and Tachiki, 1992; Yoost and Fisher, 1996; Forster, 1996; Tully, 1998). Another reason for the importance of these results is that they support a multidimensional view of the decision-making process used in making RHQ location choices. The identification of such a broad range of common dimensions as described in Table 5.5 is important because it provides the means by which variability in location decision schemas can be observed, measured and compared across different contextual conditions. The IB literature indicates that there are numerous issues that need to be considered when deciding where to locate RHQs. These factor results demonstrate that firms relate to a complex set of location decision factors when making location selection decisions.

Variability in location decision priorities

This study has used factor score means to examine how location decision priority structures vary under different contextual conditions. Our results have shown that location decision factors have different levels of relevance to different firms thereby revealing decision priority structures that configure differently across subgroups within the two contextual conditions examined, as Figure 5.1 portrays. The evidence associated with these two classification categories demonstrates an empirical link between the firms' contextual characteristics and variability in location decision priorities.

Comparing the strategic purpose data reveals the close relationship between strategic objective and decision criteria in RHQ location selection. Our data confirm the reasonable expectation that the purpose for which an RHQ is established is linked to a specific set of decision priorities. The nationality of company origin data, on the other hand, reveals how cultural distance influences RHQ location decisions. In so doing, it supports the cross-cultural literature which argues that differences in cultural perceptions arise where large cultural distances occur (Adler, 1995). The finding that the Mann–Whitney procedure reveals no difference in location decision priorities between US and European firms does confirm the culture distance argument. In other words, while differences are observed between US and European decision priorities, the small cultural distance between these two cultural orientations explains the Mann–Whitney conclusion of no significant differences between the priority structures. The strong statistical difference between US and Asian firms decision priorities also supports the cultural distance argument. While statistical support for this hypothesis is not found in the Asian and European comparison, the reason for this may be due to sample size. By increasing the sample size, future research may find that the distance between the mean ranks will increase.

In addition to illustrating the impact of strategic purpose and cultural distance on influencing location selection processes, our study also draws attention to the underlying mechanism that drives location choice. The evidence presented in this study demonstrates the interface between the contextual conditions specific to firms and the particular set of location decision factors that shape firms' RHQ selection criteria. The association demonstrated in this study supports the argument that firms' contextual conditions operate as organizing mechanisms that determine the mindset that drives firms' location selection strategies.

Research and policy implications

There are important implications that arise from this study for both researchers and policy makers. The trend is clearly towards establishment of more RHQs and greater levels of RHQ relocation and such changes raise a number of questions. Our results confirm the need for more systematic study into the decision-making dynamics of multinationals' RHQ location selection process as more HQ activities are expected to be relocated to RHQs (and shared service centres) in the future. In order to advance knowledge and theory on the RHQ location decision processes, two areas of research need to be further addressed. First, there is a basic need to confirm the dimensionality of the location decision factors identified in this study across a broader sample of MNEs who have headquartered in other global regions. Second, and more important, there is a need to develop our understanding of the task of RHQs thus capturing the variation in RHQ roles. At one end of the spectrum some RHQs have small numbers of staff and only assume limited co-ordination activities in the region, while at the other end some RHQs manage sales, production, purchasing, finance and research and development for the whole region. There is a need to understand the differentiated roles and capabilities assigned to each level of geography (the regional level as well as the local and global level) with differing degrees of importance corresponding to different dimensions of activities.

For MNCs, the challenge is to be able to access the full costs and benefits of RHQ location rather than focusing narrowly on efficiency gains, and here our research provides a way of thinking through the drivers and helps to frame the choice in a more structured way. The implications that arise from this study for policy makers are twofold. Not only does this study inform policy makers of the complexity and contingent nature of the RHQ location decision process, it also provides insight about the choice criteria associated with specific contextual mechanisms. Such knowledge and its refinement will assist policy makers to be more strategic in their design of RHQ location policies for attracting and maintaining MNEs' RHQ location commitment.

Conclusion

In conclusion, we point out three ways in which our study extends the current RHQ literature, although it should be emphasized that our findings are exploratory being based on a small sample of CEO respondents from RHQs located in Europe and the Asia-Pacific (specifically Australia). First, our study adds to the literature which sees the RHQ phenomenon as an important co-ordination mechanism used by MNEs as they respond to globalization pressures (e.g., Porter, 1986; Martinez and Jarillo, 1989; Aoki and Tachiki, 1992). We show how organizational context appears to interface with the responsiveness–integration trade off multinationals make when deciding where to locate RHQs. Secondly, the conventional RHQ literature views the choice process associated with RHQ location predominantly from a "competing incentives" perspective (e.g., Boddewyn and Brewer, 1994; David, 1994). Our study indicates that we should move beyond a preoccupation with the simple notion of incentive regimes and focus attention on the multidimensional nature of location decision processes. In so doing, this study suggests a more comprehensive view of the complex interface between firms' contextual characteristics and location selection strategies than that provided in previous studies. Finally, perhaps the foremost contribution this exploratory study makes to the literature is that it provides a way of explaining the linkage between firms' contextual conditions and firms' variability in location decision priorities. In particular, it shows how a specific set of location decision priorities that are *relevant* to one group of firms sharing similar contextual conditions may be *irrelevant* to another group of firms having different contextual conditions. In the light of the complexity of this association, we would argue, along with Doty and Glick (1994) and Ketchen et al. (1993), that a configurational research approach is best suited to guide future research and theory development of this important and emerging strategic issue.

References

Adler, N. (1995), Competitive Frontiers: Cross-Cultural Management in the 21st Century. *International Journal of Intercultural Relations*, 19(3): 523–537.

Aoki, A. and Tachiki, D. (1992), Overseas Japanese Business Operations: The Emerging Role of Regional Headquarters, *Pacific Business and Industries*, 1: 26–39.

Barkema, H. G. and Vermeulen, F. (1997), What Differences in the Cultural Backgrounds of Partners are Detrimental for International Joint Ventures, *Journal of International Business Studies*, 28(4): 845–864.

Bartlett, C. and Ghoshal, S. (1989), *Managing Across Borders: The Transnational Solution* (Boston: Harvard Business School Press).

Birkinshaw, J., Braumerhjelm, P., Holm, U., and Terjesen, S. (2006), Why Do Some Multinational Corporations Relocate their Headquarters Overseas? *Strategic Management Journal*, 27: 681–700.

Boddewyn, J. and Brewer, T. (1994), International Business Political Behavior: New Theoretical Dimensions, *Academy of Management Review*, 19 (1): 119–133.

Doz, Y. (1986), Government Policies and Global Industries, in M. Porter (ed.), *Competition in Global Industries*, (Boston, Mass.: Harvard Business School Press).

Doz, Y. and Ghohal, S. (1994), Organising for Europe: One Size does not Fit All! *Working Paper, INSEAD*.

David, P. (1994), Clio and the Economics of QWERTY, *American Economic Review Proceedings*, 75: 332–337.

Doty, D.H. and Glick, W.H. (1994), Typologies as a Unique Form of Theory Building: Toward Improved Understanding and Modelling, *Academy of Management Review*, 19(2), 230–251.

Economist Intelligence Unit (EIU). (2002), *Business Asia* (London: EIU).

Forster, C. (1996), A Down Under Perception on Asia, *Journal of Business Strategy*, 17(3): 38–39.

Ghoshal, S. (1986), Global Strategy: An Organising Framework, *Strategic Management Journal*, 8(5): 425–440.

Guisinger, S. (1985), *Investment Incentives and Performance Requirements*, (New York: Praeger).

Heenan, D. and Perlmutter, H.V. (1979), *Multinational Organizational Development*, (Reading, Mass.: Addison-Wesley).

Hennart, J.-F. and Larimo, J. (1998), The Impact of Culture on the Strategy Of Multinational Enterprises: Does National Origin Affect Ownership Strategy, *Journal of International Business Studies*, 29(3): 515–538.

Hodgetts, R.M. and Luthans, F. (1999), *International Management*, (Maidenhead: McGraw-Hill).

Hofstede, G. (1994), The Business of International Business is Culture, *International Business Review*, 3(1): 1–14.

Howell, D.C. (1982), *Statistical Methods for Psychology* (Boston, Mass.: Duxbury Press).

Jarrett, I. (1994), Pushing to be Southern Tiger, *Asian Business*, 30 October: 40–44.

Johanson, J. and Vahlne, J.E. (1977), The Internationalization Process of the Firm: A Model of Knowledge Development and Increasing Foreign Market Commitments, *Journal of International Business Studies*, 8(1): 23–32.

Ketchen, D.J., Thomas, J.B., and Snow, C.G. (1993), Organizational Configurations and Performance: A Comparison of Theoretical Approaches, *Academy of Management Journal*, 36(6): 1278–1333.

Kogut, B. (1985), Designing Global Strategies: Comparative and Competitive Value Chains, *Sloan Management Review*, 26(4): 15–28.

Kogut, B. and Singh, H. (1988), *Journal of International Business Studies*, 19(2): 411–432.

Lasserre, P. (1996), Regional Headquarters: The Spearhead for Asia Pacific Markets, *Long Range Planning*, 29(1) February: 30–37.

Lasserre, P. and Schutte, H. (1999), *Strategies for Asia Pacific: Beyond the Crisis*, (South Yarra: Macmillan), Ch. 9.

Lehrer, M. and Asakawa, K. (1995), Regional Management and Regional Headquarters in Europe: A Comparison of American and Japanese MNCs, *INSEAD Working Paper*, 95/01/SM, 19.

Lehrer, M. and Asakawa, K. (1999), Unbundling European Operations: Regional Management and Corporate Flexibility in American and Japanese MNCs, *Journal of World Business*, 34(3): 267–286.

Loree, D W. and Guisinger, S. (1995), Policy and Non-Policy Determinants of US Equity Foreign Direct Investment, *Journal of International Business Studies*, Second Quarter: 26(2): 281–299.

Martinez, J. and Jarillo, J. (1989), The Evolution of Research on Coordination Mechanisms in Multinational Corporations, *Journal of International Business Studies*, 22(3): 489–514.

Meddis, R. (1984), *Statistics Using Ranks*, (New York: Basil Blackwell).

Mendenhall, W., McClave, J.T., and Ramey, M. (1977), *Statistics for Psychology*, (North Scituate, Mass.: Duxbury Press).

Morosini, P. and Singh, H. (1994), Post-Cross-border Acquisitions: Implementing 'National Culture-Compatible' Strategies to Improve Performance, *European Management Journal*, 12(4): 390–400.

Morrison, A.J. and Roth, K. (1992), The Regional Solution: An Alternative to Globalization, *Transnational Corporations*, 1(2) August: 37–55.

Morrison, A., Ricks, D., and Roth, K. (1991), Globalization Versus Regionalisation: Which Way for the Multinational? *Organizational Dynamics*, 19: 17–29.

Norusis, M.J. (1993), *SPSS for Windows Professional Statistics R 6.0*, (Chicago, Ill.: SPSS Inc.).

Ohmae, K. (1990), *The Borderless World: Power and Strategy in the Interlinked Economy* (London: Collins).

Perlmutter, H. V. (1969), The Tortuous Evolution of the Multinational Corporation, *Columbia Journal of World Business*, 4: 9–18.

Porter, M. (1986), *Competition in Global Industries*, (Boston: Harvard Business School Press).

Prahalad, C. K. and Doz, Y. (1981), An Approach to Strategic Control on MNCs, *Sloan Management Review*, Summer 22(4): 5–13.

Schutte, H. (1997), Regional Headquarters of Japanese and Western MNCs: A Comparative Study, *INSEAD Working Paper*, 97/18/ABA, 44.

Sullivan, D. (1992), Organization in American MNCs: The Perspective of the European Regional Headquarters, *Management International Review*, 32: 237–250.

Tully, K. (1998), Kudos Count More Than Cost, *Corporate Location*, March/April: 14–17.

UNCTAD. (2003), *World Investment Report*, (Geneva: UN).

Yoost, D. and Fisher, J. (1996), Choosing Regional HQs in Asia, *International Tax Review*, 7(3): 35–39.

6

A Signaling Theory Investigation of How to Overcome Negative Country-of-Origin Effects

Lance E. Brouthers, John W. Story, and John Hadjimarcou

Signaling theory, which finds its roots in information economics and relies on the idea of information asymmetry (Spence, 1973), may provide some guidance with respect to possible ways firms may ameliorate the effects of negative country stereotypes. The concept of information asymmetry simply suggests that one party in an exchange (e.g., manufacturers) possesses information about the product that the other party (e.g., consumers) does not have (Rao et al., 1999; Kirmani and Rao, 2000). In the case of products associated with Developing Countries (DCs), the consumer and marketer may possess not only asymmetrical information, but information that is strongly contradictory.

Signaling theory helps us understand the role country of origin (COO) plays in consumer evaluations of DC products and offers various avenues on how to reduce negative COO effects, thus allowing DC companies to compete with MNCs in first world markets.

What makes this chapter unique is that we depart from previous studies that tend to treat COO as if it were a brand (Tse and Gorn, 1993; Verlegh and Steenkamp, 1999). According to the signaling theory, brands contain a bonding component (Rao et al., 1999). Therefore, we surmise that because COO labels lack a bonding component they cannot be treated similar to brands. They actually represent the static or noise that prevents consumers from arriving at objective product judgments.

Using signaling theory as an analogy, our exploratory study examines three strategies DC firms may use to tackle the issue of negative stereotypes in first world markets: reducing the noise caused by negative COO through multiple country-of-origin labels, strengthening the signal through the use of brands, and by using familiar brands and multiple COO labels).

Conceptual framework

The development of signaling theory has its roots in information economics (Spence, 1973). The basic premise underlying this theory is that an exchange between two parties is often associated with information asymmetries.

Specifically, signaling theory suggests that there is a gap or asymmetry between the information firms commonly possess and the product knowledge consumers actually have such as (similar quality products') price ranges or concrete product quality information (Rao et al., 1999; Kirmani and Rao, 2000). Hence, consumers are unable to arrive at informed product decisions, unless they expend the time and effort to either obtain information about products of comparable nature or develop decision models that "fill in" the missing data.

For example, when American and European consumers are faced with DC products and lack specific information concerning product quality or value, they tend to either seek out additional information/cues or infer information concerning important product characteristics from the cues that are available to them.

Signaling theory suggests that one way to alleviate information asymmetry is to communicate information by displaying a valid signal (Kirmani and Rao, 2000). This signal can only be accepted as true, if it is clearly associated with a cost to the sender for signaling false information. This cost serves as a bond which the company is willing to forego if it provides false information. Brand names are frequently used as guarantees to convey a bonding component for high product quality (Keller, 2003). Brand equity is damaged if the signal turns out to be false or when a guarantee or warranty is paid the firm loses money. In either case the bond is forfeited.

Signaling theory's definition of a brand does not fit the conceptualization of the COO phenomenon, despite previous scholarship treating COO as if it were a brand (Tse and Gorn, 1993; Verlegh and Steenkamp, 1999). Simply put, a COO cue is neither clearly nor directly associated with a bond. There is no guarantee associated with a COO.

Instead, we suggest that since consumers cannot surmise the bond associated with a given COO, negative country stereotypes act as a "static" in the system. They interfere with the consumer's ability to accurately perceive positive "signals" the developing country firm (DCF) is attempting to send through product attributes or through developing a brand.

Signaling theory and branding

According to signaling theory, in order to remove the "DC static," firms need to: (1) signal to the consumer that the information is valid, and (2) convey a clear cost to the firm (or bonding component) associated with an invalid signal (Kirmani and Rao, 2000). For DC product offerings at least one potential signal to validate information exists, the brand.

Marketers are using brands not to merely separate their products from others, but, more importantly, to reassure consumers about their unobservable quality. In order to be able to make such strong statements, companies invest in brand equity up front through advertising, product design, and packaging that incorporates the sort of image they are projecting.

Keller (2003) suggests that the mere presence of a brand (familiar or unfamiliar) increases consumers' expectations about the quality of the branded product because consumers readily perceive the risks, financial and otherwise, the company may face by providing a product of inferior quality. Therefore, branded products are expected to be perceived more favorably by consumers in the absence of other salient cues.

It is conceivable, for example, that the COO information may not be available to consumers when they watch a commercial or read a print ad unless the marketer makes such information an essential element of the message presented to them. Therefore, consumers may infer the initial quality of an offering from brand information alone.

Not surprisingly, familiar brands allow consumers to make easier decisions because consumers are simply more knowledgeable about them. This knowledge may be comprised of such useful information as performance, quality, image, and risk avoidance expectations. This intimate knowledge that consumers have developed about certain brands can be considered as a type of bond or pact (Keller, 2003). Familiar brands are reassuring to consumers, whereas unfamiliar ones may convey little or no expectations (good or bad).

For the above reasons we suggest that one way that DC firms could increase their international success is to pursue their own branding strategy as long as consumers are familiar or become familiar with their brands. It is important to emphasize that even unfamiliar brands with their perceived bonding information may reduce strong unfavorable COO effects.

Yet, the majority of DC firms compete on low price alone, rather than by attempting to develop a well-known brand name (Stiglitz, 1997; Ashley, 1998; Brouthers and Xu, 2002). This is perhaps due to them lacking the substantial resources required to invest in brand building and management (Hussain and Jian, 1999).

Although brands, in general, convey a bonding component, we should also acknowledge that the strength of the bond itself is also pertinent. In other words, consumers see little or no risk associated with a well-known brand name because they may have either direct or indirect knowledge of the brand, but they may also feel that the company behind the brand will honor all commitments to its customers. Known brands are, therefore, associated with strong bonds.

Conversely, while unknown brands carry a weak bond, consumers would still be more receptive to products that offer a perceived bond via the less familiar brand. For these reasons signaling theory suggests that emerging country firms would be better off with a branding strategy as opposed to a commodity product strategy.

Signaling theory and COO

Although consumers may neither be aware of a product's COO nor actively seek it, most countries require companies to imprint the "made in" information on their products or packaging. In the case of DCs' products, American and European consumers who may possess limited information typically infer *negative* product information as a result of the country stereotype.

For example, one study investigated consumer and industrial buyers' perceptions of electronic equipment manufactured in Canada, Japan, and Mexico (Ahmed and d'Astous, 1995). The findings not only showed that products made in Mexico were favored the least among buyers, but also products from newly industrializing countries were perceived as the least favorable.

Negative country stereotypes clearly lead consumers to perceive products as being of lower quality (Han and Terpsta, 1988; Hong and Wyer, 1989, 1990; Cordell, 1992; Roth and Romeo, 1992; Tse and Gorn, 1993; Maheswaran, 1994; Lampert and Jaffe, 1998; Verlegh and Steenkamp, 1999). For this reason, DC firms are at a disadvantage with American and European consumers because COO information is always available to consumers in one form or another. Therefore, the task of increasing the perceived value of DC products is rather difficult.

A realistic scenario, then, is the investigation of consumers' evaluations of products in the presence of COO information. COO research suggests that products from Japan, the United States, and the EU are almost always considered to be superior to products originating in DC markets. This appears to hold for both branded and unbranded products.

COO as a signal

Two problems associated with COO as a valid signal exist. First, COO as a valid signal can create a "free rider" dilemma; some firms may use COO to send invalid signals with limited risk to their own profits. Specifically, a COO cannot be realistically held accountable for either the perceived reputation or the actual quality of its products.

Unlike brands which are associated with specific entities that consumers can readily identify in the marketplace, the COO cue is less vulnerable to retaliation by consumers. For this reason, consumers may not perceive a salient bonding component associated with COO cues.

Second, preexisting emerging market country stereotypes create an additional impediment to COO as a positive signal in the market; potential positive signaling value of country information is likely to be superseded by inference resulting from the existing negative stereotypes. Thus, it appears that that COO acts more like a "static" in the system than as a brand. In the case of a DC market like China it conveys negative information and reduces the ability of the European or American consumer to accurately process the quality of the DC product. In the case of Japanese, American, or EU products it conveys positive information.

Three strategies to overcome negative COO stereotypes

How may DC firms compete in western markets if they lack strong brand signals and/or their COO is perceived negatively? Here we suggest three potential strategies firms may use to overcome negative COO stereotypes: (1) use multiple COO labels, (2) use a brand, or (3) use both a brand and multiple COO labels. Each is discussed below.

The use of brands and DC product evaluations

We suggest that DC product evaluations may be improved by employing a branding strategy (Campbell et al., 2003). As discussed previously, consumers perceive products associated with a brand (familiar or unfamiliar) as more favorable than products without it. Could an unfamiliar brand, however, overcome the negative stereotype associated with products from DC firms? While we expect the brand to improve product evaluations, the weak bond associated with such brands may not overcome DC negative stereotypes.

The use of multiple COO labels and DC product evaluations

In today's global marketplace the COO of a product appears to be less unambiguous than it was once considered. It is not unusual, for example, to find products that are designed in one country, assembled in another from parts and components made in yet another country, and which are marketed by corporations often associated with a different country (Chao, 2001).

Given the increasing multinationality of international products one possible way to reduce COO static/noise thereby improving the evaluation of DC products is to use multiple COO labels. Categorization theory suggests that the presence of multiple incongruent signals (such as various COOs) causes people to reduce the importance of or ignore the signals (Fiske and Pavelchak, 1986). This results in less extreme product evaluations.

The use of brands and multiple COO labels

Our discussion, so far, has focused on the impact of a brand signal and COO information in isolation from one another. In this study, we are interested in helping DC firms overcome the effect of COO stereotyping.

Although DC firms may not be able to afford to develop their own strong brands, they may engage in collaborative agreements with other companies in order to "piggyback" their products with familiar brands. We suggest that in the presence of a strong bond and the high predictive value associated with familiar brand names, the multidimensional COO cue will become less pertinent in product evaluations.

Categorization theory indicates that consumers knowingly choose the most efficient, least complex way to evaluate a product (Sujan, 1985). This means that the presence of a familiar brand name and the perceived diluted predictive value of a multidimensional COO would induce consumers to rely more on the familiar brand name cue and less on the various COO dimensions. Therefore, it appears that combining a familiar brand name with multiple COO cues results in higher DC product evaluations than pursuing either strategy in isolation.

Method and findings

We assessed the efficacy of the three strategies to overcome the COO static issue using three separate experiments. The first experiment investigates how the introduction of unfamiliar brands may affect product judgments in the context of the COO label. The next experiment is designed to addresses the multinationality of international products and the possibility that the presence of multiple COOs may clear the static associated with a negative COO label. The last experiment addresses the use of familiar brands and multiple COOs to overcome negative COO stereotypes.

Experiment 1

The first experiment was designed to investigate the effects of adding unfamiliar brand names to products with no country association, products associated with advanced industrial nations (AINs) (Canada and the USA) and products associated with our DC of choice, China. In particular, we were interested in observing product evaluation differences between products that were not associated with any brand (none) vs products associated with unfamiliar brand(s) and how those evaluations were influenced across the three COO conditions as described below.

Participants

Students in undergraduate business and economics classes were recruited to participate in an online study in exchange for nominal class credit. Three separate evaluation sessions were conducted with approximately 156 participants in each session for a total 468 evaluations. Six of the evaluations were incomplete resulting in 462 usable observations.

Design, stimuli, and measures

The experimental design was a 4 (COO) $\times$ 2 (BrPr) full factorial. The four levels of the COO variable were none, DC (China), AIN (Canada), and home (USA). Fictitious brands were created using a random number generator to select from lists of syllables. Out of approximately 20 brands generated, Calaran, NuLad, and Prisan were selected. Searches were performed to ensure that these brands were, in fact, fictitious and not currently being used.

A pretest was performed to test for differences in perceptions between the three unfamiliar brands. Participants were presented with a list of 60 actual and fictitious brands and asked to rate each brand on quality, service, technology-employed, and craftsmanship. There was no significant difference between the three unfamiliar brands on any of the four dependent measures. Given the similarity in perception for the three brands, the brand variable was collapsed to brand absent or present (BrPr) with values of 0/1.

Each respondent viewed three products, a wallet, a wine glass, and an umbrella. For all three products, each subject was exposed to one of the COO conditions (None, Canada, China, USA) and one of the BrPr conditions (None or Calaran, NuLad, or Prisan). Each subject saw the same COO and brand for all three products. The dependent variable was perceived quality, measured by four items – how attractive, well made, durable, and satisfying the product is. Participants responded to each of the quality items using a seven-point semantic differential scale.

Analysis and results

Responses to the four quality items were examined for their efficacy as a univariate measure of the quality construct. The bivariate correlations between the four measures ranged from .59 to .73. Reliability analysis found a Cronbach's alpha of .90. In addition, the four items were subjected to factor analysis. A single factor was extracted, explaining over 73% of the variance, with all four items having factor loadings greater than .83. Given these results, these four items were averaged and treated as a single dependent variable (QUAL).

The relevant effects were tested by a combination of regression analysis and planned contrasts. QUAL was regressed on COO, brand presence (BrPr), and their interaction. The overall model was significant ($p < .0001$), as was the main effect for country association ($p < .001$), but the main effect for branding (BrPr) and the interaction between country association and branding were not significant ($p > .30$). However, planned contrasts provided strong support for the effects of country association, branding, and their interaction. Results are summarized in Table 6.1.

As expected, when brands were added to products with no country association, the signaling value of the brand resulted in significantly higher evaluations (4.67 vs 4.31, $p < .05$). Additionally, these were found to be similar with the evaluations of either branded or unbranded products associated with Canada or the United States ($p > .10$). Further, products associated with the United States and Canada (AINs) were perceived as being of significantly higher quality than those associated with China ($p < .001$). This result was consistent for branded and unbranded products. Conversely, when comparing products associated with specific countries as opposed to no country association, the results were inconsistent for branded and unbranded products.

Table 6.1   Effects of country associations and branding on perceived quality

COO	No Brand	Unfamiliar Brand	*p*-value no. brand/brand
Canada	4.68[a]	4.60[a]	.675
China	4.02[b]	4.02[b]	.997
None	4.31[b]	4.67[a]	.008
USA	4.69[a]	4.63[a]	.736

[a] Not significantly different
[b] Not significantly different
[a,b] Significantly different, *p* < .05

Under closer scrutiny, the association of products with Canada or the United States as opposed to products with no country association did not result in higher evaluations when a brand was present. However, it clearly appears that the presence of a brand made a significant difference in evaluations in the no country association condition.

Specifically, in the absence of brand names, products with no country association were evaluated as significantly lower in quality than products associated with Canada (4.31 vs 4.68, $p < .05$) or products associated with the United States (4.31 vs 4.69, $p < .05$). In contrast, when comparing evaluations of products with no country association and products associated with China (DC firms), there was no significant difference for unbranded products (4.31 vs 4.02 $p > .10$) while perceived quality was significantly different for branded products (4.67 vs 4.02 $p < .01$).

The effects are illustrated in Figure 6.1. When products were associated with countries there was no significant difference in perceived quality between the branded and unbranded products (all p-values > .10). However, for products with no country association, the addition of a brand name resulted in significantly higher perceived quality (4.31 vs 4.67, $p < .01$). The difference in perceived quality between no country associations, AIN associations, and DC associations is contingent upon whether or not the product is associated with a brand name.

Discussion

Results of Experiment 1 provide strong support for the conceptualization of COO and brand effects in the context of the signaling theory. The signaling effect of a brand name makes a significant difference in perceived quality when no country association is present. However, the presence of a country association (whether AIN or DC) eliminates the information asymmetry required to achieve the brand effect and there appears to be no difference between perceived quality of branded and unbranded products.

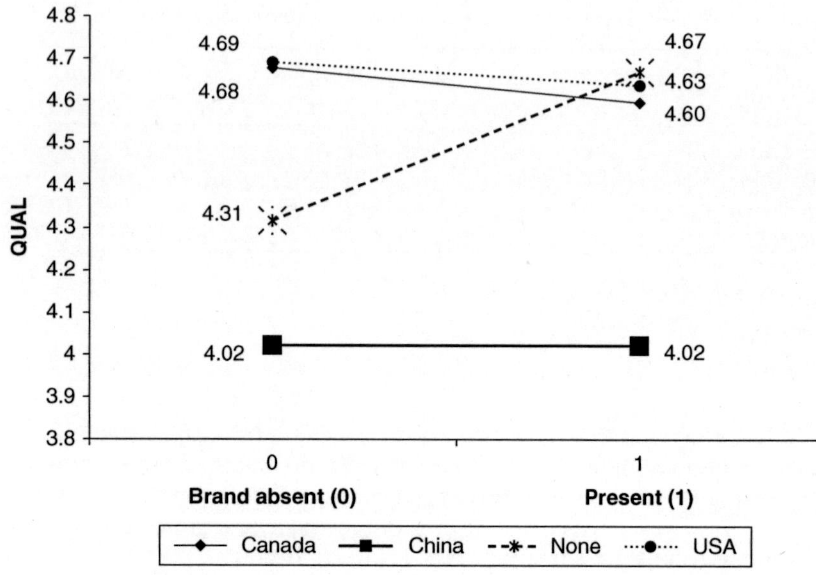

Figure 6.1   QUAL–Brand vs no brand

It is worth noting, once again, that these results were achieved with fictitious or unfamiliar brand names. The interaction between brand names and the presence or absence of country associations resulted in products with brand names, but without country associations, being perceived as of equal quality with AIN products.

Yet, for DC products, in this case associated with China, the addition of an unfamiliar brand was insufficient to overcome the negative country effects. Nevertheless, these results indicate that if consumers are unaware of, or ignore, country associations the addition of brand names results in significantly higher perceived quality.

Experiment 2

The second experiment was designed to test the effects of secondary country associations on consumers' response to DC associations. Specifically, we proposed that adding multiple secondary country associations would moderate the effect of association with DCs on perceived quality. Primary country associations were augmented with secondary associations for either AINs (USA, Canada) or DCs (Mexico, Brazil).

Participants

Students in undergraduate business classes were recruited to participate in an online study in exchange for nominal class credit. These students were different from the ones who participated in the first experiment. Three separate evaluations were performed by each of 50 participants. Five of the evaluations were incomplete resulting in 145 usable observations.

Design, stimuli, and measures

The experimental design was a 3 (COO)×2 (FROM) full factorial. The three levels of the primary COO variable were DC (China), AIN (Canada), and home (USA). The variable FROM represented the secondary COOs and the values were "Mexico, Brazil, China" and "U.S.A., Canada, China." At the bottom of each product page, respondents saw *"Product of (USA, Canada, or China), made of materials from one or more of the following countries: (Mexico, Brazil, China or USA, Canada, China)."*

Each respondent viewed three products, a wallet, a wine glass, and an umbrella. For each of the three products, each subject experienced one of the primary COO conditions (Canada, China, USA) and one of the secondary COO (FROM) conditions (Mexico, Brazil, China or USA, Canada, China). Each respondent saw the same primary and secondary country associations for all three products. The dependent variable was perceived quality (QUAL), measured by the same four items as in the first experiment – how attractive, well made, durable, and satisfying the product is. Participants responded to each item using a seven-point semantic differential scale.

Analysis and results

A combination of regression analysis and planned contrasts between cell means from both experiments were employed in order to test the relevant effects. QUAL was regressed on primary COO, secondary country association (FROM), and their interaction. Unlike the results of the first experiment, the overall model was not significant ($p > .10$). The main effect for COO, the only significant effect in the previous experiment, became insignificant when secondary country associations were added to the product descriptions. The results of Experiment 2 are summarized in Table 6.2.

Table 6.2 Effects of primary and secondary country associations on perceived quality*

		Secondary Country Association	
		USA, Canada, China	Mexico, Brazil, China
Primary	Canada	4.59	4.74
Country	China	4.43	4.55
Association	USA	4.50	4.58

* No significant differences between cells ($p > .30$)

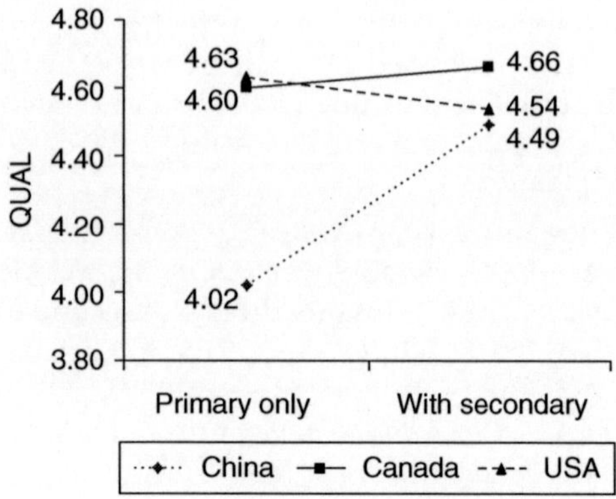

Figure 6.2   Primary COO effects with and without secondary country associations

Figure 6.2 contrasts the results of Experiment 1 and Experiment 2. In the absence of secondary country associations, there are significant differences between AIN and DC product evaluations. Yet, when secondary country associations were included, all products were perceived to be of similar quality. This provides strong support for the "multiple-COO" strategy which suggested that the addition of secondary country associations would moderate the effects of primary country associations on consumers' perceptions.

Further, results from the two experiments were combined and QUAL was regressed on primary country association (COO), secondary country associations (FROM), and their interaction. The overall model was significant ($p < .01$) as well as the main effect for COO ($p < .01$). The interaction between COO and FROM was only marginally significant ($p = .094$).

As anticipated, there was not a significant main effect for FROM ($p > .10$). A further test was provided by planned contrasts between the two levels of secondary associations (USA, Canada, China and Mexico, Brazil, China). There was no significant difference between the two levels of secondary country associations for any of the three primary countries (cell means shown in Table 6.2, all p-values $> .10$).

Given the lack of difference between the two levels of secondary country association, the interaction between primary and secondary country associations are better revealed if secondary association is treated as dichotomous. The secondary association variable (FROM) was recoded as a dichotomous variable, 0 – no secondary association, 1 – with secondary association.

Data from the two experiments were combined and QUAL was regressed on primary country association (COO) and dichotomous secondary country association (SECONDCO) along with their interaction. The overall model was significant, as expected ($p < .01$).

The main effect for country was significant ($p < .01$) and the main effect for secondary country association was not significant ($p > .05$). However, the interaction between primary and secondary country association was significant ($p < .05$), thereby indicating that COO main effects are dependent upon the presence of multiple country information. In fact, the addition of multiple countries (in comparison to Experiment 1) seems to have eliminated any significant differences attributed to COO alone, especially in the case of China.

Discussion

Experiment 2 explored one strategy for reducing the impact of negative country stereotypes associated with products from less developed countries. Specifically, we tested the effectiveness of adding secondary country associations in moderating the negative effects of DC associations. We hypothesized that adding multiple country associations to product descriptions would compel consumers to put less emphasis on the various COO cues, thereby moderating their product evaluations.

The results clearly showed that introducing multiple COO cues influences product evaluations in a favorable manner for DC firm products. As such, DC firms may improve consumer product evaluations by following this relatively inexpensive strategy under the assumption that multiple COOs are already involved in the development, design, and production of such products.

Experiment 3

We conducted the last experiment to examine the impact of introducing familiar or reputable brands in DC firm product evaluations as well as to assess the combined effects of familiar brands and multiple COO labels. As discussed earlier, one recommended strategy for improving AIN consumer product evaluations of DC firm products was to employ brands.

Signaling theory would suggest that the perceived *strong* bond attached to familiar brands may help DC firms overcome negative COO effects. This is in contrast to the first strategy and experiment which showed that unfamiliar brands do little if anything to alleviate DC stereotyping.

Method, stimuli, and measures

Participants, different from the ones who participated in the previous two experiments, were recruited from undergraduate business classes. A total of 149 participants completed the experiment. Each respondent viewed three products, a wallet, a wine glass, and an umbrella.

For each product, subjects received information on a primary COOs (Canada, China, USA, None) and secondary COOs (Mexico, Brazil, China; United States, Canada, China; or None). All products were associated with familiar or reputable brands (Polo Wallet, Waterford Glasses, Samsonite

Umbrella). Familiar brands were selected based on a pretest. Subjects, similar to the ones who participated in the actual experiment but not the same, were asked to indicate the most reputable, familiar brands associated with each of the three products employed in this study.

As in the previous experiments, the dependent variable was perceived quality (QUAL), measured by four items – how attractive, well made, durable, and satisfying the product is. Participants responded to each of the quality items using a seven-point semantic differential scale.

Analysis and results

Table 6.3 summarizes the results of this experiment. Whereas the main COO effect was not significant ($p > 10$), the results indicated a significant main effect with regard to brand ($p < .05$).

A closer examination of the results shows the pervasive impact or signaling power of a familiar brand name, especially in the case of our DC, China. Evaluations of products from China associated with a familiar, reputable brand are significantly higher than those under either the no brand condition or the unknown brand condition ($p < .05$). Not surprisingly, the addition of a well-known brand name resulted in the most dramatic increase in product evaluations across all three brand conditions under the "none" COO condition ($p < .01$), although AIN product evaluations seem to have benefited from well-known brand names as well.

Lastly, we examined the strategy of using familiar brands and multiple COOs. According to this strategy, the combination of familiar brand names with multiple COO labels should dramatically increase product evaluations of DC firm products. The results clearly show that DC firm product evaluations improve significantly ($p < .01$) under the multiple country–familiar brand condition. Table 6.4 shows the results from this analysis. These effects are also illustrated in Figure 6.3.

Table 6.3   Effects of familiar brands on product evaluations*

	Brand		
	None	**Unfamiliar**	**Familiar**
Canada	4.68	4.60	5.12
China	4.02	4.02	4.69
None	4.31	4.67	5.59
USA	4.69	4.63	5.10

*$n = 444$

Table 6.4 Effects of familiar brands and multiple COOs on product evaluations

		China	China-MBC	China-UCC
	Unfamiliar	4.02	4.56	4.46
Brand	Familiar	4.69	4.81	4.97
	None	3.95	4.54	4.38
		Canada	Canada-MBC	Canada-UCC
	Unfamiliar	4.60	4.59	4.71
Brand	Familiar	5.12	5.24	5.06
	None	4.68	5.13	4.34
		USA		
		None	MBC	UCC
	Unfamiliar	4.63	4.56	4.48
Brand	Familiar	5.10	5.09	4.73
	None	4.69	4.81	4.54

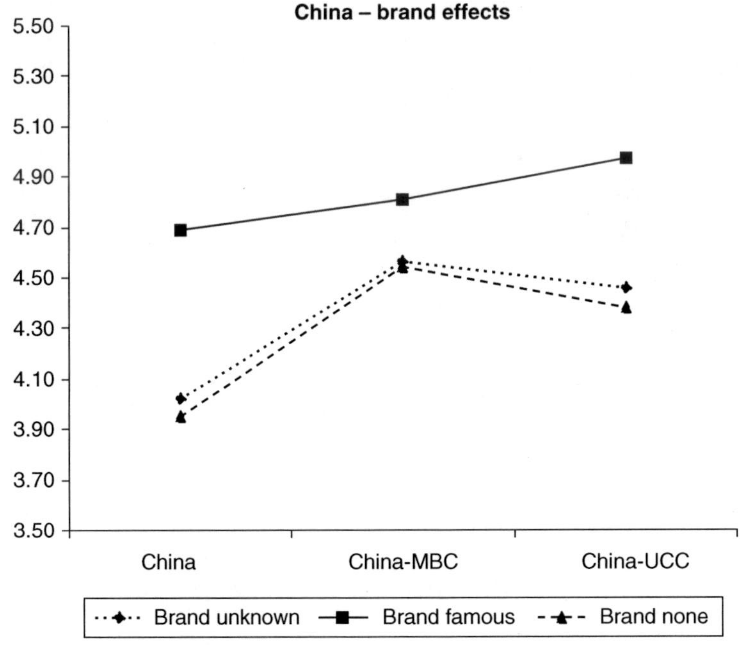

Figure 6.3 Multiple COO and well-known brand effects

Discussion

By employing the signaling theory and categorization frameworks, we posited that, perhaps, the most effective strategy for DC firms to follow in order to alleviate the inherent burden associated with their negative country stereotypes in first world markets would be the use of multiple COO labels along with a brand strategy.

Our findings overwhelmingly showed that this appears to be a rather prudent strategy for DC firms. While the multiple COO condition would be rather easy to implement, identifying and developing reputable, familiar brand associations is more of an onerous task because of the involvement of outside entities and firms. Yet, in the pursuit of cheaper sources of production, AIN or other firms possessing such reputable brands may, in fact, pursue DC firm product alliances.

General discussion

We began this study by asking whether DC firms can prosper in Triad nation markets. Conventional wisdom suggests why this is so difficult for DC firms. Typically DC firms (1) have substantially less international experience than multinational enterprises (MNEs); (2) tend to be quite smaller than MNEs and as a consequence; (3) have very limited resources compared to MNEs (Hussain and Jian, 1999).

Developing country firms commonly (4) operate from weak and/or shallow home country "Diamonds of Advantage" (Porter, 1990) which pushes them away from differentiation strategies and toward competing on price, often resulting in lower levels of performance (Lecraw, 1993; Brouthers and Xu, 2002; Gao et al., 2003). Last, Triad nation markets tend to be mature, saturated and as a result, highly competitive. Each of these factors diminishes the likelihood of DC firm Triad nation success.

Previous literature also suggests that DC firms that attempt to replace the typical commodity low price strategy with some type of differentiation product strategy commonly confront negative COO effects (Baughn and Yaprak, 1993; Liefeld 1993; Wood and Darling 1993; Johansson et al., 1994; Manrai et al., 1998). Negative COO stereotyping makes it very difficult for DC firms to move from price leadership to differentiation-based product strategies.

So what can DC firms do to overcome their negative COO effects? Here we drew upon signaling theory (Spence, 1973; Rao et al., 1999; Kirmani and Rao, 2000) to develop and test a new paradigm of how DC firms may be able to reduce negative COO effects allowing them to compete with MNEs in first world markets. We used signaling theory's definition of a brand (brands contain a bonding component) and concluded that COO labels lack a bonding component and therefore are actually "noise" in the system.

More specifically, we proposed and tested three strategies DC firms could use to reduce negative COO influences in first world markets: (1) boosting the signal (through using brands); (2) reducing the noise caused by negative COO (through multiple country-of-origin labels); or (3) using familiar brands and multiple COO labels. These strategies were tested through a series of experiments on first world consumers.

We found that by employing signaling theory and categorization frameworks, the use of familiar brands and multiple COO associations (separately or combined) reduced negative COO effects and improved consumer evaluations of products. We showed that, perhaps, the most effective strategy for DC firms to follow was the use of multiple COO labels *in combination with* familiar brand associations.

While the multiple COO condition seems comparatively easy to implement, identifying and developing reputable (familiar) brand associations is more of an onerous task because of the involvement of outside entities and firms. Yet, it is possible that in the pursuit of cheaper sources of production, AIN or other firms possessing such familiar brands may, in fact, pursue DC firm product alliances. Alternatively, it may be possible for DC firms to purchase defunct, but familiar brands as was the case when a Taiwanese bicycle manufacturer bought the Schwinn bicycle brand.

Limitations and future research

This study has a few limitations. First, it was an experiment. As such the question of external validity is always present. Second, we used student samples. Although the products used in the study are familiar to them, there is always the question of whether students represent typical consumers.

Third, we only examined a handful of COO labels. For this reason our findings may not generalize to other DCs. Fourth, since this study is cross-sectional in nature, future efforts may wish to determine whether our results are supported in a longitudinal context.

Fifth, we are not suggesting that all DC firms pursue the same negative COO reduction strategies. All we are suggesting is that two of our proposed strategies, on average, appear to work. Future efforts need to propose and test additional strategies DC firms can use to successfully penetrate Triad nation markets.

Finally, it should be pointed out that while our theory appears to reduce negative COO "noise" in the system, it is quite likely that additional factors play a significant role in the success of DC firms in penetrating Triad nation markets. Future research efforts examining DC firm performance in first world markets may wish to incorporate our theory into their hypotheses and analyses.

Conclusion and managerial implications

Our findings have at least two implications for DC firms targeting Triad nation markets. First, our empirical results found that DC firms that use either multiple COO labels and/or familiar brand associations achieve, on average, higher average product evaluations. These results provide initial evidence that our theory may be normative and for that reason, may help to guide DC firms as they formulate product strategies for Triad nation markets.

For example, China's largest computer manufacturer, Lenovo, chose to enter the US market by acquiring the venerable ThinkPad brand from IBM in recent years. Following an initial co-branding strategy, Lenovo has recently begun selling computers under its own brand name. Haier, a famous Chinese "white goods" company who tried to acquire the "Maytag" brand name represents an illustration that larger, more successful Chinese firms are beginning to understand the power of a familiar brand name.

Second, because our theory and results provide an alternative to the conventional wisdom (use a low price strategy) given to DC firms wishing to do business in Triad nation markets, this study offers the possibility that other alternatives to the low price commodity strategy also exist. We do not suggest that all DC firms attempting to enter a specific Triad nation will or should have identical product strategies or use our suggested strategy. What we have shown is one method that appears to yield superior product evaluations for DC firms. We believe that other equally successful strategies may exist and encourage future research efforts to discover them.

One such strategy has been offered by Brouthers et al. (1995). They hypothesized and found that DC firms that imitated the dominant price–quality relationship found in the Triad nations (the European Union, the United States, and Japan) performed better than DC firms that employed other strategies.

A second possible strategy is to target segments of AIN populations where DC brands may be more attractive than AIN brand names. For instance, certain ethnic food brand names or cosmetic brands may appeal to recent immigrant populations. Such brands represent an inexpensive way for "strangers in a strange land" to feel more at home, by buying familiar brand name products. Such strategies unfortunately are less likely to work with the majority native-born AIN populations.

In our study, the introduction of brands did not alleviate the negative stereotyping associated with DC products. It nonetheless pointed out the idea that a branding strategy leads to significantly higher evaluations than a no branding strategy. This was especially true in the case where the COO was not present. Could we, then, extrapolate from this that if a DC firm is successful in downplaying the noise emanating from its negative COO can it realize higher product evaluations? Then, the issue remains of how you can actually "hide" or "muffle" this unwelcome noise.

Thus, we view our efforts here as being research opening. In this chapter we examined merely one approach for DC firms to use to compete in Triad nation markets. Other exploitable strategies for DC firms likely exist as well; we encourage future research efforts to discover them.

References

Ahmed, S.A. and d'Astous, A. (1995) "Comparison of Country-of-Origin Effects on Household and Organizational Buyers' Product Perceptions", *European Journal of Marketing*, 29(3): 35–51.

Ashley, S.R. (1998) "How to Effectively Compete Against Private-Label Brands", *Journal of Advertising Research*, 38(1): 75–82.

Baughn, C.C. and Yaprak, A. (1993) "Mapping Country-of-Origin Research: Recent Developments and Emerging Avenues", in N. Papadopoulos and L.A. Heslop (eds), *Product-Country Images*, Binghamton, NY: International Business Press, pp. 89–115.

Brouthers, K., Brouthers, L. E., and Wilkinson, T. (1995). "Strategic Alliances-Choose Your Partners", *Long Range Planning*. 1995, 28(3): 18–25.

Brouthers, L.E. and Xu, K. (2002) "Product Stereotypes, Strategy and Performance Satisfaction: The Case of Chinese Exporters", *Journal of International Business Studies*, 33(4): 657–677.

Campbell, M.C., Keller, K.L., Mick, D.G., and Hoyer, W.D. (2003) "Brand Familiarity and Advertising Repetition Effects", *Journal of Consumer Research*, 30(2): 292–314.

Chao, P. (2001) "The Moderating Effects of Country of Assembly, Country of Parts, and Country of Design on Hybrid Product Evaluations", *Journal of Advertising*, 30(4): 67–81.

Cordell, V.V. (1992) "Effects of Consumer Preferences for Foreign Sourced Products", *Journal of International Business Studies*, 23(2): 251–269.

Fiske, S.T. and Pavelchak, M.A. (1986) "Category-Based Versus Piecemeal-Based Affective Responses: Developments in Schema-Triggered Affect", in R.M. Sorrentino and E. Tory Higgins (eds), *Handbook of Motivation and Cognition: Foundations of Social Behavior*, New York, NY: Guilford, pp. 167–203.

Gao, P., Wortzel, J.R., and Wu, Y. (2003) "Can Chinese Barnds Make it Abroad?", *McKinsey Quarterly*, 4: 54–65.

Han, C.M. and Terpstra, V. (1988) "Country-of-Origin Effects for Uni-National and Bi-National Products", *Journal of International Business Studies*, 19 (Summer): 235–255.

Hong, S.-T. and Wyer, R.S. Jr. (1989) "Effects of Country-of-Origin and Product Attribute Information on Product Evaluation: An Information Processing Perspective", *Journal of Consumer Research*, 16 (September): 175–187.

Hong, S.-T. and Wyer, R.S., Jr. (1990) "Determinants of Product Evaluation: Effects of Time Interval between Knowledge of a Product's Country-of-Origin and Information about its Specific Attributes", *Journal of Consumer Research*, 17 (December): 277–288.

Hussain, A. and Jian, C. (1999) "Changes in China's Industrial Landscape and their Implications", *International Studies of Management and Organization*, 29(3): 5–20.

Johansson, J.K., Ronkainen, I.A., and Czinkota, M.R. (1994) "Negative Country-of-Origin Effects: The Case of the New Russia", *Journal of International Business Studies*, 25(1): 157–176.

Keller, K.L. (2003). *Strategic Brand Management: Bulding, Measuring, and Managing Brand Equity*, Upper Saddle River, NJ: Prentice Hall.

Kirmani, A. and Rao, A. (2000) "No Pain, No Gain: A Critical Review of the Literature on Signaling Unobservable Product Quality", *Journal of Marketing*, 64 (April): 66–79.

Lampert, S.I. and Jaffe, E.D. (1998) "A Dynamic Approach to Country-of-Origin Effect", *European Journal of Marketing*, 32(1/2): 61–78.

Lecraw, D.J. (1993) "Outward Direct Investment by Indonesian Firms: Motivation and Effects", *Journal of International Business Studies*, 24(3): 589–600.

Liefeld, J.P. (1993) "Experiments on Country-of-Origin Effects: Review and Meta-Analysis of Effect Size", in N. Papadopoulos and L.A. Heslop (eds), *Product-Country Images*, Binghamton, NY: International Business Press, pp. 117–156.

Maheswaran, D. (1994) "Country of Origin as a Stereotype", *Journal of Consumer Research*, 21(2): 354–64.

Manrai, L.A., Lascu, D.-N., and Manrai, A.K. (1998) "Interactive Effects of Country of Origin and Product Category on Product Evaluations", *International Business Review*, 7(6): 591–616.

Porter, M.E. (1990) "The Competitive Advantage of Nations", *Harvard Business Review*, 68(2): 73–93.

Rao, A.R., Qu, L., and Ruekert, R.W. (1999) "Signaling Unobservable Product Quality Through a Brand Ally", *Journal of Marketing Research*, 35 (May): 258–268.

Roth, M. and Romeo, J. (1992) "Matching Product Category and Country Image Perception: A Framework for Managing Country-of-Origin Effects", *Journal of International Business Studies*, 23(3): 477–498.

Spence, M. (1973) "Job Market Signaling", *Quarterly Journal of Economics*, 87 (August): 355–374.

Stiglitz, J.E. (1997) *Principles of Microeconomics*, NY: W.W. Norton & Company.

Sujan, M. (1985) "Consumer Knowledge: Effects on Evaluation Strategies Mediating Consumer Judgments", *Journal of Consumer Research*, 12: 31–46.

Tse, D.K. and Gorn, G.J. (1993) "An Experiment on the Salience of Country-of-Origin in the Era of Global Brands", *Journal of International Marketing*, 11: 57–76.

Varlegh, P.W.J. and Steenkamp, J.-B.E.M. (1999) "A Review and Meta-Analysis of Country-of-Origin Research", *Journal of Economic Psychology*, 20: 521–546.

Wood, V.R. and Darling, J.R. (1993) "The Marketing Challenges of the Newly Independent Republics: Product Competitiveness in Global Markets", *Journal of International Marketing*, 1(1): 77–202.

7

Institutions and Organizational Socialization: Integrating Employees in Cross-Border Mergers and Acquisitions

Ruth V. Aguilera, John C. Dencker, and Zeynep Y. Yalabik

Mergers and Acquisitions (M&As) have been a major strategic tool for business growth and repositioning in recent decades (Hitt et al., 2001; Schweiger, 2002; Anand et al., 2005), yet they are often beset by problems during the integration phase (Kitching, 1967, 1973; Shanley and Correa, 1992; Daniel, 1999; Larsson and Finkelstein, 1999; Hitt et al., 2001; Marks and Mirvis, 2001; Capron and Pistre, 2002). Many of these problems trace to difficulties in effectively integrating the human side of merging organizations (Buono and Bowditch, 1989; Haspeslagh and Jemison, 1991), resulting, for example, from clashes between organizational cultures of merging organizations (Nahavandi and Malekzadeh, 1988; Marks, 1991; Weber and Schweiger, 1992; DeVoge and Spreier, 1999; Overman, 1999; Morosini, 2004), as well as national cultures in cross-border M&As (Marks, 1991; Belcher and Nail, 2001) especially during the post-merger period. Although these studies have generated numerous important findings, a challenging task is to extend this research to specify how organizational systems, values, and work processes become stabilized in newly merged organizations and to do so in ways that are relevant to practitioners.

In this chapter, we develop a theoretical framework to help maximize effectiveness of the integration during post-acquisition.[1] We define integration as socio-cultural integration of groups of people (Gunter et al., 2005). There are a variety of factors that help create successful post-acquisition integration, with success defined according to different criteria, such as value creation for the acquiring firm or low stress level among acquired employees. However, perhaps the most difficult challenge in M&A integration is to minimize the negative effects that the acquisition process has for *acquired employees* (Buono and Bowditch, 1989; Schweiger and Walsh, 1990; Schweiger and DeNisi, 1991; Marks and Mirvis, 2001). We believe that effective socialization of the *acquired employees* is likely to result in a more successful post-acquisition integration. Thus, we focus primarily on how value can be created by understanding and managing the socialization process of *acquired employees* more effectively in the post-acquisition integration stage.

We conceptualize effective post-acquisition integrations as those that achieve an effective cooperation between acquiring and acquired employees, and explore what conditions enhance employee socialization. Our framework combines organizational socialization and institutional theory in the context of M&As by drawing on the phenomenological view of early institutional scholars who argued that socialization plays an important role in the institutionalization process (e.g., Berger and Luckmann, 1967; Barley and Tolbert, 1997). An important step in obtaining a better understanding of the social side of cross-border M&As is the inclusion of the agency role in structural theories (Oliver, 1991; Emirbayer and Mische, 1998), which allows institutions to act not only as constraints or enablers of certain forms of organizational action, but also to provide value by generating accepted ways of behavior in increasingly diverse and sometimes conflicting work groups.

By better understanding their roles, managers (i.e., agents) can implement different systems, practices and values to cope with organizational change more rapidly and thoroughly, thereby increasing the firm ability to make effective use of its structures and institutions (Eisenhardt, 1989; Judge and Miller, 1991; Forbes, 2005). Moreover, because social reality is the product of human construction and social interaction among individuals, socialization entails the construction of common meaning systems and shared knowledge. Our approach to these systems and knowledge is in terms of "institutions." Following Berger and Luckmann (1967), we suggest that the culmination of socialization is when socially constructed reality and institutions are internalized to such a degree that then they become institutionalized.

While we rely on the earlier view of socialization as a mechanism of institutions and institutionalization, our discussion in this study will be on the other side of socialization process that is on the "domains" or "content," in other words, on "what is being learned" during the organizational socialization and what this means in terms of institutions and institutionalization.[2] In this sense, we draw on the three pillars of institutional theory – regulative, normative, and cognitive (Scott, 2001) – to explain the enhancement of integration effectiveness through six domains of organizational socialization – individual work roles, organizational goals and values, people, language, organizational politics, and organizational history (Chao et al., 1994).

Objectives and expected contributions

The goal of this chapter is to explain post-M&A integration first as an ideal type (which allows us to develop the conceptual framework) and then apply this framework to cross-border M&A. The first part, or our propositions, evaluates each socialization domain in relation to the three institutional pillars. Our assumption is that as the merging firms understand such relationship, the integration of both organizations will be more effective. For acquiring firms, such understanding means an easier "replication" (Barley and Tolbert, 1997) of its institutions in the merged firm and "imposition" of its values, rules, and norms on the newly acquired employees. We believe that learning about one of the socialization domains – such as organizational jargon and slang, power structures, formal and informal goals and values, and so on – relates to one of the institutional pillars, which in itself symbolizes a different way of behaving, interpreting, coding, or rewarding. In a word, learning about one domain means more than learning that domain in absolute terms since it will be internalized differently under various institutional pillars. As acquiring and acquired firms acknowledge this relationship, they might integrate their employees in the merged entity faster and more effectively by choosing the most productive strategic tools and human resource management practices that achieve the best employee socialization.

Although socialization occurs regardless of whether there are policies and practices designed to aid it, guidance by management can be critical for organizational success in order to maintain and lead organizational norms, characteristics, and togetherness (Ahuja and Galvin, 2003). That is, integration effectiveness is a function of the speed by which socialization can be accomplished for the majority of employees in an acquisition, with M&A integration more effective the more quickly the process is completed (Schweiger, 2002). The implication is that firms that socialize employees into the newly merged organization more rapidly are likely to reap numerous benefits.

There are a number of roadblocks to effective socialization in acquisition integration, assuming that merging firms require a medium to high level of integration to effectively pursue the goals of the M&A. Managers are often ambiguous during the acquisition process (Jemison and Sitkin, 1986), thereby increasing the complexity of post-acquisition integration. In addition, the integration process involves changes in the organizational practices and structures, and demands some degree of cooperation between the two firms to develop the necessary joint firm capabilities (Cartwright and Cooper, 1992). This ambiguity is sometimes reduced because the acquiring firm in an M&A is typically more dominant than the acquired firm, and uses its power to transform the newly merged organization during the integration stage (Haspeslagh and Jemison, 1991; Bower, 2001; Schweiger, 2002; Schuler et al., 2004). For example, Pablo (1994: 806) notes that "change is frequently one-sided, occurring primarily within the acquired organization." Because M&As are rarely mergers of equals (i.e., one firm is usually dominant) (e.g., Weston et al., 2001; Carey et al., 2004), in constructing our framework, we focus on how acquiring firms can more effectively integrate acquired employees.

Our proposed theoretical model makes several contributions to existing research. First, we respond to Scott's (2001) call for the need to give more attention to how the three institutional types (pillars) are distinct from each other. We do so by identifying what types of institutions are most salient and likely to be internalized in each socialization domain. This is important because integration managers, as key decision-makers, will give different weight to available information in making their integration decisions (Stahl and Zimmerer, 1984; Duhaime and Schwenk, 1985). Second, we assess the "value" of human resources of the merging organizations relative to the entire M&A deal. Indeed, following an M&A, uncertainty raises in the organizational environment and employees experience anxiety regarding their future (e.g., Marks and Mirvis, 1986; Buono and Bowditch, 1989; Schweiger and DeNisi, 1991; Schweiger et al., 1993; Larsson and Finkelstein, 1999). Consequently, employees will seek to gain information about the transforming issues in their organization. If the organization is not sensitive to this uncertainty and anxiety, then it is likely to experience a loss of some valuable firm human capital.

In effect, as Stanwick and Stanwick (2001) highlight the value merging organizations attach to each other is closely related to the skills and knowledge the other organization's employees possess. In this regard, if merging firms are not capable of keeping at least their best performing employees, then the premium value attached to the entire merger is overestimated. We assume that most merging organizations will not want to lose what is most valuable to them due to the merging uncertainty and therefore they will seek ways to reduce employees' anxiety in the new organization. It is also critical, during the post-M&A integration, to understand what kind of information and knowledge merging employees are looking for and how this information seeking might affect their behavior and attitudes toward the new organization so that they will be willing to stay in the new firm. While various studies on M&As discuss these issues from different points of view, our focus will be on the perspective of organizational socialization of acquired employees. In addition, even though as mentioned, we focus on "absorption", our framework might be easily applied to other contexts involving change and in turn requiring socialization such as joint ventures.

Third, at the theoretical level we integrate two literatures that have been disconnected, in part because institutional studies take the organization as the level of analysis, and socialization studies take the individual as the level of analysis. In contrast, we agree that organizational socialization, as a mechanism, helps institutions perform and reproduce. However, by looking at what type of institution is internalized within each socialization domain, we bridge both levels of analysis while examining a different aspect of socialization process, that is, domains, in addition to seeing it only as a mechanism. Instead of focusing on socialization and institutionalization processes as pure mechanisms, we focus on the link between what is being institutionalized (i.e., regulative, normative, and cognitive institutions) and what is being learned through socialization (i.e., socialization domains or content). Fourth, we shed additional light on the M&A integration process by focusing not only on the human side of the equation, but also by looking at the process from the social interaction point of view with socialization theory.

The rest of this chapter is designed as follows. We begin by discussing structural and institutional concepts in the M&A context. Second, we describe organizational socialization, highlighting key concepts and specifying the importance of the socialization process in the post-acquisition integration stage. Third, we develop systematic theoretical links between organizational socialization domains and the pillars of institutionalism in the context of acquisition integration. Finally, we discuss how our framework can be modified to capture the additional complexity arising in cross-border M&As and provide practical implications on how integration managers can implement our proposed model.

Structures, institutions, and the M&As context

Institutions are typically defined as "multifaceted, durable social structures, made up of symbolic elements, social activities, and material resources" (Scott, 2001), with the central ingredients of institutions being rules, norms, and beliefs. Tensions between environments and institutions can arise as environments are transformed, as in the case of technological innovations, or when different organizational environments interact, as in the case of M&As. Because M&As involve more than taking control of hard firm assets in that they require the combination of two organizations with unique histories, practices, and leaders (Marks, 1991; Daniel, 1999), when two organizations merge they are likely to face new rules, new norms, and new beliefs (i.e., institutions with which they might not be familiar with). A key challenge, then, lies in the integration of various structures, processes, and cultures (Daniel, 1999; Schuler and Jackson, 2001; Aguilera and Dencker, 2004). Furthermore, Strebel (2004) argues that when a merger takes place the managers of the joining companies tend to asses the other side on the basis of "clichés" rather than on the basis of institutions (i.e., the explicit organizational relationships). However, as he emphasizes, it is important to go beyond these clichés in that the merging organizations should understand the institutional side of each others' organizational culture as well as how these institutions interact with values, beliefs, and behaviors for a better integration.

We develop our integration logic around the type of acquisition that will require full consolidation of operations, organizational practices, and culture of both entities, that is, an absorption acquisition. According to Haspeslagh and Jemison (1991), absorption acquisitions are "those in which the strategic task requires a high degree of interdependence to create the value expected but has a low need for organizational autonomy to achieve that interdependence" (p.147). Integration of this type of M&A will, therefore, imply that the acquiring firm will seek to transfer and implement most of its practices into the acquired firm (Schweiger and Walsh, 1990; Pablo, 1994). We propose that the transfer and internalization of new practices by the employees in the acquired firm is done through a socialization process.

Institutional pillars

Regardless of institutional level, "the institutionalization of practices and behavioral patterns depends on how long an institution has been around as well as how widely and deeply it is accepted by the members of a collective" (Barley and Tolbert, 1997: 100). Once institutionalized, institutions are taken for granted (cognitive), supported by the public (normative), or enforced by law (regulative). These are the three pillars of institutions (Scott, 2001) that we conceive of as a continuum ranging from rigid approaches to subtle interventions. Our theory development (propositions section) will focus on these three types of institutions and explain their relationship with organizational socialization domains.

The *Regulative* institutional pillar represents the rules and the laws of the institutional environment (Kostova and Roth, 2002). Regulative institutions directly relate to "rule-setting," "monitoring," and "sanctioning" activities in an organization (Scott, 1998, 2001) such as laws stating which behaviors are allowed (Palmer and Biggart, 2002). Power, coercion, and authority play an important role in the enactment of regulative institutions. Since regulative institutions reflect "rules," "regulations," or "formal rules," failing to obey them results in legal sanctioning.

The *Normative* institutional pillar refers to values, beliefs, norms, and assumptions existing in the institutional environment (Kostova and Roth, 2002) that captures prescriptive, evaluative, and obligatory dimensions in social life (Scott, 2001) and provides structures regarding acceptable behavior (Palmer and Biggart, 2002). Normative institutions encompass "rules-of-thumb, standards, operating procedures, occupational standards and educational curricula" (Hoffman, 1999) and are based on social interactions and obligatory parts of these interactions (Wicks, 2001). They comprise values (proper ways) and norms (ways that are supposed to be followed) (Scott, 1998, 2001). Their ability to influence employees and firm behavior comes from seeking conformity, enforcing social obligation, social necessity, and shared understandings of what is proper in the organization (Wicks, 2001; Palmer and Biggart, 2002).

The *Cognitive* institutional pillar refers to widely shared social knowledge and cognitive categories such as stereotypes and schemata (Markus and Zajonk, 1985) that represent the models of "individual behavior based on subjectively constructed rules and meanings that dictate appropriate thought, feeling and action" (Wicks, 2001: 665). Cognitive institutions embody "symbols-words, signs, and gestures—as well as cultural rules and frameworks that guide understanding of the nature of reality and the frames through which that meaning is developed" (Hoffman, 1999: 353) that are reproduced through mimetic processes (i.e., through mimicry of successful practices or implementations of others) (Palmer and Biggart, 2002). Compliance with cognitive components of the institutional environment occurs because of "taken for granted" traits of routines (Scott, 2001). Organizations and organizational members follow these cognitive institutions without any conscious thought (Zucker, 1983).

Internalization of institutions

It is important to differentiate among these three types of institutional pillars because as Scott (2001: 52) points out, they move from the conscious to the unconscious, and from being legally sanctioned to being taken-for-granted. Hence, in the context of M&A integration, if managers know that a given socialization domain entails predominantly the internalization of cognitive institutions, then these managers can develop and implement the necessary socialization tactics to ensure an effective socialization that it is likely to lead to effective M&A integration. In other words, integration managers can develop an ability to engage in the socialization process through obtaining knowledge about the salient institutions in this context.

We focus primarily on institutions that exist at the organizational level and examine how individuals (employees) internalize these institutions first in the context of domestic M&As and then in cross-border M&As. Recent approaches argue that institutions surrounding an organization operate at three levels: organizational, industry (inter-organizational), and national (Scott, 2001). Although national and industry-level institutions influence organizational level institutions, organizational institutions are absorbed and diffused in an organization and become unique over time (Zucker, 1987; Morosini et al., 1998).

Similarly, even though routines and repertoires implemented by an organization co-evolve with that organization's history and institutional environment, such co-evolution fabricates a unique and firm-specific set of routines and repertories (Barney, 1986; Collis, 1991; Morosini, 1999). For example, the interaction between a focal organization and other organizations in its industry or country may lead to similar patterns of institutions across a number of organizations, yet relationships between a focal organization and foreign industry competitors can trigger the development of unique sets of routines and repertories within specific organizations (Collis, 1991; Morosini et al., 1998). These unique set of routines might be difficult to imitate by other firms since they did not experience the same pattern of development nor had access to the similar institutional environment. In M&As, then, access to and appreciation of such uniqueness is likely to bring competitive advantage to the merging organizations because the organization does not need to forecast future valuable routines and repertories that are not immediately available to a firm (Morosini, 1999).

In terms of understanding why the employee information shared during an M&A overlaps with certain institutions, we suggest that socialization is one of the mechanisms by which institutions are internalized in an organization. Checkel (2005), although he refers to the socialization of nations, argues that compliance of socialization depends on the internalization of new rules and institutions. The shift to internalization occurs whenever there is "change," and at this point, socialization starts triggered by different mechanisms (i.e., strategic calculation, role plating, and normative suasion) (Checkel, 2005). This argument is also applicable to organizational level socialization.

Furthermore, as a result of organizational socialization process, employees in an organization are channeled to think and behave similarly (Schneider, 1987; Ostroff and Rothausen, 1997). Equally, institutions in an organization reinforce related values and behaviors (Strebel, 2004). Therefore, the fit between organizational socialization and institutional theory helps us to recognize the synergies in the underlying integration M&A processes. In addition, Morosini (1999) argues that following a merger, "social fabric" of the merging organizations suffers seriously. How to build "common glue" or "connective tissue" between these organizations is the only answer if these merging firms want to create value.

In order to create such the social glue or fabric, it is important for the merging sides to understand each other's values, goals, and practices. We believe that understanding the link between socialization and institutional theory in the M&A context provides such "glue." In sum, understanding institutions helps both merging firms to know better the "social fabric" of the joining organizations which is crucial for a successful integration. Following this logic, we develop our propositions, which explore the relationships between organizational socialization domains and institutional pillars. In other words, we argue that as the acquired firms' employees socialize in their work roles, organizational values, and so on (i.e., socialization domains), they internalize the different institutions – regulative, cognitive, or normative – of the acquiring firm. Before we analyze the relationship between domains and institutions, we discuss the overall organizational socialization process and its place in M&A context.

Organizational socialization process

Socialization is the process by which people learn to cope with social norms (Parsons, 1959; Berger and Luckmann, 1967). In organizations, socialization involves the acquisition of social knowledge and skills necessary to assume an organizational role (Van Maanen and Schein, 1979; Fisher, 1986). When individuals enter into an organization, they reevaluate their assumptions while seeking information to decrease uncertainty and anxiety, and easing these *negative feelings* is their main goal (Van Maanen and Schein, 1979; Louis, 1980; Jones, 1986; Miller and Jablin, 1991; Ashforth and Saks,

1996). Organizational socialization therefore facilitates the adjustment of newcomers to organizations (Ashforth and Saks, 1996) because upon entering into an organization, employees tend have less information, and organizational socialization helps to shape (mold) employees' attitudes and behaviors in the organization's desired way (Allen and Meyer, 1990). More importantly, organizational socialization ensures that organizational values and norms are continuously transmitted and maintained (Bauer et al., 1998; Fogarthy and Dirsmith, 2001; Chow, 2002; Evans et al., 2002).

Earlier perspectives on organizational socialization emphasize a reactive role of newcomers while more recent perspectives agree that newcomers have a proactive role (i.e., information seeking) (Morrison, 1993a; Ashforth and Saks, 1997; Thomas and Anderson, 2002; Hsiung and Hsieh, 2003). As Ashforth and Saks (1996) explain, the newcomers are distressed about getting information and they are open (and vulnerable) to being influenced. Such worrisome leads them to acquire information about their roles as well as about the organization through various ways whether their organization provides the information or not in a structured way (Miller and Jablin, 1991). This situation makes organizational socialization more complex since newcomers' learning might be directed not only by the organization but also by other sources (i.e., coworkers, staff, social activities, etc.) inside the organization. As a result, organizations need to be careful about the multiple sources as well as what kind of information these sources might provide to their employees.

In considering these key characteristics of the socialization process, we discuss three main parts of organizational socialization: tactics, practices, and the domains, although our main emphasis is on socialization domains since our propositions seek to understand the relationship between "what is being learned" during socialization (i.e., domains) and the institutional pillars. The other two dimensions of the socialization process, tactics and practices, are included in our discussion, albeit not as a central driver, because organizational socialization draws mainly on these two dimensions when its role as a mechanism of the institutionalization is considered. These practices and tactics are also combined with domains and institutional pillars in the cross-border M&A section. Because in the literature, organizational socialization mostly refers to the adoption of *newcomers* to new environments, we discuss why we believe that the organizational socialization process is relevant in the M&As' context for the employees of the merging organization who are actually different from newcomers.

Socialization tactics, practices, and domains

The socialization process has been conceptualized in terms of socialization tactics, practices, and domains, as synthesized in Figure 7.1. The main difference between socialization *tactics* and *practices* is that the former describes the general organizational attitude regarding the socialization process while the

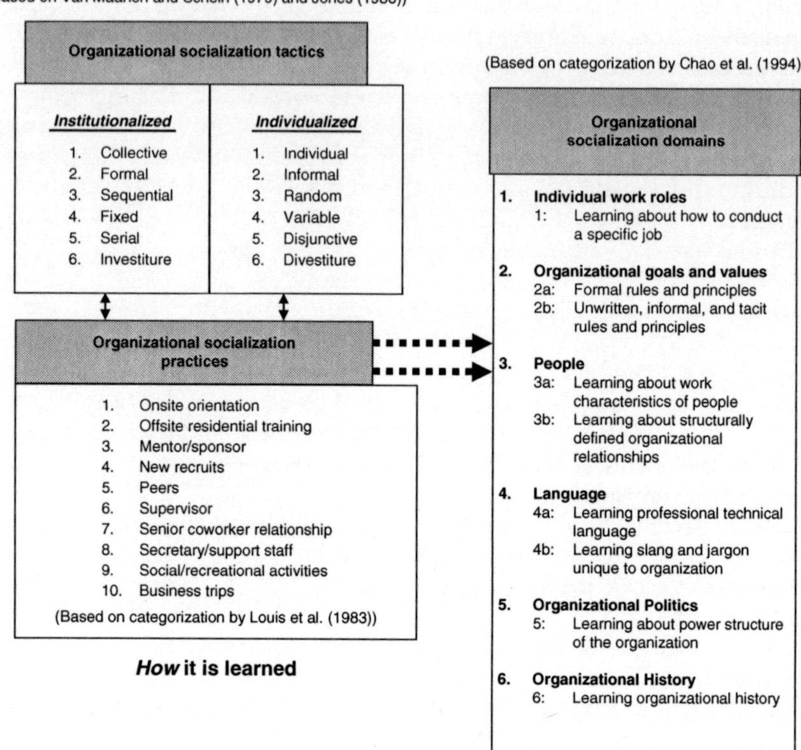

Figure 7.1   The organizational socialization process

latter refers to the actual ways organizations use to bring newcomers on track. Ashforth and Saks (1996: 151) note that "institutionalized tactics reflect a more structured program of socialization while individualized tactics might occur by default rather than design." In other words, socialization tactics are like the "ideology" or general orientation of organizations about the socialization process, whereas practices define the mechanisms this ideology is implemented in organizations. Organizations utilize socialization tactics to structure the socialization experiences of their individual actors (Ashforth and Saks, 1996). Certain organizational socialization tactics affect positively individual level outcomes such as intentions to quit, organizational commitment, job satisfaction, and role orientation, while other tactics affect such individual level outcomes negatively (e.g., Jones, 1986; Ashforth and Saks, 1997). Similarly, some organizational socialization practices (i.e., orientation, training, mentor, peers/coworkers) are found to be more effective than others in terms of affecting individual level attitudes and behaviors (e.g., Louis et al., 1980; Ostroff and Kozlowski, 1992).

Organizational socialization tactics are reflected in daily organizational life through organizational socialization practices (Louis et al., 1983). Chao et al. (1994) specify that learning content, or socialization domains, clarifies the link between organizational socialization tactics and attitudinal outcomes. Socialization tactics and practices help individuals learn *how* to become members of an organization. *What* is learned through these tactics are the organizational socialization domains. Socialization domains refer to the various aspects of the organization with which individual actors need to be familiar. It has been supported that the content of the information acquired by newcomers is positively related to job satisfaction, organizational commitment, intentions to quit, and stress (e.g., Ostroff and Kozlowski, 1992; Chao et al., 1994; Thomas and Anderson, 2002). We draw on Chao et al.'s (1994) typology of six key organizational socialization domains: individual work roles, organizational values and goals, people, language, organizational politics and organizational history, which are summarized in Figure 7.1 and discussed in detail in our framework below.

In general, individual actors (employees) must master each socialization domain in order to become effective organizational members (Schein, 1968; Feldman, 1981; Fisher, 1986; Kraimer, 1997). For example, research has shown that organizational members who acquire more knowledge of organizational domains through various socialization tactics and practices tend to be more adjusted to the organization and display higher positive attitudes (Kraimer, 1997).

M&As and the socialization process

Even though there is no prior research applying the organizational socialization process to the M&As' context, we propose that the following characteristics of organizational socialization and M&As' context show that the socialization process is important in organizational change efforts, such as during an (absorption) M&A, because it helps reduce the ambiguity created in this process. Organizational socialization tactics and practices are relevant in M&As, particularly during due diligence (pre-announcement) and in the announcement to completion stage of a merger, in no small part because the socialization process is a "continuous" process. In the due-diligence stage, information about the potential merger is normally limited to top-level executives and managers. As negotiations become more serious, information usually spreads to lower levels in the organization. At this point, employees of the merging organizations start thinking about the possible positive or negative changes and consequences that might occur to them as a result of the merger, a stage that can be called anticipatory socialization. The idea here is that not everything to be learned is new: employees will have a knowledge base and will build on it.

The merger process involves the combination of two organizations in order to effectively create a new organization in which none of the predecessor organizations are fully dominant (Shapiro, 1992). An M&A, hence, neither implies a full change in prior group membership nor a full continuation to it (Van Knippenberg et al., 2002). Unlike the newcomers, the employees of the new organization will carry over their former beliefs and values while learning new ones. Therefore, how these members will be integrated into the newly merged organization is vital since the perception of employees about the merged organization will be different from what the newcomers experience (van Knippenberg et al., 2002).

Once a M&A is announced, employees seek to learn about their roles, but aside from planned systems and practices, the ultimate nature of these practices will not be fully understood until the M&A integration stage. This "major passage" nevertheless communicates to acquired employees that they will need to socialize new rules and ways of behaving since employees in different organizations likely have substantially "different orientations to one another, their roles and organizational mission," with the "process of leaving an old situation" influencing the "process of entering the new situation" (Louis, 1980: 864–865).

The socialization process, particularly as it relates to socialization domains, is relevant during the M&A integration phase (Haspeslagh and Jemison, 1991; Child et al., 2001; Schweiger, 2002) because it highlights the norms, values, and rules that employees must learn. In other words, it specifies *what* institutions acquired employees internalize. We suggest that the "what" or "the kind of information acquired" will vary depending on the institutions internalized in each domain, and hence we propose to identify the different types of institutions involved in each socialization domain. Hence, understanding whether the rule or value to be learned is learned through the internalization of regulative institutions as opposed to cognitive institutions has important consequences for how integration managers should help acquired employees to learn the new rules and practices in the newly merged entity. In the next section, we provide the logic for the salience of specific institutions in each relevant socialization domain.

Institutional pillars and socialization domains in the context of M&As

Organizational socialization is a dynamic process in which individual actors and organizations change over time (Fisher, 1986). This trait helps an organization to accommodate changing institutional rules and affords an organization the chance to adapt and transform its structure without disturbing the inertia it has created. From this angle, organizational socialization provides continuous isomorphism to the institutional environment.

Socialization is seen as a main mechanism that facilitates the internalization of institutions by the earlier institutional views (e.g., Berger and Luckmann, 1967; Barley and Tolbert, 1997). Since organizational socialization ensures the continuity of organizational norms and values, it helps to internalize institutions into the organizational structure over the time (Inzerille and Rosen, 1983; Meek, 1988; Fogarty and Dirsmith, 2001). The socialization process ensures that existing institutional rules shaping organizational structure are diffused repeatedly. For merging organizations, the importance of this step comes from realizing that institutions – namely, values, beliefs, norms, and rules – that are part of an organization's institutional environment (internal or external) are transferred and internalized through the organizational socialization process. Hence, utilizing and understanding the organizational socialization process as a mechanism of institutionalization while considering the type of institutions involved in each socialization domain will help acquiring organizations integrate employees of acquired organizations more effectively. As pointed out, the focus of our study is on the effect of the relationship between types of institutions and socialization domains on the M&As' integration effectiveness.

In M&A integration, employees in merging organizations need to learn rules, values, norms, and standards that shape organizational structures and practices (Morosini et al., 1998). Through socialization, rules, principles, standards, and values become increasingly internalized into the organizational structure of the merged organization (Fogarthy and Dirsmith, 2001). In our framework, this process entails the transmission of institutions from the acquiring firm by acquired firms' employees through organizational socialization. Instead of the pure transmission process, we are interested in explaining the substance that is, institutional pillars and organizational socialization domains.

In the next section, we identify the dominant institutional pillar/s that tend to be internalized in each of the six socialization domains (see Table 7.1). We evaluate whether learning about socialization domains means internalization of a specific institutional pillar. The relationships we recommend between a particular socialization domain and an institutional pillar are perceived as the ideal-types for more effective M&A integration. When developing the proposed relationships between domains and institutional pillars, we have first focused on the explicit and implicit nature of the information gained thorough socialization process. While it might be easier for explicit or technical knowledge (e.g., regulative institutions) to be documented and made available, the social information is more ambiguous and informal in nature (e.g., normative and cognitive institutions); they are harder to code through written means (Morrison, 1993a; Ahuja and Galvin, 2003). Second, we have considered the degree of sanctioning in case of incompliance with a certain rule or institution while establishing the links between domains

Table 7.1 Institutional pillars and socialization domains internalized by acquired employees during M&A integration

	Three Pillars of Institutionalism		
Organizational Socialization Domains	**Regulative (Sanctioned by rules)**	**Normative (Socially conditioned)**	**Cognitive (Taken-for-granted)**
Individual work roles (P1)	Formal job characteristics	Job processes	
Organizational goals and values (P2)			
Formal rules and principles	Formal rules relating to the integrity of the acquiring organization	Socially defined principles of what the acquiring organization represents	
Unwritten, informal, and tacit rules and principles			Taken-for-granted employee behavior and action
People (P3) Informal relationships			Informal social networks among employees
Structurally defined relationships	Formally specified links among jobs in the acquiring organization		
Language (P4) Technical language		Culturally specific accepted language of a profession	Universally accepted language of a profession
Slang and jargon			Socially accepted language unique to the acquiring organization
Organizational politics (P5)	Formal power structures specified by job hierarchies		Informal power structures revealed by dynamic decision-making processes
Organizational history (P6)			Artifacts related to the history of the acquiring organization

and three pillars. Drawing on previous literature, Hart and Miller (2005: 297) note that "informal initiations and rituals" are not punished by management during socialization of a newcomer. Moreover, Morrison (1993a: 559) mentions that newcomers seek for information about expected behaviors and attitudes, which are referred as *normative* information by her, in their job and organization. Similar to these arguments, our logic of differentiating between the types of institutions comes from the difference between direct and definite as opposed to indirect and possible sanctions that might be forced on the employees in relation to a specific socialization domain. Overall, if a domain has formally defined characteristics then we argue that it helps more to the internalization of regulative institutions while domains with informal substance, we believe, are related more to the internalization of normative or cognitive institutions. The differentiation between normative and cognitive institutions comes from their definitions. We have basically paid attention to the morally sanctioning characteristics of the domain as opposed to being taken-for-granted.

Even though we do not claim that institutional pillars are mutually exclusive, we assume for the sake of theoretical clarity that some institutional types (pillars) will be more salient in a given socialization domain than others. Being aware of what type of institutions are internalized therefore sheds light into the socialization process and will allow for a more effective M&A integration as we discuss in the managerial implications.

Individual work roles

The first socialization domain, "individual work roles," indicates that individual actors need to learn how to perform tasks on the job (Fisher, 1986; Chao et al., 1994). This domain has been divided into job characteristics (what is to be done) and job processes (how it should be done) (Van Maanen and Schein, 1979). Job characteristics are often designed and formalized by human resource managers in the firm. During socialization process the employees have to be given instructions, explanations, and guidance in order to help their adjustment to their organization (e.g., Louis, 1980; Ostroff and Kozlowski, 1992; Saks and Ashforth, 1997). Especially at earlier stages, employees will need detailed information on what their job entails and how they should perform it (e.g., Ostroff and Kozlowski, 1992). In many organizations, human resource managers define jobs in terms of their skill requirements and create formal performance management systems and pay structures that are specific to certain jobs (Gerhart and Rynes, 2003). Job processes, by contrast, involve on-the-job learning of effective ways to accomplish work tasks.

Job descriptions, requirements, and characteristics will need to be explicitly made known to acquired employees. Even though they discuss it for teams, Ahuja and Galvin (2003) mention that the information about tasks that are "technical" in nature should be made explicit and available though documentation or training to all employees, who are members of a group, during socialization process. In return, all employees are obliged to follow what is involved in their job description.

Since formal job characteristics vary across organizations, newly merged organizations need to provide formal guidelines about the requirements of individual roles and tasks during the M&A integration process. For example, if a job has been defined according to certain educational requirements (e.g., a mechanical engineering degree) and has specific rules governing performance evaluation and reward systems, these requirements and the consequences of not meeting them will need to be made known not only to acquired employees who may occupy such jobs, but also to employees who will be filling future job vacancies and to those managers evaluating and rewarding employees who occupy the positions. In this case, the socialization of individual work role domains will involve the internalization of regulative institutions by acquired employees (Scott, 1998, 2001). Therefore, in the context of M&A integration, this socialization domain is likely to be more effectively learned by acquired employees when managers know that some of the institutions being internalized are regulative, and consequently set the right strategies in place to achieve the socialization of this domain. In other words, learning about job characteristics imply internalization of regulative institutions of the acquiring firm since there will be organizational measures taken formally against failure to comply with these characteristics. Hence, we propose

Proposition 1a: As acquired employees are socialized in terms of formal job characteristics of individual work roles, they internalize regulative institutions of the acquiring firm. If this is the case, then M&A integration will be more effective.

Learning about job processes, such as how to deal with a job crisis, is often accomplished through advice from peers, supervisors, mentors, and on-the-job learning (e.g., Ostroff and Kozlowski, 1992; Morrison, 1993a). That is, although characteristics of a job are formally defined and governed by rules of an organization, how each job is to be performed by an employee is based on norms specific to the organization, and perhaps the work group within the organization. Work norms in some work groups will encourage an open-door approach, with employees able to solicit just-in-time advice from their peers. By contrast, work norms in other work groups may promote tasks to be performed primarily by the individual due to the confidentiality or the knowledge-specificity of the job task.

The integration of job processes in M&A integration process therefore relates to the internalization of normative institutions that are not necessarily coercive rules but that involve binding expectations on how employees should learn about the job processes. This implies that firms need to specify and transfer normative institutions surrounding the employees' job position in the new organization. For example, while learning the job responsibilities in the newly merged organization, employees of the acquired firm will need to recognize what constitutes respectful behavior, whether they need to be experts or problem solvers, and how they should evaluate and deal with uncertain situations. Following this logic, we argue that M&A integration is more effective when integration managers are aware that employee knowledge of job processes (or socialization domain) also entails employees' understanding of what is appropriate (normative institutions). Hence, by increasing their awareness of this aspect of integration, integration managers can set up the necessary mechanisms that help internalization of such normative institutions. In other words, normative information meaning what is being accepted and valued and what behaviors are normal are being learned (Ahuja and Galvin, 2003). Hence, we propose

Proposition 1b: As acquired employees are socialized in terms of job processes of individual work roles, they internalize normative institutions of the acquiring firm. If this is the case, then M&A integration will be more effective.

It is also worthwhile to discuss the institutional pillars that we do not see as predominant within a given socialization domain. In the individual work roles domain, we do not suggest a relationship between individual work roles and the cognitive institutional pillar because we believe that individual roles related to organizational tasks are seldom taken for granted or learned without any formal or socially enforced framework. Work roles are explicitly codified by the organization or defined by the profession in which work roles are exercised. As a result, employees are expected to follow them to a certain degree. Finally, we also know that individual work roles are constructed and communicated to acquired employees through different organizational mechanisms, such as training, orientation, coworkers, and so on that we will discuss in the managerial implications section.

Organizational goals and values

The second socialization domain, "organizational goals and values," refers to the institutions that maintain the integrity of organizations (Schein, 1968). Organizational goals and values are divided into two different categories: formal rules and principles and unwritten, informal, and tacit rules and principles (Chao et al., 1994). Formal rules are written codes and regulations that guide employee behavior such as a mission statement or a code of ethics. They can be formal rules relating to the integrity of the acquiring organization, or socially defined principles of what the acquiring organization represents. For example, an acquiring firm in the electronics industry is likely to have some rules about minimum quality standards or complying with ISO9000. By contrast, unwritten, informal, and tacit rules and principles reflect taken-for-granted behavior and action among employees in a given organization (Fisher, 1986). For example, acquiring employees know that they should not engage in certain practices simply because such behavior and action is not done in that firm. This knowledge is embedded in a firm's history.

We suggest that the socialization of formal rules in a new organization will require the internalization of regulative institutions by acquired employees since formal rules are sanctioned by organizations and organizations expect these rules to be followed carefully. Thus, the acquiring organization needs to ensure that acquired employees will follow and understand these formally specified organizational goals and values. In particular, organizational members are explicitly required to learn and know the formal rules and principles of the newly merged organization because they are general firm laws or standard rules. For example, if the codified definition of "what fair business practices" differs between merging organizations, the newly merged organization will need to use a regulative institution to define expediently what a fair business practice is and to specify the reprimands faced from its violation. Or, if an acquiring investment brokerage firm explicitly prohibits "churning," while the acquired firm has no such formal policies, acquired employees will need to be informed and held accountable that such behavior is not allowed, and can result in sanctions such as termination of the employment contract. Following this logic, we propose that when integration managers are aware of the type of institution that needs to be internalized at each socialization domain, they are more likely to design and implement the integration strategies and practices leading to a more effective M&A integration process. In case of formal organizational values and norms, the institutional pillar that will be internalized consists of regulative ones. Hence, we propose

Proposition 2a: As acquired employees are socialized in terms of formal rules relating to organizational goals and values, they internalize regulative institutions of the acquiring firm. If this is the case, then M&A integration will be more effective.

The second component of organizational goals and values, unwritten, informal, and tacit rules, is learned via the emulation of others in the newly merged organization. While some of these informal rules might be learned without any conscious recognition, some of them are socially forced. Morrison (1993b) mentions newcomers, as they learn about organizational goals and values, also seek for feedback about how their social behaviors are socially perceived. Such feedback seeking behavior supports the possibility of moral sanctioning in relation to organizational goals and values. Moreover, socially defined principles of an organization laid out, for example, in mission statements relate to the internalization of normative institutions. These are principles stating accepted social behavior that is sanctioned not by specific rules, but rather by socially accepted norms. Norms governing what constitutes proper employee behavior will be internalized through employee interaction and can be made salient through social sanctions of improper behavior. Thus, as acquired employees learn about these principles and procedures they internalize normative institutions.

We propose that these particular organizational goals and values are likely to mean internalization of cognitive and normative institutions as opposed to regulative institutions. The employee adoption of these norms and values cannot be achieved through regulative institutions because they are unwritten and tacit which makes them harder to codify. As a result, employees are expected to comply with them to a degree but they are not sanctioned through formal means for incompliance. As Louis (1980) argues, norms and assumptions in an organization emerge interactively and are performed rather than explicitly recognized. Moreover, they are less likely to mean internalization of normative institutions because unwritten goals and values reflect certain procedures and standards that are the result of social interaction. For instance, the supervisor–subordinate relationship toward achieving organizational goals might differ across organizations. The determining features of such a relationship would probably not be written in any document or codified, nor would they involve social sanctions because it is a dyadic relationship on how to behave according to organizational goals and values. Instead, these goals and values that are shared between a supervisor-subordinate would most likely be learned cognitively over time. We argue that in the M&A integration process, the socialization of informal organizational goals and values also mean internalization via cognitive institutions. Knowing the main institutional pillar involved in the socialization domain can help integration managers to more effectively socialize acquired employees, particularly in absorptive M&As, as opposed to seeking socialization through writing what usually is unwritten code. Hence, we propose

Proposition 2b: As acquired employees are socialized in terms of unwritten, informal, and tacit rules and principles relating to organizational goals and values, they internalize cognitive and normative institutions of the acquiring firm. If this is the case, then M&A integration will be more effective.

People

The third socialization domain, "people," is defined as learning about the work groups with which the individual actors interact (Fisher, 1986). It underscores becoming familiarized with informal work relationships among employees as well as the structurally defined employee relationships within the organization (Chao et al., 1994).

Learning about informal relationships includes interaction with other employees, learning about relevant norms and values, as well as work group's normative structure (Ostroff and Kozlowski, 1992: 852). Informal employee relationships will occur through daily organizational life without formal intervention by the organization. Acquired employees will likely learn the nature of different types of social networks over time, such as to whom they can turn to for task advice, and with whom they can form friendship ties. Interaction with coworkers has been found to provide important information particularly about group domain in the literature (e.g., Miller and Jablin, 1991; Ostroff and Kozlowski, 1992). Because such traits will be taken for granted and will be accepted as they are, without much questioning, understanding informal social networks among employees in the acquiring firm, we believe, will involve the internalization of cognitive institutions. Most of the time, organizational members will assimilate this knowledge without even recognizing it. For example, characteristics such as whether coworkers are fair, responsible, and timely in their decisions will be learned over time during the M&A integration process as employees address various organizational challenges and perform every-day tasks.

The socialization of people's informal relationships is not related to regulative institutions because it is not imposed on the newcomer through formal mechanisms, nor does it relate to normative institutions because their assimilation has nothing to do with accepted norms or standards resulting from social interaction and socially accepted behavior. Employees will self-select whom they see as the helpful source to get information about group dynamics and other related issues. Then, they internalize such knowledge either by learning from coworkers or through observation overtime without any official enforcement. Hence, we propose

Proposition 3a: As acquired employees are socialized in terms of informal relationships, they internalize cognitive institutions of the acquiring firm. If this is the case, then M&A integration will be more effective.

The second component of the "people" socialization domain, learning about the structurally defined organizational relationships of organizational members, entails knowing how jobs in the acquiring organization are linked, both horizontally and vertically. These relationships among positions in an organization will be explicitly defined and communicated to employees in the newly merged organization. They therefore can be considered as requiring the adoption of formal rules and regulations. That is, employees will be expected to follow the formal structure during the everyday functioning of the newly merged organization, such as knowing the reporting relationships associated with certain jobs, respecting others due their position in the organization, and so on. Thus, this component of the people domain will entail internalization of regulative institutions because they are introduced to organizational members in order for them to follow and function according to the new organizational relationships which at the same time introduce the formal hierarchical structure of the organization.

The socialization of the structurally defined relationships of organizational members in the newly merged organization relates neither to the internalization of cognitive institutions nor to normative institutions, since this learning is not left to the discretion of organizational members and does not reflect social norms or procedures of the organization. Employees in the newly merged organization will immediately need to learn to whom they need to report, with whom they will work, and who will be accountable to them. In addition, employees will learn their boundaries of responsibilities as well as those of others. Since most of these responsibilities are formally defined and determined, they will have to be learned in the detail required by the acquiring organization. We propose that integration managers seeking to socialize acquired employees in the structurally defined relationships of the newly merged entity will be more effective when they consider the regulative institutions that are internalized at the same time. Hence, we propose

Proposition 3b: As acquired employees are socialized in terms of structurally defined organizational relationships relating to people's work characteristics, they internalize regulative institutions of the acquiring firm. If this is the case, then M&A integration will be more effective.

Language

The fourth socialization domain, "language," refers to the communication tools needed to transfer and acquire the necessary information to perform a job task. Language as a socialization domain has two dimensions: learning the technical language that is necessary to perform a task (Chao et al., 1994) and becoming familiar with a given organization's slang and jargon. The first component is often related to learning technical language specific to a given profession. Although technical language is common to employees across organizations, as it is universally accepted within professions, there can be differences in certain organizations due to broader organizational cultural differences. For example, if a Japanese automobile firm acquired an organization from another country, the Japanese firm would want the acquired employees to understand technical language such as "Kanban," "just in time," and "quality circles" which might not be common in the acquired firm.

We suggest that culturally specific language that needs to be learned by the acquired employees during the M&A integration process is largely related to the internalization of normative institutions, although there may be a cognitive component if language is not essential to performing effectively. For example, if a British printed news firm acquires a US firm, there might be slight differences in technical language. In some instances, these differences will be minor, such as using an "s" rather than a "z" in written communication which can be quickly learned. Eventually, the language of the acquiring firm will become taken-for-granted as acquired employees are exposed to the language differences and realize that a single language form is accepted. Normative sanctions can still be applied to assist in institutionalizing acquired employees, such as through the use of humor, in cases where it is important that language be similar, as might occur when writing legal documents related to a deal. In rare cases, when language similarity is absolutely crucial, acquiring firms may find it to be cost effective to create explicit policies regarding the use of language. However, in general, it will be most effective to use norms and principles to ensure that acquired employees integrate specific technical language.

In effect, if an acquired employee is integrated into an organization where the professional norms and standards regarding language related to the acquiring organization's culture differs from the norms they experienced in the past, he or she will be expected to know and follow the skills and standards this profession obliges. These standards will most likely not be legally sanctioned. Nevertheless, they are often important for functioning in the organization and therefore cannot be learned over long periods of time. Thus, they will relate to the internalization of normative institutions, rather than regulative or cognitive institutions. Hence, we propose

Proposition 4a: As acquired employees are socialized in terms of culturally specific technical language, they internalize normative institutions of the acquiring firm. If this is the case, then M&A integration will be more effective.

Universally accepted language of a profession will be related to the internalization of cognitive institutions. That is, acquired employees will bring a shared knowledge of professional language to the acquiring firm, which will result in a taken-for-granted aspect during M&A integration. For example, terminology related to engineering processes will be institutionalized in universities and professional meetings/associations and will therefore be common to employees in both acquiring and acquired firms. Technical language will not be related to the internalization of regulative institutions because such language is not legally sanctioned: rather, it is unconsciously used since it is part of the individual meaning set. Its normative component will generally be institutionalized by employees prior to joining either firm through professional associations and/or accreditation associations, and therefore this technical language will have a taken-for-granted status, as Berger and Luckmann (1967) relate in their discussion of the transmission of norms across generations in societies.

In light of this discussion, when managers seek to socialize acquired employees in terms of their technical language domain, they should rely on cognitive institutions where constitutive schema and shared understanding exist. Hence, we propose

Proposition 4b: As acquired employees are socialized in terms of universally accepted technical language, they internalize cognitive institutions of the acquiring firm. If this is the case, then M&A integration will be more effective.

The second component of the language socialization domain is learning the slang and jargon unique to the merging organizations. Similar to the case for learning culturally specific technical language, acquiring firms will desire that acquired employees know the informal language specific to the acquiring firm in order to be able to work effectively. However, in contrast to learning culturally specific formal language, it is unlikely that potential negative harm to firms will result if informal language is learned over time. One possible exception would be the case of informal language that is considered inappropriate such as behavior that is viewed as harassment in the acquiring firm and not in the acquired firm. In this case, acquiring firms will need to sanction language, either through regulations or perhaps through normative sanctions if there are myriad ambiguities associated with the language differences.

Thus, acquired employees' learning of informal language primarily relate to the internalization of cognitive institutions over time. In rare instances, the acquiring firm may need to create formal regulations, or use normative sanctions, to communicate to employees what is proper language and behavior. Hence, we propose

Proposition 4c: As acquired employees are socialized in terms of slang and jargon relating to language, they internalize cognitive institutions of the acquiring firm. If this is the case, then M&A integration will be more effective.

Organizational politics

The fifth socialization domain, "organizational politics," refers to learning the power structures within the organization (Fisher, 1986) so that employees comprehend the political dimension between individual employees and organizational structures. The power structure of an organization might be revealed to an individual actor formally – such as through an organizational level schema – or informally through peers or observation (e.g., Ostroff and Kozlowski, 1992). In other words, individual employees may learn about formal hierarchical power structures through sources such as an organizational level schema relating to job hierarchies (regulative institutions) and informal power structures that are revealed over time through decision-making processes and interaction with employees in different informal networks (cognitive institutions).

Learning about formal power structures can be accomplished through reference to organizational schema. Organizations formally give some sense of these different hierarchical dynamics, although in some instances employees will discover some of them over time. Power structures specified in employee handbooks often cover a wide range of rules and regulations. Important rules and regulations will be highlighted, while others may be discovered over time as specific cases motivate employees to refer to the handbook to understand their rights and liabilities. Learning about which employees have more knowledge and/or power than others allows for a more efficient learning and adjustment process during socialization (e.g., Louis, 1980; Chao et al., 1994).

In general, we suggest that learning about formal power structure of an organization by the acquired employees will mean internalization of regulative institutions. For example, the VP of a group or function will have certain rights, such as establishing pay guidelines for their group or function. She or he will also have formally specified responsibilities by higher level superiors, such as meeting specific goals. These rules cover a wide variety of political issues, such as who determines and allocates rewards to employees. Pay decisions for upper-level managers may be determined in committees of peers and superiors, while pay decisions for middle-managers may be determined directly by superiors. We suggest that when integration managers understand that acquired employees learn the organizational politics, which simultaneously will mean internalization of regulative institutions, the M&A integration process will be more effective. Hence, we propose

Proposition 5a: As acquired employees are socialized in terms of formal power structures, they internalize regulative institutions of the acquiring firm. If this is the case, then M&A integration will be more effective.

Learning about informal power structures will generally occur over time. Acquired employees will learn about the key decision-makers or influential leaders in their new units or departments through interactions with these influential individuals or through informal discussions with peers. Power stemming from informal structures such as networks will be revealed through repeated actions, such as promotions provided to subordinates. Thus, acquired employees may be able to assess the power structure by observing differences in the ability of managers at the same level to confer rewards on their subordinates or by hearing about past actions from colleagues. Learning about the organizational power structure is generally not associated with normative institutions because it has little to do with organizational standards or procedures that are governed by social sanctions. As mentioned, knowing who has more power and knowledge will overall benefit the employee; however, lacking such understanding is hardly punishable through moral or formal means. Understanding that employees will learn the informal organizational politics through shared understandings that relates to the internalization of cognitive institutions will help managers in achieving more effective M&A integrations. Hence, we propose

Proposition 5b: As acquired employees are socialized in terms of informal power structures, they internalize cognitive institutions of the acquiring firm. If this is the case, then M&A integration will be more effective.

Organizational history

The sixth socialization domain, "organizational history," is described as learning the organizational traditions, customs, myths, and rituals that are part of the organizational culture (Ritti and Funkhouser, 1987), as well as learning about an organization's background. In many cases, organizational history is observed in artifacts unique to an organization, such as dress codes, the way people address each other, and the physical layout of the organization (Schein, 1990). These artifacts are typically unique to organizations.

Although some artifacts can be socially sanctioned, such as norms regarding the appropriateness of facial hair, in general they are seen as taken-for-granted aspects of an organization. For example, dress codes in a business school setting may differ according to whether classes are in session. Thus, an employee who joins a department in the summer may come to perceive that informal dress is the norm in the organization. However, once classes start, they may be pleasantly surprised when they show up for work and their experienced colleagues are wearing suits.

In general, artifacts, traditions, rituals, and culture will be learned over time as a result of repetition, with acquired employees internalizing cognitive institutions at the same time. Employee behaviors are internalized almost subconsciously. They do not directly reflect regulative institutions since they tend to be taken for granted rather than being legally sanctioned, and for the most part, do not reflect normative institutions since they are learned over time.

In the context of M&A integration, the organizational traditions and customs will generally not be tangible. Conversely acquired employees will understand over time the shared meanings of organizational history and be able to differentiate those that matter from those that do not. In this regard, integration managers need to realize that the socialization of the organizational history domain is likely to be related to the internalization of cognitive institutions through exposing acquired employees to common beliefs. Hence, we propose

Proposition 6: As acquired employees are socialized in terms of organizational history, they internalize cognitive institutions of the acquiring firm. If this is the case, then M&A integration will be more effective.

Country institutional profiles and socialization in cross-border M&As

In this section, we expand our post-acquisition integration framework to discuss how national contextual characteristics influence the different organizational socialization domains. The national level is critical in research on cross-border M&As, not only because of the increasing importance of mergers across borders, but also due to their complexity vis-à-vis domestic M&As. Developing a connected workforce in a newly merged organization is more challenging in cross-border M&As, particularly when organizations differ in terms of their language, national culture, institutional, and social contexts (Greenberg et al., 2005). A great deal of the hindrance to integration success for cross-border M&As is the neglect of differences in societal customs and norms with the other side of the merger during the integration process (Olie, 1994; Belcher and Nail, 2001). However, empirical studies examining the role of management in the process of post-acquisition integration are rare (Uhlenbruck and DeCastro, 2000; Child et al., 2001; Piske, 2002).

Access to unique organizational routines and repertories might provide competitive advantage (Morosini, 1999). In the case of cross-border M&As, these unique organizational routines and repertories are more likely to be supported by different industry and national level institutions, which surround the merging organizations separately. It is important to recognize that organizational level institutions are created as a result of an organization's interaction with its institutional environment (i.e., national and industry level). Following Morosini's (1999) argument about gaining competitive advantage through accessing unique routines, cross-border M&As seem more advantageous. However, it is hard to negate that these M&As will also face more complexity, at least initially. The link between what kind of information the employees of the acquired organization obtain and through which institutional pillars such information diffused is not straightforward.

Differences in cross-national management practices are often attributed to national culture, and tend to be drawn from Hofstede's (1980) ubiquitous four-fold categorization. We find that national culture is too broad of a concept for analyzing cross-border M&A integration practices and instead draw on Scott's (1998, 2001) three institutional pillars, wherein the former dimensions are conceptually and empirically distinct. Kostova (1999) offers a novel theoretical solution to this conceptual conundrum using institutional rather than cultural characteristics of countries to create a construct called a country institutional profile (CIP). As Kostova (1999: 314) notes, "a country's social environment can be characterized by its CIP: a three-dimensional construct defined as the set of regulatory, cognitive, and normative institutions in that country." As such, this construct fits nicely with our theoretical framework because it allows us to retain our focus on the internalization of Scott's (2001) three institutional pillars in various socialization domains.

There is, of course, some overlap between Kostova's CIP construct and national culture – for example, both cognitive and normative dimensions have similarities to culture – but the CIP is broader and has unique elements. For instance, the regulatory dimension is unique to CIP but not to national culture. Moreover, as Kostova notes, the CIP allows for analysis at multiple levels in addition to the national level, and can be constructed at different levels of specificity. More importantly, there are a number of elements of the CIP that lend themselves to an analysis of cross-border M&As. For example, Kostova (1999) demonstrates the relevance of the CIP construct in understanding the transfer of organizational practices across borders. Clearly, a cross-border M&A can be seen as involving the transfer of a number of practices from the acquiring firm to the acquired firm, the more so the more integrated the companies become. An important factor is that there may be inconsistencies in the transfer of some of these practices across borders that can lead to conflict, with the greater the difference in CIP between countries, the greater the likelihood of misfit between the transfer of practices across borders, and hence the need for greater effort in the socialization process.

In effect, the link between CIP and the transfer of organizational practices across nations via cross-border M&As is fairly straightforward. In particular, assuming at least some degree of integration in a cross-border M&A,[3] the greater the institutional distance between countries of the merging firms, the greater is the difficulty in diffusing the regulative, normative, and cognitive institutions through organizational socialization domains. Thus, the greater the institutional distance, the greater the emphasis a firm will need to place on socialization by internalizing the most salient institutions.

Transactions across borders are rarely as straightforward as the above illustration suggests, as is evident in empirical research based on Kostova's (1999) CIP showing how CIP plays out in different contexts, such as entrepreneurship (Busenitz et al., 2000) and the adoption of an organizational practice by subsidiaries of multinational corporations (Kostova and Roth, 2002). Existing empirical research on CIPs also indicates that firms may need to allocate more resources to internalizing different institutions in each organizational socialization domain.

Based on the CIP research, we argue, as shown in Table 7.2, that when large differences in the regulatory dimension between the countries of two merging firms exist (assuming little or no differences in normative and cognitive institutions), the newly merged entity will need to spend a significant amount of time and energy in socializing employees in the socialization domain of formal rules and principles.[4] By contrast, if the institutional difference between countries is greatest for the normative dimension, the newly merged entity will need to focus on internalizing these norms by socializing employees on the following domains: individual work roles, structurally defined relationships, and the history and politics of the organization. Finally, if the two countries diverge primarily in the cognitive institutional dimension, then managers in the acquiring firm should pay particular attention in socializing employees about the unwritten, informal, and tacit rules and principles, informal relationships, and language domains.

As we have suggested, reality is more complex than what our model indicates. For example, if cross-border M&As involve the transfer of practices that are associated with different CIP, firms will need to vary the socialization

Table 7.2 Key socialization domains to take into account in cross-border M&As when institutional distance is high

	High Regulatory Difference	**High Normative Difference**	**High Cognitive Difference**
Socialization Domain Emphasized	Formal rules and principles	Individual work roles	Unwritten, informal, and tacit rules and principles
		Structurally defined relationships	Learning about work characteristics of people
		Organizational politics	Language
		Organizational history	

domains they use for each different practice. While such management techniques can become increasingly complicated – for example, if the degree of integration is high, rather than medium or low, or if firms are in radically different industries – the nature of CIP and our post-acquisition integration framework can provide substantive guidance and thereby minimize potential difficulties in cross-border M&As. For the case of different industry groups, this outcome can be resolved by developing an industry institutional profile, as Kostova (1999) notes is possible.

Managerial implications

We have identified what type of institution (institutional pillar) is most dominant in each socialization domain and developed a set of propositions to specify how M&A integration can be made more effective. This allows us to take the next step in which we suggest specific implications of our propositions for managers seeking to effectively integrate acquired employees. An important factor in a successful M&A integration is, therefore, that managers understand which types of rules, norms, and values are circulating in the newly merged organization. This fine-grained understanding will allow managers to choose the most effective strategic tools and human resource practices to effectively socialize employees, and hence pursue a better post-merger integration. For example, regulative institutions might be codified during employee orientation and training so that formal job characteristics are clearly communicated to all employees. Normative institutions might be articulated through supervising, mentoring, peers, secretary/support staff so that employees learn the necessary professional technical language to conduct their organizational roles. Finally, cognitive institutions might be facilitated through social/recreational activities so that employees understand the power structure of the newly merged organization. We next discuss the managerial implications for each socialization domain.

Individual work roles

Managers will need to specify clearly the characteristics associated with specific jobs, a role traditionally performed by the human resource management function. Nevertheless, managers in different departments and business units will have an important role to play in ensuring that employees clearly understand the requirements of the jobs that they hold. Managers can do so by taking a proactive role in transferring knowledge of job processes to acquired employees, for example, by providing information about jobs to employees, either from employee handbooks or through easily accessible internal websites. Managers can also help ensure that there are open lines of communication between employees in similar jobs, thereby facilitating the integration of peers from the acquiring company with those in the acquired firm.

Organizational goals and values

Managers can provide acquired employees with specific formal rules about what behavior is not acceptable and subject to being sanctioned. Managers can also help acquired employees to understand the norms governing values and goals of the acquiring organization, for example, by highlighting values in the mission statement that are desired and by illustrating behaviors that have been socially sanctioned in the past. Although it is more difficult that acquired employees internalize unwritten goals and values of the acquiring firm given the time needed to become taken-for-granted, managers can speed up the post-acquisition integration process by sponsoring social functions that highlight desired behavior. If they can convince the firm's leaders to participate in these functions, acquired employees will see more clearly the importance of following certain tacit rules and principles. Thus, managers may need to persuade leaders of the benefits that their participation will bring to the firm.

People

Managers can facilitate the exposure of acquired employees to a variety of informal networks by placing them strategically into multi-function and multi-level teams in the newly merged organization. Doing so will help to integrate acquired employees and allow them to build their own effective informal networks. Conversely, structurally defined employee relationships can be communicated to acquired employees, for example, by distributing relevant organizational charts or by having supervisors or peers in the acquiring firm provide insight into the different reporting relationships within business units and divisions of the new organization. As in the case of individual work roles, managers can also make available information on structural relationships contained in handbooks or on internal web-based systems to acquired employees.

Language

Managers can integrate acquired employees more effectively by specifying the important culturally specific language of a profession that is required to work effectively in the acquiring firm. They can also involve human resource managers in specifying what is considered to be inappropriate language, and clearly relating possible sanctions from violating informal codes of conduct, particularly if such behavior goes against the legal rules of a society. Many other language differences will be revealed through interaction, as well as through written and informal communication related to work activities. Managers can therefore help to integrate acquired employees by ensuring that they are exposed to a variety of activities, particularly for employees who may be telecommuting, or who engage in a significant amount of off-site travel.

Organizational politics

Managers can assist in the socialization of acquired employees by specifying clearly the job hierarchies and the reporting relationships associated with different jobs in the firm and its component groups. By so doing, acquired employees can better understand which employees are supervisors, which are subordinates, and to whom do they report. By communicating this formally specified information to acquired employees, acquiring firms can reduce much of the uncertainty associated with M&A integration, such as who evaluates their performance, how they do so, and more importantly, how they will be rewarded.

Specifying formal power structures not only involves a description of job bands and grade level structures, but also a presentation of how hierarchically related jobs fit within other organizational structures, such as functional and matrix structures. For example, acquiring firms with matrix structures will need to specify to the acquired employees whether they will have one or more bosses and which one has the ultimate authority over certain work tasks they might perform. In effect, managers in acquiring firms will want to make it clear to acquired employees who their bosses are, what responsibilities they have to them, and what determines important career outcomes for these employees, such as promotions, bonuses, and salaries.

Managers will have less ability to influence the socialization of informal power structures characteristic of organizational politics in acquired employees, since this information is generally learned over time. Nevertheless, as in other instances where cognitive institutions are being socialized, managers can enhance integration effectiveness by increasing acquired employees' exposure to organizational actions that reveal informal authority, as well as exposure to managers and colleagues who can and will impart such information to them. For example, placing acquired employees in a number of work groups can give them a better sense of who has the informal power in network structures of the acquiring organization.

Organizational history

Managers can increase the effectiveness of the integration process by exposing acquired employees to a variety of artifacts that thereby help to further socialize them into the acquiring organization. For example, although many employees will experience the acquiring organization's history on a daily basis as they experience a variety of artifacts such as the organization's layout, they may not internalize them quickly due to the cognitive nature of these institutions. Thus, while being cognizant of overloading acquired employees with information, managers may be able to assist these employees by putting them in contact with peers or mentors who can provide answers to questions that they feel are important, as well as to provide them with an understanding of what role the acquiring organization's history has in determining the way the acquiring organization appears.

In sum, managers in acquiring firms can take a variety of managerial actions to help ensure effective integration of acquired employees into the newly merged firm. A crucial task for upper-level managers and leaders is to sell the idea of effective integration to the managers who are best situated to impart knowledge to acquired employees of the myriad policies, values, systems, and practices important to the organization's success. In particular, deal makers (boards and top management teams) will need to convince integration managers that integration is not simply a task to be performed by human resource management practices and guidelines, but depends critically on their ability to socialize acquired employees in their work groups effectively and quickly.

These implications are also applicable to cross-border M&As. However, as we discussed, the case of cross-border M&As is more complex in that one needs to account for the differences in industry and national level institutions in addition to the organizational level ones. Such complexity makes understanding the implications of acquiring various kinds of information more important. In other words, even though differences between the merging organizations seem to exist at organizational level, grasping differences within a context will be beneficial to the managers of the merging organizations. While there are unique organizational level routines, the creation of such routines is influenced by environmental characteristics surrounding the organization. Therefore, understanding broader contextual characteristics might help merging organizations make more sense of organizational level differences. For example, for the individual work roles domain, we propose that managers might provide information about jobs to employees by using handbooks, intra-organizational network, and open communication. If we assume that two organizations from collectivist and individualistic cultures (i.e., differences at national level institutions) merge, the perception of the employees of a specific job task might be different. Employees of the collectivist organization might perceive their performance in relation to their peers while the employees of an individualist-oriented organization might try to stand out more individually. If such differences are not taken into account, then the evaluation of employees might create misperceptions on the side of managers in terms of, for example, the performance of that employee. Therefore, in cross-border M&As differences in organizational, industry, and national level institutions should be considered as a whole.

Discussion and Conclusion

In this chapter, we analyzed the relationship between the three pillars of institutions and the six domains of socialization in the context of the integration phase of M&As. Our main assumption is that the organizational socialization process entails the internalization of different types of institutions (e.g., Inzerille and Rosen, 1983; Meek, 1988; Fogarty and Dirsmith, 2001) and thus it is critical to identify what types of institutions will be most salient in to each socialization domain. We propose that post-acquisition integration will be more effective when the socialization process is coupled with the internalization of the necessary institutions.

Our examination of what type of institution will be internalized in each socialization domain has generated theoretical propositions arguing that the use of a given institution in the socialization process will lead to a more effective integration. For the sake of theory development, we have identified what we argue are the most prominent institutions in each domain. However, we do not categorically deny that all types of institutions might be present in each socialization domain. We simply argue that the ones that we identify should be recognized and utilized in the socialization process.

Notes

1. For the purposes of theory building, we focus exclusively on acquisitions as opposed to mergers, where the acquiring firm obtains ownership and control over the acquired firm. Depending on the literature we believe that this is legitimate to do since M&As are seen as a whole and the terms used interchangeably most of the time (e.g., Child et al., 2001; Houghton et al., 2003). Even though we discuss only one side of the medallion, our discussions might be very well extended to both sides albeit not attributing the same weight.
2. Depending on the literature, we present our perception of the organizational socialization process in Figure 7.1. We discuss the relationships drawn in the Figure 7.1 in the organizational socialization literature review section.
3. Most cross-border M&As involve some integration, the exceptions being perhaps those involving Japanese acquiring firms (Child et al., 2001) or M&As as substitutes for research and development (Bower, 2001). Even in these cases, the acquiring firm will need to communicate its intentions and likely diffuse its institutions over time.
4. This assumes that the difference in the regulatory dimension is not very large. As Kostova (1999) notes, if a practice is perceived to be in conflict with the regulatory institutions of the recipient country, there is a high likelihood that the practice will not be transferred and implemented.

References

Aguilera, R. V. and Dencker, J. 2004. The role of human resource management in cross-border mergers and acquisitions. *International Journal of Human Resource Management*, (15) 8: 1357–1372.

Ahuja, M. and Galvin, J. 2003. Socialization in virtual groups. *Journal of Management*, 29 (2): 161–185.

Allen, N. J. and Meyer, J. P. 1990. Organizational socialization tactics: A longitudinal analysis of links to newcomers' commitment and role orientation. *Academy of Management Journal*, 33 (4): 847–859.

Anand, J., Capron, L., and Mitchell, W. 2005. Using acquisitions to access multinational diversity: Thinking beyond the domestic versus cross-border M&A comparison. *Industrial and Corporate Change*, 14: 191–224.

Ashforth, B. E. and Saks, A. M. 1996. Socialization tactics: Longitudinal effects on newcomer adjustment. *Academy of Management Journal*, 39 (1): 149–178.

Ashforth, B. E. and Saks, A. M. 1997. A longitudinal investigation of the relationships between job information sources, applicant perceptions of fit and work outcomes. *Personnel Psychology*, 50 (2): 395–426.

Barley, S. R. and Tolbert, P. S. 1997. Institutionalization and structuration: Studying the links between action and institution. *Organization Studies*, 18 (1): 93–117.

Barney, J. B. 1986. Organizational culture: Can it be a source of sustained competitive advantage? *Academy of Management Review*, 11 (3): 656–665.

Bauer, T. N., Morrison, E. W., and Callister, R. P. 1998. Organizational socialization: A review and directions for future research. *Research in Personnel and Human Resource Management*, 16: 149–214.

Belcher, T. and Nail, L. 2001. Culture clashes and integration problems in cross-border mergers: A clinical examination of the Pharmacia-Upjohn merger. *Issues in International Corporate Control and Governance*, 15: 353–370.

Berger, P. L. and Luckmann, T. 1967. *The Social Construction of Reality*. NY: Doubleday.

Bower, J. L. 2001. Not all M&As are alike – and that matters. *Harvard Business Review*, March: 93–101.

Buono, A. F. and Bowditch, J. L. 1989. *The Human Side of Mergers and Acquisitions: Managing Collisions Between People, Cultures, and Organizations*. San Francisco, CA: Josey-Bass Publishers.

Busenitz, L., Gomez, C., and Spencer, J. 2000. Country institutional profiles: Unlocking entrepreneurial phenomena. *Academy of Management Journal*, 43: 994–1003.

Capron, L. and Pistre, N. 2002. When do acquirers earn abnormal returns? *Strategic Management Journal*, 23 (9): 781–795.

Carey, D. C., Ogden, D., and Roland, J.A. 2004. The human side of M&As: Leveraging the most important factor in deal making. New York, NY: Oxford University Press, Inc.

Cartwright, S. and Cooper, C. L. 1992. *Mergers and Acquisitions: The Human Factor*, Oxford: Butterworth-Heinemann.

Chao, G. T., O'Leary-Kelly, A. M., Wolf, S., Klein, H. J., and Gardner, P. D. 1994. Organizational; Socialization: Its content and consequences. *Journal of Applied Psychology*, 79 (5): 730–743.

Checkel, J. T. 2005. International institutions and socialization in Europe: Introduction and framework. *International Organization*, 59 (4): 801–826.

Child, J., Faulkner, D., and Pitkethly, R. 2001. *The Management of International Acquisitions*, Oxford: Oxford University Press.

Chow, I. H. 2002. Organizational socialization and career success of Asian managers. *International Journal of Human Resource Management*, 13 (4): 720–738.

Collis, D. 1991. A resource based analysis of global competition: The case of the bearings industry. *Strategic Management Journal*, 12: 49–68.

Daniel, T. A. 1999. Between trapezes: The human side of making mergers and acquisitions work. *Compensation & Benefits Management*, 15 (1): 19–37.

DeVoge, S. and Spreier, S. 1999. The soft realities of mergers. *Across the Board*, 36 (10): 27–33.

Duhaime, I. M. and Schwenk, C. R. 1985. Conjunctures on cognitive simplification in acquisition and divestment decision making. *Academy of Management Review*, 10: 287–295.

Eisenhardt, K. 1989. Making fast strategic decisions in high-velocity environments. *Academy of Management Journal*, 32: 543–576.

Emirbayer, M. and Mische, A. 1998. What is agency? *American Journal of Sociology*, 103: 962–1023.

Evans, P., Pucik, V., and Barsoux, J-L. 2002. *The global challenge: Frameworks for International Human Resource Management*. New York, NY: McGraw Hill.

Feldman, D. C. 1981. The multiple socialization of organizational members. *Academy of Management Review*, 6: 309–319.

Fisher, C. D. 1986. Organizational socialization: An integrative view. *Research in Personnel and Human Resource Management*, 4: 101–145.

Fogarthy, T. J. and Dirsmith, M. W. 2001. Organizational socialization as instrument and symbol: An extended institutional theory perspective. *Human Resource Development Quarterly*, 12 (3): 247–266.

Forbes, D. P. 2005. Managerial determinants of decision speed in new ventures. *Strategic Management Journal*, 26: 355–366.

Gerhart, B. and Rynes, S. L. 2003. *Compensation: Theory, Evidence, and Strategic Implications*. Thousand Oaks, CA: Sage.

Greenberg, D. N., Lane, H. W., and Bahde, K. 2005. Organizational learning in cross-border mergers and acquisitions. In G. K. Stahl and M. E. Mendenhall (Eds), *Mergers and Acquisitions: Managing Culture and Human Resources*. Stanford, CA: Stanford University Press.

Gunter, K. S., Mendenhall, M. E., Pablo, A. L., and Javidan, M. 2005. Sociocultural integration in mergers and acquisitions. In: G. K. Stahl and M. E. Mendenhall (Eds), *Mergers and Acquisitions: Managing Culture and Human Resources*. Stanford, CA: Stanford University Press.

Hart, Z. P. and Miller, V. D. 2005. Context and message context during organizational socialization: A research note. *Human Communication Research*, 31 (2): 295–309.

Haspeslagh, P. and Jemison, D. B. 1991. *Managing Acquisitions*. New York: The Free Press.

Hitt, M. A., Harrison, J. S., and Ireland, R. D. 2001. *Mergers and Acquisitions: A Guide to Creating Value for Stakeholders*. New York, NY: Oxford University Press.

Hoffman, A. J. 1999. Institutional evolution and change: Environmentalism and the U.S. chemical industry. *Academy of Management Journal*, 42 (4): 351–371.

Hofstede, G. 1980. *Culture's Consequences: International Differences in Work-Related Values*, Beverly Hills, CA: Sage Publications.

Houghton, J. D., Anand, V., and Neck, C. P. 2003. Toward a framework of corporate merger processes and outcomes: A behavioral perspective. *International Journal of Public Administration*, 26: 97–117.

Hsiung, T. L. and Hsieh, A. T. 2003. Newcomer socialization: The roles of job standardization. *Public Personnel Management*, 32 (4): 579–589.

Inzerille, G. and Rosen, M. 1983. Culture and organizational control. *Business Research*, 17: 281–292.

Jemison, D. B. and Sitkin, S. B. 1986. Corporate acquisitions: A process perspective. *Academy of Management Review*, 11(1): 145–163.

Jones, G. R. 1986. Socialization tactics, self-efficacy, and newcomers' adjustments to organizations. *Academy of Management Journal*, 29 (2): 262–279.

Judge, W. and Miller, A. 1991. Antecedents and outcomes of decision speed in different environmental contexts. *Academy of Management Journal*, 34: 449–463.

Kitching, J. 1967. Why do mergers miscarry? *Harvard Business Review*, 45 (6): 84–107.

Kitching, J. 1973. *Acquisitions in Europe: Causes of Corporate Success and Failures*, Geneva: Business International.

Kostova, T. 1999. Transnational transfer of strategic organizational practices: A contextual perspective. *Academy of Management Review*, 24: 308–324.

Kostova, T. and Roth, K. 2002. Adoption of an organizational practice by subsidiaries of multinational corporations: Institutional and relational effects. *Academy of Management Journal*, 45 (1): 215–233.

Kraimer, M. L. 1997. Organizational goals and values: A socialization model. *Human Resource Management Review*, 7 (4): 425–447.

Larsson, R. and Finkelstein, S. 1999. Integrating strategic, organizational, and human resource perspectives on mergers and acquisitions: A case survey of synergy realization. *Organization Science*, 10 (1): 1–26.

Louis, M. R. 1980. Surprise and sensemaking: What newcomers experience in entering unfamiliar organizational settings. *Administrative Science Quarterly*, 25: 226–248.

Louis, M. R., Posner, B. Z., and Powell, G. N. 1983. The availability and helpfulness of socialization practices. *Personnel Psychology*, 36: 857–866.

Marks, M. L. 1991. Merger management HR's way. *HR Magazine*, 36 (5): 60–66.

Marks, M. L. and Mirvis, P. H. 1986. The merger syndrome. *Psychology Today*, 20: 36–42.

Marks, M. L. and Mirvis, P. H. 2001. Making mergers and acquisitions work: Strategic and psychological preparation. *Academy of Management Executive*, 15 (2): 80–94.

Markus, H. and Zajonk, R. B. 1985. The cognitive perspective in social psychology. In G. Lindsey and E. Aronson (Eds), *Handbook of Social Psychology*, 137–230. New York: Random House.

Meek, V. 1988. Organizational culture: Origins and weaknesses. *Organization Studies*, 9: 453–473.

Miller, V. D. and Jablin, F. M. 1991. Information seeking during organizational entry: Influences, tactics, and a model of the process. *Academy of Management Review*, 16 (1): 92–120.

Morosini, P. 1999. *Managing cultural differences: Effective strategy and execution across cultures in global corporate alliances*, Oxford, UK: Pergamon.

Morosini, P. 2004. Are mergers and acquisitions about creating values? In P. Morosini and U. Steger (Eds), *Managing Complex Mergers: Real World Lessons in Implementing Successful Cross-Cultural Mergers and Acquisitions*, UK: Prentice Hall.

Morosini, P., Shane, S., and Singh, H. 1998. National cultural distance and cross-border acquisition performance. *Journal of International Business Studies*, 29 (1): 137–158.

Morrison, E. W. 1993a. Newcomer information-seeking: Exploring types, modes, sources, and outcomes. *Academy of Management Journal*, 36: 557–589.

Morrison, E. W. 1993b. Longitudinal study of the effects of information seeking on newcomer socialization. *Journal of Applied Psychology*, 78 (2): 173–183.

Nahavandi, A. and Malekzadeh, A. R. 1988. Acculturation in mergers and acquisitions. *Academy of Management Review*, 13: 79–90.

Olie, R. 1994. Shades of culture and institutions in international mergers. *Organization Studies*, 15 (3): 381–405.

Oliver, C. 1991. Strategic responses to institutional processes. *Academy of Management Review*, 16: 145–179.

Ostroff, C. and Kozlowski, S. W. J. 1992. Organizational socialization as a learning process: The role of information acquisition. *Personnel Psychology*, 4 (4): 849–874.

Ostroff, C. and Rothausen, T. J. 1997. The moderating effect of tenure in person-environment fit: A field study in educational organizations. *Journal of Occupational & Organizational Psychology*, 70 (2): 173–188.

Overman, S. 1999. Learning your merger's ABCs. *HR Focus*, 76 (8): 7–8.

Pablo, A. L. 1994. Determinants of acquisition integration level: A decision-making perspective. *Academy of Management Journal*, 36 (4): 803–836.

Palmer, D. A. and Biggart, N. W. 2002. Organizational institutions. In Joel A. C. Baum (Ed.), *Companion to Organizations*. Oxford, UK: Blackwell.

Parsons, T. 1959. The school class as a social system. *Harvard Educational Review*, 29: 297–318.

Piske, R. 2002. German acquisitions in Poland: An empirical study on integration management and integration success. *Human Resource Development International*, 5 (3): 295–312.

Ritti, R. R. and Funkhouser, G. R. 1987. *The Ropes to Skip and the Ropes to Know*. New York: Wiley.

Saks, A. M. and Ashforth, B. E. 1997. Organizational socialization: Making sense of the past and present as a prologue for the future. *Journal of Vocational Behaviour*, 51: 234–279.

Schein, E. H. 1968. Organizational socialization and the profession of management. *Industrial Management Review*, 9: 1–16.

Schein, E. H. 1990. *Organizational Culture and Leadership*. San Francisco: Jossey-Bass.

Schneider, B. 1987. People make the place. *Personnel Psychology*, 40: 437–453.

Schuler, R. S., Jackson, S. E., and Luo, Y. 2004. *Managing Human Resources in Cross-Border Alliances*. London: Routledge-Taylor.

Schuler, R. and Jackson, S. 2001. HR issues and activities in mergers and acquisitions. *European Management Journal*, 19 (3): 239–253.

Schweiger, D. M. 2002. M&A integration: A framework for executives and managers. USA: McGraw Hill.

Schweiger, D. M. and DeNisi, A. S. 1991. Communication with employees following a merger: A longitudinal field experiment. *Academy of Management Journal*, 34: 110–135.

Schweiger, D. M. and Walsh, J. P. 1990. Mergers and acquisitions: An interdisciplinary view. *Research in Personnel and Human Resources Management*, 8: 41–107.

Schweiger, D. M., Csiszar, E. N., and Napier, N. K. 1993. Implementing international mergers and acquisitions. *Human Resources Planning*, 16 (1): 53–70.

Scott, W. R. 1998. *Organizations: Rational, Natural and Open Systems*, Upper Saddle River, NJ: Prentice-Hall, Inc.

Scott, W. R. 2001. *Institutions and Organizations*. Thousand Oaks, CA: Sage Publications.

Shanley, M. T. and Correa, M. E. 1992. Agreement between top management teams and expectations for post-acquisition performance. *Strategic Management Journal*, 13: 245–266.

Shapiro, M. S. 1992. Mergers of professional practices: Managing the process. The Canadian Institute of Chartered Accountants, Canada.

Stahl, M. J. and Zimmerer, T. W. 1984. Modeling strategic acquisition policies: A simulation of executives acquisition decisions. *Academy of Management Journal*, 27: 369–383.

Stanwick, P. A. and Stanwick, S. D. 2001. Human resources: Your secret weapon for post-merger success. *The Journal of Corporate Accounting & Finance*, 12 (2): 9–14.

Strebel, P. 2004. Institutional factors are critical in cross-cultural M&As. In P. Morosini and U. Steger (Eds), *Managing Complex Mergers: Real World Lessons in Implementing Successful Cross-Cultural Mergers and Acquisitions*, UK: Prentice Hall.

Thomas, H. C. and Anderson, N. 2002. Newcomer adjustment: The relationship between organizational socialization tactics and information acquisition and attitudes. *Journal of Occupational and Organizational Psychology*, 75: 423–437.

Uhlenbruck, K. and DeCastro, J. 2000. Foreign acquisitions in Central and Eastern Europe: Outcomes of privatization in transnational economies. *Academy of Management Journal*, 43: 381–402.

Van Knippenberg, D., van Knippenberg, B., Monden, L., and de Lima, F. 2002. Organizational identification after a merger: A social identity perspective. *British Journal of Social Psychology*, 41: 233–252.

Van Maanen, J. and Schein, E. 1979. Toward a theory of organizational socialization. *Research in Organizational Behavior*, 1: 209–264.

Weber, Y. and Schweiger, D. 1992. Top management culture conflict in mergers and acquisitions: A lesson from anthropology. *International Journal of Conflict Management*, 3 (4): 285–302.

Weston, J. F., Siu, J. A., and Johnson, B. A. 2001. *Takeovers, Restructurings and Corporate Governance*, 3rd edition. Upper Saddle River, NJ: Prentice Hall.

Wicks, D. 2001. Institutionalized mindsets of invulnerability: Differentiated institutional fields and the antecedents of organizational crisis. *Organization Studies*, 22 (4): 659–692.

Zucker, L. 1983. Organizations as institutions. In S. B. Bacharach (ed.), *Research in Sociology of Organizations*, Greenwich, CN: Jai Press.

Zucker, L. G. 1987. Institutional theories of organizations. *Annual Review of Sociology*, 13: 443–464.

8
Multi-Firm Collaboration and International Competitive Dynamics

Craig Crossland, David J. Ketchen, Jr., and Charles C. Snow

A new form of organizing is emerging in the world of international business (IB) called the multi-firm collaborative network (Miles *et al.*, 2005). Its core competence is the ability to collaborate among a group of firms in both the creation and application of knowledge. For firms that have, or can develop, the ability to collaborate across organizational, geographical, and cultural boundaries, this new means of organizing will allow them to pursue strategies and grow in a manner that has heretofore been largely unattainable.

The multi-firm collaborative network has been slow to evolve because there are many barriers that stand in its way, including large institutional, societal, and philosophical challenges. However, in various places around the world, pieces of the overall organizational model for multi-firm collaboration already exist. In those innovative organizational arrangements, some of which we describe below, several of the most troublesome barriers have been overcome. Therefore, we believe that it is only a matter of time before a full-blown multi-firm collaborative network will appear somewhere in the world, and it will serve as both a model and as inspiration for other firms to follow.

In this chapter, we first describe the multi-firm collaborative network and why it is needed – indeed demanded – by the global economy. Our description is based on a fictional organization called OpWin Global Network which contains all of the key ingredients of the new organizational model. We then discuss how this means of conducting international business will affect future competitive dynamics, both for firms inside the network and for their external rivals.

Innovation, collaboration, and economic development

Innovation has long been considered the primary determinant of economic development (Schumpeter, 1934). This belief has been recently substantiated by Baumol (2002), whose large empirical study demonstrated that firm and inter-firm ability to innovate explains why capitalist economies on average have had much stronger growth records than other economic systems. However, despite its usefulness for firm and economic development, innovation is not an easy task for the typical firm to perform. Indeed, one survey estimated that CEOs believe their firms utilize only 15–25% of their innovation capacity (Käser and Miles, 2002).

Historically, even the most innovative firms have not been able to fully utilize their innovation capacity. Whether one focuses on Hewlett-Packard in the 1950s and 1960s, Xerox in the 1970s, Rubbermaid in the 1980s, or Intel or Cisco Systems today, none of these firms has been able to figure out how to innovate on a consistent and efficient basis. Various organizational arrangements have been tried – cross-functional business teams, internal venture capital processes, creating or acquiring new business units, spinning off new ventures, and forming alliances with or investing in partner firms (Burgelman and Sayles, 1986; Block and MacMillan, 1993; Miles and Woolridge, 1999) – but the best outcome from all of these approaches appears to be the capability to engage in periodic innovation that is mostly limited to the firm's existing industries. What is needed – and, fortunately, what is becoming increasingly feasible (Chesbrough, 2003) – is an organizational process that will enable innovation to be *continuous* and occur *outside* a firm's traditional industry boundaries (Miles *et al.*, 2005).

Using the logic of the resource-based view of business strategy (Penrose, 1959; Wernerfelt, 1984; Barney, 1991), many observers today suggest that the most underutilized resource among firms in advanced economies is knowledge (cf. Friedman, 2005). The drive to turn knowledge and other underutilized resources into economic wealth is what pushes managers to experiment with new ways of reconfiguring strategies, structures, and processes in order to make their firms more effective and valuable. We believe that the search for continuous innovation, currently taking place within many firms, will result in the appearance of the multi-firm collaborative network organization.

Collaboration is a process whereby two or more parties work with each other to achieve mutually beneficial outcomes (Emery and Trist, 1965; Appley and Winder, 1977). Collaboration can be directed toward any mutually desired objective: solving a problem, resolving a conflict, creating a new product or business, and so on. The concept of collaboration that we see taking hold in an increasing number of business firms and other types of organizations is collaborative entrepreneurship: the creation of something of economic value based on new, jointly generated ideas or knowledge (Miles *et al.*, 2005).

Collaboration to create and apply knowledge is very sophisticated behavior as it is based on deep competence and experience, trust among individuals and across organizations, heavy investments in intellectual and relational capital, and efficient, open sharing of ideas and information. Nevertheless, as with any behavior, collaboration can be taught, learned, and studied, and thus it can eventually diffuse throughout a society to the point where it becomes a widely abundant resource or meta-capability (Miles *et al.*, 2005). Collaboration among individuals and groups is widespread in advanced economies, occurring among scientists, scholars, doctors, engineers, and other professionals. Large-scale inter-firm collaboration, on the other hand, is a fairly recent phenomenon, but its origins can be seen in several real-world examples. For example, beginning in the early 1990s, the small Danish city of Kalundborg has been the site of an evolving, successful program of industrial–municipal collaboration that has been referred to as industrial symbiosis (Jacobsen and Anderberg, 2001). As of 2003, this cross-sector collaboration has created financial returns of over $200 million on an investment of approximately $90 million – an average annual return of over 16%. The source of these returns is annual savings from symbiotic exchanges across a network of municipal agencies and private businesses. This alliance offers evidence that a voluntary, self-directed experiment can lead to the growth of an expanding collaborative search for creative value-adding approaches to utilizing resources.

Across the firms and government agencies that make up the US civil construction industry, a collaborative process has emerged that has produced less carefully measured but quite probably larger percentage returns than those of the Kalundborg experiment (Associated General Contractors of America, 1991). Moreover, the growing competence of US construction firms in partnering has increased their ability to engage in new approaches to large construction projects, and partnering has become both a firm and an industry asset. Though limited to a single industry, the investments in collaborative capability being made by civil construction industry agencies, firms, and professional and educational institutions show the way for other organizations that wish to engage in large-scale inter-organizational collaboration.

Neither the Danish industrial–municipal alliance nor the American partnering process in civil construction represents an example of collaboration as a true joint enterprise. Although both examples involve business situations, neither group of organizations is focused primarily on new products, services, or markets – and certainly not on continuous innovation. The firm that perhaps comes closest to practicing continuous innovation through collaboration on a large scale is the Acer Group (Mathews and Snow, 1998; Mathews, 2002). Based in Taiwan, Acer has thousands of employees, operations in 44 countries, and dealer relationships in more than a hundred countries. With revenues of nearly $5 billion, Acer is the world's fifth-largest personal computer manufacturer, and it is in the process of transforming itself into a complete global information technology company that in recent years has started many successful e-business services.

Acer is a worldwide federation of companies held together by mutual interest and collaboration. Some units of Acer are wholly owned by the firm, while others (mainly marketing and distribution firms) are jointly owned by Acer and local investors. Both types of firms work willingly with the other companies in the federation because all firms have worked hard to become the preferred provider in their particular specialty or market. Acer helps its partner firms in other countries to develop professional management, obtain investment funding, and become publicly owned if they desire to do so. Acer's type of "collaborative capitalism" is steadily increasing in the global economy, particularly in emerging markets. However, while Acer is almost able to be continuously innovative up and down its value chain, it is still not especially adept at innovating outside of the global IT business.

OpWin Global Network

These three examples indicate that inter-firm collaboration to produce continuous innovation on a large scale is practically feasible. Therefore, it requires only a small conceptual leap to imagine and then describe an organization composed of firms from different industries whose collaborative abilities allow them to pursue a joint strategy of continuous innovation. That envisioned organization we call OpWin Global Network (Miles *et al.*, 2005).

OpWin is a dynamic network of 60 member firms and their temporary affiliates. The network is dynamic in that none of its members has a fixed role, and the resources each firm has assembled are often shared in business ventures with other firms, usually but not always within the network. It is also dynamic in that its membership has expanded dramatically since its founding, and the process of adding new members is ongoing.

Each member firm joined OpWin as a profitable independent entity, and it is each firm's responsibility to maintain its ability to support and grow its own resources and generate significant income for itself and its network partners. Firms vary in size from less than a hundred staff members to a few thousand, and each firm is expected to serve all of its stakeholders in an exemplary manner, in line with OpWin's stated pledge to set the highest standards of customer satisfaction, human resource management, and natural environment sustainability. Each member firm measures its own (a) net wealth creation, (b) human resource growth and retention (including educational and skill upgrades of staff), and (c) annual customer satisfaction, and members send this information to OpWin's Central Services Office (which provides educational, training, information technology, and other services to the member firms).

Member firms are expected to create products and services for their own markets and work with other firms in the network on innovation projects. Within their own markets, firms pursue organic growth through market penetration with existing products or services while attempting to meet the expectation that at least half of their revenues will be generated via continuous innovation. Innovations in a given firm's market come not only from ideas and efforts within the firm but also from the continuous scanning of ideas and innovations from other network firms. Each firm describes product ideas, development projects, and product-service upgrades in OpWin's Innovation Catalog, an electronic database accessible only by member firms. Not only do member firms post potential value-generating information in the catalog, they are also expected to proactively contact other firms that might have an interest in their ideas, projects, or new models.

Firms in related markets regularly send design, marketing, and operating staff to OpWin's Market Exploration Workshops that are held periodically. Moreover, firms also collaborate across the network on development projects that do not have obvious connections to their own markets. Staff specialists may be invited by another member firm to visit and discuss a listed idea or project, and they may in turn request additional meetings to provide elaboration and possibly joint pursuit of an idea or project. In some instances, a staff member from Firm A may work with Firm B on a particular project even though it has been determined not to have relevance in Firm A's usual market. When this occurs, Firm B pays for the staff member's time and effort. Further, if the contributions from Firm A are later incorporated into a profitable product or service, Firm B is expected to provide an appropriate return for Firm A such as a royalty or one-time payment.

In all cases, OpWin member firms are expected to engage in joint development efforts and contribute needed skills and abilities to other firms without strict calculation of costs, benefits, or potential returns. It is the responsibility of the user to recognize contributions and initiate equitable payment and make certain that the provider is satisfied with the outcome. On joint projects, it is the market "owner's" responsibility to propose a schedule of returns that is seen as equitable by its project partner(s). Where new or shared markets are served by a jointly designed product or service, the participating parties draw lots in advance to determine which firm will take the lead in proposing market-delivery responsibility and an equitable distribution of returns.

The heavy focus of OpWin firms on continuous innovation often limits their interest in taking an active role in creating wealth via the long-term production of goods or services. In those cases, OpWin firms work with outside partners to produce components or even complete products for OpWin markets. After assuring the market success of a product or service, OpWin firms may license designs to outside partners for their own long-term sales and service. Licensees, too, are required to meet OpWin's customer satisfaction and environmental standards.

To become a member of OpWin, a firm must demonstrate its competence and trustworthiness. This can often be achieved by the successful completion of a single collaborative project. At any point, a firm can apply for membership, which must be voted on by all members after an OpWin review team has assembled a sponsorship document. Alternatively, a firm may be affiliated with OpWin on a temporary or infrequent basis, typically as a licensee or other type of contractual provider.

In summary, OpWin member firms operate independently in their own markets and in alliances of one sort or another with members of the network to design and take to market a continuous stream of innovative products and services. However, OpWin's alliances differ from other alliances in several important ways. First, OpWin alliances are usually generated by ideas and activities that are viewed as open – available to all member firms, with users responsible for acknowledging the source of the ideas and the contributions of their partners. Also, OpWin alliances are open-ended rather than special-purpose, and rewards are determined after the fact rather than in advance. Lastly, roles, responsibilities, and returns are governed not so much by contracts (though these are widely used) as by norms of equity and collegiality, aided by an agreed-on set of explicit operating protocols (such as user responsibility for provider equity and satisfaction). Overall, OpWin member firms have enjoyed great success to date by working collaboratively with each other to find applications for their ideas and knowledge in markets outside their traditional industries.

The multi-firm collaborative network and international competitive dynamics

Up to this point, our characterization of the multi-firm collaborative network has been largely anticipatory. We are not aware of any worldwide collaborative network of firms that approximates the size and scope of OpWin Global Network. However, if the embryonic collaborative networks outlined above – those in Denmark, the US construction industry, and Taiwan's Acer Group – continue to develop and perhaps inspire other similar networks, we believe that one or more fully fledged OpWin-style collaborations are feasible within the next decade (Miles *et al.*, 2006). If this vision of the future does indeed develop, what are the implications for international competition? How will competition change and evolve? More importantly, will firms engaging in OpWin-style collaboration experience a competitive advantage over those that do not?

We believe that the unique dynamics of the multi-firm collaborative network, exemplified by the OpWin group, suggest a number of important implications for international competitive dynamics, specifically in the areas of multi-point competition, co-opetition, and virtual clustering.

Multi-point competition

Multi-point competition concerns the competitive interactions between firms that compete simultaneously in more than one product-market category (see Ketchen *et al.*, 2004 for a review). The study of multi-point competition arose from the recognition that competition within a single market is influenced by external elements, such as concurrent competition within other markets. Central to multi-point competition is the notion of mutual forbearance, the idea that firms may avoid acting aggressively if they believe that their competitors will retaliate (Golden and Ma, 2003). For example, a firm competing in the same markets as its major rival might cede control of one market in exchange for a reciprocal cessation of control by that rival in a different market.

One implication of the rise of the multi-firm collaborative network is a significant increase in complexity in multi-point competition. Multi-point competition is currently conceptualized as occurring between two or more firms in two or more markets. The rise of multi-firm collaboration will complicate such linkages. First, there will continue to be multi-point competition between independent firms, similar to current competitive dynamics, or between the non-collaborative components of OpWin-like firms. Also, there will be competition between single stand-alone firms and OpWin collaborations, consisting perhaps of transient alliances among several firms. Third, there may be competition between collaborating partners within OpWin. Lastly, and most complex of all, consider two OpWin member firms, A and B, which participate in collaborations X and Y, respectively. As OpWin member firms are likely to come from related industries, it is possible that firms A and B may be competing with one another in several markets as well as simultaneously competing with each other, through their respective collaborations, in several different markets. Each of these scenarios increases the complexity of multi-point competition for a given firm and hence the complexity of its strategizing.

Multi-point competition also will become more complex because on average competitive rivalries are likely to become more transient. One element that reduces complexity in multi-point competition is the mutual forbearance that often develops between long-term competitors (Gimeno, 1999). We envisage OpWin-like collaborations as short-term, innovation-centered projects rather than long-term stable alliances. Hence Firm A may face multi-point competition from Collaboration Project I in one period, Project J in a second period, and Project K in a third period. Such transient relationships will tend to reduce the development of mutual forbearance compared to how it currently works.

Lastly, multi-point competition will become more complex because a firm within a given domain will face a larger range of potential competitors. Using the logic above, we see the multi-firm collaborative network as a source of multiple, short-term, innovation-oriented collaborations within a particular domain, each of which may challenge established industry firms and each reflecting a different set of competitive dynamics.

There are several specific implications for executives of firms that face more complex multi-point competition. First, executives in independent firms, and in OpWin-like firms as well, will need to broaden their environmental scanning in order to be effective (Elenkov, 1997). As threats are likely to arise with less notice, in myriad fashion, and from a greater variety of sources, it will behoove executives to keep closer tabs on changes, innovations, and opportunities in industries that might become related to their own industry and do more scenario planning. For example, immediate industry-level concerns will become relatively less important compared to broader concerns in adjacent industries and regional markets. OpWin-like collaborations are likely to bring together firms that did not previously operate in the same competitive niche, thus resulting in innovations at the interstices of traditional industry boundaries.

At the same time that they attempt to develop more sensitivity to external challenges, however, executives will need to continue to ensure that their firms' own internal capabilities, particularly in areas related to innovation management, remain efficient (Miles *et al.*, 2005). The rise of OpWin-style collaborations cannot help but heighten competition based on continuous innovation as well as shorten product life cycles and push the cost-quality frontier further out. Thus, firms wishing to remain competitive will need to become better at both external scanning *and* internal innovation.

Another implication for executives is that as mutual forbearance becomes less pervasive, it will provide less of a competitive "crutch" for firms than it has in the past. As discussed earlier, the reciprocal cessation of control inherent in mutual forbearance often arises when two firms have a long-term competitive relationship in multiple markets (Golden and Ma, 2003). This will become less likely if multi-point competition is coming not from an established single firm but from a short-term, project-focused collaboration among temporarily interlocked firms. Thus, if the multi-firm collaborative network becomes a reality, executives facing such competition will need to become better at dealing with simultaneous, concerted multi-market changes and threats.

When the multi-firm collaborative network becomes a marketplace reality, firms that do not participate in such collaborative ventures may be at a significant competitive disadvantage relative to those that do. This should be particularly true for smaller firms and those that operate in turbulent, high-velocity environments (Bourgeois and Eisenhardt, 1988). In such firms, the economies of scope arising from greater access to knowledge will give an edge to those firms able to work collaboratively with their partners (Kogut and Zander, 1992). Furthermore, firms that engage in OpWin-style collaborations will have a number of means of buffering the increased complexity of multi-point competition that are not available to independent firms, such as access to the resources and knowledge of other member firms as well as more opportunities for developing their internal innovation capabilities. These and other implications discussed below are summarized in Table 8.1.

Table 8.1 Practical implications of the multi-firm collaborative network

Multi-point competition	Co-opetition	Virtual clustering	Overall implications
Firms will be less able to rely on mutual forbearance	Firms will become more effective at simultaneously managing exploration and exploitation	Firms will have access to the benefits of agglomeration without the need to geographically collocate	Executive focus will shift from firm-to-firm competition toward network-to-network competition
Firms participating in multi-firm collaborations may possess a competitive advantage	Executives will show a greater commitment to the value of collaboration	Firms will have greater latitude in deciding where to locate and seeking collaborative partners	The level of hyper-competition in the business environment will increase
Firms will broaden their environmental scanning	Executives will develop a more nuanced understanding of intra- and inter-industry competitive dynamics	Firms will be able to pursue shorter, riskier collaborations and partnerships	

Co-opetition

The rise of the multi-firm collaborative network will increase the prevalence of co-opetition, which occurs when two or more firms simultaneously engage in cooperation and competition (Gee, 2000). We foresee that collaborative networks such as OpWin will place rough limits on the amount of a firm's business that can come from within the collaborative network (say, 50%). Thus, firms will join OpWin as an established business – a set of products, markets, suppliers, customers, and competitors. As firms within OpWin are often linked across adjacent industries, it is reasonable to assume that some of the firms entering OpWin will already be competing with other OpWin member firms. Inevitably, collaborations will develop between competitors, the essence of co-opetition. Moreover, the multi-firm collaborative network also raises the interesting possibility of co-opetition between more than two firms.

Firms that enter OpWin-like alliances are, by their nature, more likely to seek collaborative relationships and less likely to be influenced solely by their own self-interest. One study found that co-opetition is less successful when a partner firm appropriates a disproportionate share of alliance benefits (Khanna *et al.*, 2000). Such a situation is less likely to occur within the bounds of a multi-firm collaborative network, given its emphasis on the joint creation of economic value and the equitable sharing of returns. Similarly, firms that engage in an OpWin-type alliance tend to be those interested in pursuing innovation-oriented "prospector" strategies (Miles and Snow, 1978). This means that collaborative alliances are likely to focus on new, growing markets, where a larger number of firms can simultaneously succeed, instead of mature markets which tend to favor defender-type strategies.

A greater prevalence of co-opetition in the future has implications for managerial decision making and behavior. For example, successful firms in a multi-firm collaborative relationship will need to be ambidextrous (O'Reilly and Tushman, 2004). At the same time that a firm tries to protect and grow its existing business, including focusing on how to exploit its current market position, a considerable portion of that firm's resources will be devoted to working collaboratively with other firms toward the objective of continuous innovation, an exploratory orientation (March, 1991). Executives in such "coopetive" situations will need to possess or develop a level of cognitive dexterity that can accommodate the coexistence of competing resource allocation demands.

Also, managers will not only need to understand and reflect in their actions the variety of their firms' internal processes, but they will need to develop a cognitively complex understanding of the multifaceted competitive dynamics within their industry and those industries represented in future collaborations (Calori *et al.*, 1994). Here, executives will need a strong belief in, and commitment to, the value of collaboration. This portends a major shift from the prevailing business philosophy built on maximizing one's self-interest to a philosophy based on communitarian values (Yankelovich, 1999; Rifkin, 2004).

Virtual clustering

The competitive dynamics literature has examined the concept of regional clustering, whereby a number of similar firms colocate in one geographic area to obtain the benefits of abundant factor inputs or increase customer access and collective demand (Porter, 1998). By locating close to factor inputs, such as raw materials or specialized labor, firms in some clusters benefit from better access and lower costs (Russo, 2003). Alternatively, another type of regional cluster, used by restaurant chains, shopping centers, and car dealerships, provides firms easier access to customers and helps promote overall demand for the product or service (Canina *et al.*, 2005). While the first type of benefit might be called input-based agglomeration, the latter could be called demand-based agglomeration. Both types of clustering, however, derive their benefit from geographic colocation.

One of the main benefits of OpWin-like collaborative networks is that member firms can gain innovation-generating benefits without necessarily having to geographically colocate. Elements of OpWin, such as its Innovation Catalog and the activities of the Central Services Office, facilitate the transfer, integration, and recombination of knowledge, critical processes in the pursuit of continuous innovation (Kogut and Zander, 1992). We call this collective access to knowledge resources "virtual clustering," as the agglomerative benefits derive primarily from electronic rather than geographic proximity. The emergence of virtual clusters has several potential consequences for competition.

Virtual clustering gives the member firms within a collaborative network considerable latitude in deciding where to locate. Because firms will obtain the benefits of clustering irrespective of their geographic location, they can select their physical location based on factors such as a favorable regulatory environment, location-contingent financial assistance, adjacency to a key component of the supply chain, or a region with desirable lifestyle opportunities. Unlike firms in regional clusters, which benefit from clustering but are also constrained by it, member firms of a virtual cluster have considerable geographic flexibility.

Virtual clustering will substantially increase member firms' access to knowledge-based resources, a prime motivator of firm-to-firm alliances (Mowery *et al.*, 1996). Freed of the requirement to use geographically based resources, firms can search worldwide for collaboration partners and can more easily justify short-term, riskier collaborations. Moreover, membership in a virtual cluster will reduce the need for engaging in formal alliances such as international joint ventures which tend to restrict the search for, and engagement with, collaboration partners.

Future research directions

We have discussed a new species of network organization and its implications for international competition. If our prediction comes true, and multi-firm collaborative networks appear and spread, then there will be many research opportunities to study this type of organization and how it will compete in the international arena.

One promising line of research will be to focus on the network – or supply chain – as the unit of analysis. The supply chain is the central organizing unit in today's global industries. Over the last three decades, supply chains have evolved through three cumulative stages (Miles and Snow, 2007). In the first stage, the primary focus was on how to make operations throughout the supply chain more efficient. In the second stage, the focus shifted from efficiency to effectiveness as leading firms began to incorporate the ideas and expertise of their suppliers and partners into the management of the supply chain. In the current stage, some networks (such as OpWin described above) are beginning to explore how supply chains can be extended across industries in addition to operating efficiently and effectively within industries.

The most sophisticated supply chain organizations will play an increasingly prominent role in the global economy. Collaborative and other knowledge-based supply chains are different from traditional goods-based supply chains, and they have more potential to contribute to the long-term economic development of a country or region. For example, shared knowledge can be a rapidly expandable resource and may show increasing rather than diminishing economic returns. Thus, interactions between US information technology firms and their network partners in India and China have produced valuable knowledge spillovers across the economies of these countries (Engardio, 2005). Also, because knowledge-based supply chains can grow laterally across industries, they can create product and market innovations that traditional networks have not been able to achieve on a consistent basis. Such innovation-driven supply chains will ultimately prove to be more valuable to a country's economic development than cost-driven supply chains because they have the capability to move knowledge across as well as within industries and thereby generate new business.

At some point in the future, collaboration-based supply chains will begin to compete with other collaborative networks. As more and more product/service innovations derive from multi-firm collaborations, the basis of competition will shift from its current firm-to-firm locus to a network-to-network basis. Some initial research has begun to identify the implications of a competitive paradigm where a network of firms, rather than a single firm, is the unit of analysis (Gimeno, 2004). To date, this research has examined the behavior of a particular industry's major competitors and their networks of suppliers and partners. In tomorrow's business environment, it will be important to study how networks composed of collaborating firms compete not only within but across industries.

In addition to the developments in multi-point competition, co-opetition, and virtual clustering discussed above, we believe that the international competitive landscape as a whole will undergo other, broader shifts if multi-firm collaborative networks appear and grow as we predict. For example, there is likely to be an increase in what has been called "hyper-competition" (D'Aveni, 1994). Although we recognize that not every innovation results in Schumpeterian "creative destruction" (Rothaermel, 2000), we believe that pursuing the goal of continuous innovation, the basis for OpWin's formation and growth, will inexorably lead to shortened product life cycles and therefore greater competitive pressure on established product lines across many industries. As argued by D'Aveni (1994), sustainable competitive advantage will derive from linking a succession of transitory quasi-monopolies (via continuous innovation) rather than stable Ricardian rents (via a favorable position in a particular industry). Recent research indicates that hyper-competition has indeed increased over time (Wiggins and Ruefli, 2005), and the emergence of the collaborative network organizational form will accelerate and perhaps alter hyper-competitive dynamics.

Conclusion

We believe that the multi-firm collaborative network is the natural outcome of the ever-increasing need for individual firms to better employ their under-utilized knowledge and innovation capacities and thus improve their ability to compete through continuous innovation. Assuming that this new organizational form develops as predicted, it will have important implications for international competitive dynamics. Specifically, multi-point competition will become more complex, co-opetition will become more prevalent, and firms will increasingly seek the competitive benefits of virtual clustering. More broadly, we believe that the multi-firm collaborative network will increase hyper-competition in the IB environment as well as increase network-to-network competition among firms.

Built on factors such as flexibility, collaboration, and innovation, in contrast to extant organizational axioms of stability, efficiency, and zero-sum competition, the multi-firm collaborative network represents the next logical step in the evolution of organizational forms. The more rapidly and effectively scholars can anticipate other new organizational forms, and how they compete, the greater will be the benefit both to the global economy and our understanding of organizations and how they are managed.

References

Appley, D. G. and Winder, A. E. 1977. An evolving definition of collaboration and some implications for the world of work. *Journal of Applied Behavioral Science*, 13: 279–291.

Associated General Contractors of America. 1991. *Partnering: A Concept for Success*.

Barney, J. 1991. Firm resources and sustained competitive advantage. *Journal of Management*, 17: 99–120.

Baumol, W. J. 2002. *The Free-Market Innovation Machine: Analyzing the Growth Miracle of Capitalism*, Princeton, NJ: Princeton University Press.

Block, Z. and MacMillan, I. 1993. *Corporate Venturing*, Boston, MA: Harvard Business School Press.

Bourgeois, L. and Eisenhardt, K. 1988. Strategic decision processes in high velocity environments: Four cases in the microcomputer industry. *Management Science*, 34: 816–835.

Burgelman, R. and Sayles, L. 1986. *Inside Corporate Innovation*, New York, NY: Free Press.

Calori, R., Johnson, G., and Sarnin, P. 1994. CEOs' cognitive maps and the scope of the organization. *Strategic Management Journal*, 15: 437–457.

Canina, L., Enz, C., and Harrison, J. 2005. Agglomeration effects and strategic orientations: Evidence from the U.S. lodging industry. *Academy of Management Journal*, 48: 565–581.

Chesbrough, H. 2003. *Open Innovation: The New Imperative for Creating and Profiting from Technology*, Boston, MA: Harvard Business School Press.

D'Aveni, R. 1994. *Hypercompetition: Managing the Dynamics of Strategic Maneuvering*, New York, NY: Free Press.

Elenkov, D. 1997. Strategic uncertainty and environmental scanning: The case for institutional influences on scanning behavior. *Strategic Management Journal*, 18: 287–302.

Emery, F. E. and Trist, E. 1965. The causal texture of organizational environments. *Human Relations*, 18: 21–32.

Engardio, P. 2005. A new world economy. *Business Week*, 22/29 (August): 52–58.

Friedman, T. L. 2005. *The World is Flat: A Brief History of the Twenty-First Century*. New York, NY: Farrar, Straus and Giroux.

Gee, E. 2000. Co-opetition: The new market milieu. *Journal of Healthcare Management*, 45: 359–363.

Gimeno, J. 1999. Reciprocal threats in multi-market rivalry: Staking out 'spheres of influence' in the U.S. airline industry. *Strategic Management Journal*, 20: 101–128.

Gimeno, J. 2004. Competition within and between networks: The contingent effect of competitive embeddedness on alliance formation. *Academy of Management Journal*, 47: 820–842.

Golden, B. and Ma, H. 2003. Mutual forbearance: The role of intrafirm integration and rewards. *Academy of Management Review*, 28: 479–493.

Jacobsen, N. B. and Anderberg, S. 2001. *The Evolution of Industrial Symbiotic Networks – The Case of Kalundborg*, Paper presented at the ISIE conference, Leiden, The Netherlands.

Käser, P. A. W. and Miles, R. E. 2002. Understanding knowledge activists' successes and failures. *Long-Range Planning*, 35: 9–28.

Ketchen, D. J. Jr., Snow, C. C., and Hoover, V. L. 2004. Research on competitive dynamics: Recent accomplishments and future challenges. *Journal of Management*, 30: 779–804.

Khanna, T., Gulati, R., and Nohria, N. 2000. The economic modeling of strategy process: Clean models and dirty hands. *Strategic Management Journal*, 21: 781–790.

Kogut, B. and Zander, U. 1992. Knowledge of the firm, combinative capabilities, and the replication of technology. *Organization Science*, 3: 383–397.

March, J. G. 1991. Exploration and exploitation in organizational learning. *Organization Science*, 2: 71–88.

Mathews, J. A. 2002. *Dragon Multinational: A New Model of Global Growth*. New York, NY: Oxford University Press.

Mathews, J. A. and Snow, C. C. 1998. A conversation with Taiwan-based Acer Group's Stan Shih on global strategy and management. *Organizational Dynamics*, 27: 65–74.

Miles, J. A. and Woolridge, J. R. 1999. *Spin-offs and Equity Carve-outs: Achieving Faster Growth and Better Performance*, Morristown, NJ: Financial Executives Research Foundation.

Miles, R. E. and Snow, C. C. 1978. *Organizational Strategy, Structure, and Process*. New York, NY: McGraw-Hill.

Miles, R. E., Miles, G., and Snow, C. C. 2005. *Collaborative Entrepreneurship: How Communities of Networked Firms use Continuous Innovation to Create Economic Wealth*, Stanford, CA: Stanford University Press.

Miles, R. E., Miles, G., and Snow, C. C. 2006. Collaborative entrepreneurship: A business model for continuous innovation. *Organizational Dynamics*, 35: 1–11.

Miles, R. E. and Snow, C. C. 2007. Organization theory and supply chain management: An evolving research perspective. *Journal of Operations Management*, 25(2): 459–463.

Mowery, D., Oxley, J., and Silverman, B. 1996. Strategic alliances and interfirm knowledge transfer. *Strategic Management Journal*, 17 (Winter Special Issue): 77–91.

O'Reilly, C. and Tushman, M. 2004. The ambidextrous organization. *Harvard Business Review*, 82 (April): 74–81.

Penrose, E. 1959. *The Theory of the Growth of the Firm*, London: Blackwell.

Porter, M. 1998. Clusters and the new economics of competition. *Harvard Business Review*, 76: 77–90.

Rifkin, J. 2004. *The European Dream: How Europe's Vision of the Future is Quietly Eclipsing the American Dream*. New York, NY: Penguin.

Rothaermel, F. 2000. Technological discontinuities and the nature of competition. *Technology Analysis and Strategic Management*, 12: 149–160.

Russo, M. 2003. The emergence of sustainable industries: Building on natural capital. *Strategic Management Journal*, 24: 317–331.

Schumpeter, J. A. 1934. *The Theory of Economic Development: An Inquiry into Profits, Capital, Credit, Interest, and the Business Cycle*, Cambridge, MA: Harvard University Press.

Wernerfelt, B. 1984. A resource-based view of the firm. *Strategic Management Journal*, 5: 795–815.

Wiggins, R. and Ruefli, T. 2005. Schumpeter's ghost: Is hypercompetition making the best of times shorter? *Strategic Management Journal*, 26: 887–911.

Yankelovich, D. 1999. The magic of dialogue: Transforming conflict into cooperation. New York: Simon and Schuster.

9
Establishing the Moral Basis of Global Capitalism: Implications for MNEs in Emerging Markets

Eden Yin

Morality is concerned with rules determining right action, identifying actions that are wrong, morally unjust, unfair, or improper (Hosmer, 1994) and is considered an important part of the institutional infrastructure of a society (Lal, 2003). It is essential to control man's self-aggrandizing instincts to garner the gains from cooperation, because "a sympathy with public interest is the source of moral approbation, which attends that virtue 'justice'" (Hume, 1740/1985: 551). Adam Smith's "Laws of Justice" further proclaims that a market economy has to depend upon the scarce virtues, like benevolence, for its efficient functioning (Smith, 1776/1991).

However, immoral and unethical behaviors have a presence in all walks of life (Behrman, 2003). This is true over much of the world, where political, business, and church scandals are reported among leaders in these fields (*The Economist*, 2002). The frequently reported global business scandals, such as *Enron*, *Arthur Anderson*, *Worldcom*, and *Global Crossing* are particularly alarming because they indicate that the modern global capitalism is built on shaky ground. This problem has tremendous implications for nearly all nations and its massive ripple effect takes place at a global scale, much more far-reaching than unethical behavior in other realms of life with the rapid advancement of globalization in today's world.

Recognizing the enormous significance of this issue, several scholars indicate the importance of analyzing and evaluating the moral basis of modern global capitalism (Buckley and Casson, 2001; Dunning, 2001). They argue that the consequence of ignoring it is likely to be the clash of civilization depicted in Huntington's work (1996), which may destroy any material gains obtained from global interdependence and undermine the long-term sustainability of global capitalism. Anti-globalization demonstrations in Davos, Prague, Seattle, Washington D.C., Cancun, and the increase in cross-border tensions further highlight the fact that the growing discontent of the world's poor can no longer be ignored by global institutions and companies (Stiglitz,

2003). These thorny problems further indicate the tremendous urgency of investigating this issue in the context of international business (IB)research.

A substantial amount of effort has been made in management and business ethics in analyzing and understanding various aspects of ethical business practices, their consequences, and implications (Hosmer, 1994; Singer, 1994; Small, 2002; Robertson and Crittenden, 2003; Carroll, 2004), yet research on global moral and ethical issues in the context of international business is rather sparse despite its paramount importance. Carroll (2004) and Donaldson and Dunfee (1999) examine the notions of global corporate social responsibility and global business ethics, respectively, and they provide useful guidance on how MNEs should deal with global ethical issues, yet their works do not address the moral basis of modern global capitalism, which should serve as the foundation for global business ethics. We attempt to investigate this issue in this chapter.

Specifically, we plan to address the following issues: First, following the previous research (Dunning, 2001, 2003) on global moral basis, we further echo the importance of establishing a global moral order in modern capitalism. Moreover, we advance this discussion by laying out some of the specifics on how MNEs should endorse this view. Second, we discuss the nature, the components of this moral basis, and the global moral imperatives. Third, we demonstrate the solid economic rationale of establishing a moral basis by indicating that MNEs' sustainable growth and competitive advantage rely on such a moral foundation. We then use the story of a highly successful MNE in China, that is, *Xi'an Janssen* Pharmaceutical, to further illustrate our points. Fourth, we advocate more research in international business on this important issue and present a potential agenda for future research.

Importance of moral basis for modern global capitalism

The importance of establishing a moral basis for business and global capitalism has been echoed by several prominent scholars (Sen, 1992, 1997, 1999; Dunning, 2001, 2003). Their key concerns are that modern business and global capitalism, without a solid moral basis, will inevitably bring in social instability, significant damage to economic gain, or even clashes of civilizations (Huntington, 1996). Therefore, having a solid moral order that emphasizes fairness and social justice can mitigate these problems and ensure that global society will endure and flourish.

These concerns are deeply grounded in the realization of the flawed nature of modern global capitalism. First and foremost, modern market capitalism is no longer "curbed by self-imposed emotional sanctions" (Buckley and Casson, 2001: 305) as the early Western capitalism was in a more religious, social, and cultural context. The excessive profit-seeking behavior, which is intrinsic to market capitalism, will then inevitably create the extremely uneven distribution of wealth. As Dunning (2001) points out, even though it is no fault of their own, a large number of participants of globalization are especially disadvantaged by globalization. Consequently, the uneven distributional effects of the global marketplace become the source of conflict and an obstacle for the further advance of modern global capitalism.

Moreover, the world and the global marketplace are becoming increasingly interdependent. At the same time, global markets today are frequently dominated by a few large firms or interest groups that have the capability to exploit market failures and engage in unacceptable social or moral behavior (Dunning, 2001). Excess greed propels institutions to seek out every possible opportunity to reap excess return without considering other participating members' interests. However, the malfunction of one part of the market due to the actions of irresponsible global capitalism often leads to a chain effect whose impact can be felt bitterly by all members in this networked ecosystem including those that are responsible for these malfunctions. In other words, market failure is prevalent and can spread out just like endemics.

If imperatives of social justice are not reconciled with such a huge wealth disparity, clashes among nations will eventually damage the gain of modern global capitalism and, more importantly, endanger the social cohesion by injecting enormous instability into this world. In the modern secular world, we believe that a solid moral basis which is not based on denominational religions for global capitalism will play a central role in establishing definite limits on the extent of profit-seeking behavior, especially when such behavior is pursued at the expense of broader social objectives. Consequently, the potential conflicts among nations caused by massive wealth disparity can be sufficiently mitigated.

Second, market capitalism has entered a new era, that is, modern global capitalism, in which knowledge and human capital are the key sources of its wealth creation. As Dunning (2001, 2003) indicates, this stage of capitalism is fundamentally different from the previous ones, such as the industrial and finance capitalism in which markets were impersonal. Modern global capitalism is knowledge based, whose source of wealth is often human capital, knowledge, and intellectual capital of all kinds. Therefore, the cultivation, development, and employment of human capital and knowledge rest on individuals' enduring motivation, commitment, and inspiration, which stem largely from a strong sense of value, principles, and self-actualization in pursuing wealth creation endeavor. In other words, modern global capitalism depends on a solid moral basis for sustainable wealth creation.

Third, this world is becoming an increasingly integrated whole in which nations are deeply intertwined with others economically, politically, socially, and even culturally. There has been a huge growth in all forms of interfirm coalitions and inter-government agreements over the past two decades (UNCTAD, 2000). No country can flourish without collaboration and cooperation with other members of this global society. Therefore, the current form of capitalism is characterized by the pervasiveness of all forms of alliances, networks, and cooperative ventures. Individuals, enterprises, governments, and other non-market institutions need to cooperate with each other in a wide variety of ways. It is here where moral virtues such as trust, reciprocity, and forbearance, which cannot easily be built into a purely contractual transaction, are the key to business success (Buckley and Casson, 2001; Dunning, 2001, 2003). A solid moral basis is essential in creating and maintaining trust, hence this crucial interdependence among participating members of global capitalism.

Yet, modern global capitalism in its current form is characterized by self-interest, greed, insensitivity, excess individualism, and unsaturated profit-seeking behavior. This is because the important insights of human nature that were embodied in early capitalism have been lost in the modern secular world (Skutch, 1970), and modern MNEs that are governed by "spiritually poor" people are primarily "concerned with aggression, procreation and the pursuit of social dominance and so on" (Buckley and Casson, 2001: 305). Consequently, global capitalism in fact "actively undermines the moral order on which it depends for its long-term survival" (Buckley and Casson, 2001: 304).

However, history repeatedly indicates that morality has been playing a central role in economic progress throughout human history. Most successful economies have been guided by a strong moral ethos and frequently, these same economies collapsed when this moral foundation was undermined (Landes, 1999), because no community can sustain itself on evil values (Dunning, 2001). As a result, the survival and growth of global market capitalism critically depends on a solid moral basis.

Hence, it is vital to provide such a moral order for modern global capitalism to make it sustainable, and business practices need a moral compass (Donaldson, 1996). Individual and organizational moral virtues should be strengthened and reconfigured in a way that is consistent with a knowledge-intensive, alliance-based, multicultural society. Perceived economic inclusiveness and social justice must be an integral part of the objectives of global capitalism if it is to flourish (Dunning, 2001).

The global moral and ethic imperatives

Dunning (2001, 2003) forcefully demonstrates that failures in the economic and institutional fields are intrinsically connected with the failure of morality, and deficiency of moral virtues lies at the core of the failure of the markets and institutions. It is important not only to advocate the endorsement of a global moral order, but also to provide specific imperatives from which participants of modern globalization can draw insights and guidance.

Despite the heated debate over whether or not a global ethic indeed exists has been ongoing, and though major religious traditions, such as Christianity, Islam, Judaism, Hinduism, and Buddhism, seem to have different value systems, there is enough in common among the major religions of the world to produce a meaningful and workable code of conduct in the global marketplace (Dunning, 2001). Therefore, we believe that it is not only possible but also crucial to develop a universally accepted moral order, that is, the so-called hypernorms (Carroll, 2004), and design an overarching global ethic, or the global moral standard (Donaldson, 1996), which can accommodate different cultural values.

Dunning's (2001) 3Cs framework for establishing a moral basis, which emphasizes creativity, cooperation, and compassion, represents the first serious attempt by IB scholars to make such an important step toward this direction. Creativity centers on values such as diligence, perseverance and emphasizes the individual's responsibility to personal self-improvement. Cooperation, being the key element of alliance capitalism, emphasizes values such as mutual trust, forbearance, and tolerance. Compassion includes such virtues as benevolence, fairness, justice, and empathy toward others' suffering.

This framework provides important insights into how we should construct a global moral order for modern market capitalism. Yet, it has several limitations. First of all, this framework fails to distinguish between virtues and their behavioral outcome. Both creativity and cooperation are not virtues per se, but the consequence or outcome of practicing certain virtues. As a matter of fact, this framework only emphasizes one virtue, that is, compassion, and it is therefore not comprehensive enough to cope with the intricacies embedded in the moral and ethical dimensions of modern global capitalism.

Second, and more importantly, this framework does not examine the foundation such virtues as compassion is based on. Virtues do not spring out from nothing. Without a clear understanding of the foundation of moral beliefs and behavior, these moral imperatives themselves are of no solid basis and, therefore, will be unlikely to be endorsed and endure. Virtues and moral beliefs should themselves be grounded firmly on a universally endorsed basis.

Some scholars argue for a biological foundation of morality and virtues stating that the creation and practices of morality systems are the biological needs of human species in maximizing the probabilities of survival for individuals and communities (Hinde, 2002; Flack and de Waal, 2004). We think that the biological needs for moral values such as reciprocity, empathy, sympathy, and so on are the origin of human morality; but we as spiritual beings should and have the capacity to move beyond this stage of moral intelligence and practices. We believe that the fundamental basis for global morality and ethics is the belief in a higher meaning and purpose, a belief that is entrenched in the mind of individuals, organizations, and societies. It is a purpose that is beyond ones' self-interest and his or her immediate relational vicinity. Individuals or organizations that possess such a higher purpose are those that transcend from their narrow "self" to pursue a higher goal, which takes into consideration the overall interests and benefits of the global society as a whole. Then, helping others who are in need, serving the global society, and working for the betterment of this world become the primary source of inspiration, development, and achievement for individuals and organizations.

Such a higher purpose rests on the realization and recognition that we human beings are all equal, all interconnected, and all part of the oneness. There is no boundary among us. This realization is the outcome of individual and organizational transcendence, which elevates human beings above the biological foundation of morality. Once an individual or organization possesses a higher purpose, he, she, or they naturally feel empathetic and compassionate about others, and this empathy and compassion come from an enormous sense of interconnectedness, which trivializes and even ridicules the superficial differences among human beings, organizations, and nations in culture, religion, ethnicity, social, and economic status. These differences therefore cease to divide and separate people.

A person or an organization that does not have the ability to transcend from the narrow "self" to a higher state of personal and organizational development can never truly be compassionate about others' suffering and interests. The natural response of a person or an organization that exists in a segmented world in which every member of it is perceived by others as being fundamentally different is to maximize the individual gains and minimize the potential threats from other "aliens," often time at the expense of other members' interests and benefits.

In order for global market capitalism to thrive and endure, it needs to transform itself into a responsible global capitalism which has a solid moral basis that itself is established on a higher meaning and purpose. With such a higher purpose as the fundamental basis, responsible global capitalism should consider itself not as an end, but as a means to provide a more satisfying and meaningful life for individuals and their families, and advance the economic objectives and social transformation of societies (Stiglitz, 2003).

With a higher meaning and purpose as the fundamental basis for a global moral order, a comprehensive moral framework can be established. Besides compassion, other essential moral values should be identified based on the most acute moral deficits at this stage of global capitalism. Previous studies indicate that the biggest moral problems that modern global capitalism have are the lack of social justice and responsibility, insensitivity, arrogance, lack of truthfulness and trustworthiness, and excessive greed (Dunning, 2001, 2003). Values that constitute a solid moral basis should directly address these moral problems.

Compassion certainly mitigates, if not eradicates, the problem of the lack of social justice and responsibility, insensitivity, and arrogance. Compassion naturally implies such virtues as the sense of social justice and social responsibility, fairness, empathy, altruism, reciprocity, and so on. Honesty and integrity, which aim at diminishing the lack of truthfulness and trustworthiness, are absolutely required for alliance capitalism to function properly.

These two virtues are the source of trust, which is a critical element for knowledge-intensive economy and alliance capitalism. A set of virtues such as trustfulness, principle, reliability, and so on follow from these central values, all of which center on interpersonal relationships, cooperation, and collaboration.

Excess greed, driven by an unsaturated desire for profit, has been the defining characteristic of modern market capitalism. At this stage of human civilization, we add unprecedented strains on the environment and its natural resources. Global warming and other forms of natural disasters loom closer. The developed world, especially the United States, filled with unsaturated consumerism, accumulates wealth at no concern over the impact on the environment and our world as a whole, while nations in the developing world are bearing the burden. Under this circumstance, preservation and self-control are critical, not only for the sustainability of modern global capitalism, but also for the entire human race. Allowing the modern global capitalism to pursue its excessive greed will make it the most formidable enemy of human beings, and we will eventually become the victim of our own creation.

Based on the above discussion, we believe that the three essential moral values, compassion, integrity and preservation, should form the moral basis for global market capitalism. These values directly confront and address the moral deficits of modern market capitalism. Our moral framework can be summarized in Figure 9.1.

Regarding the global moral and ethical framework, several important points need to be made. First, moral imperatives surpass religions. There is no need to wear a religious hat when preaching such a global moral framework. Most importantly, a global moral framework should not be labeled as Christianity-centered moral imperative even though these values are the essential building blocks of a Christian moral system, because we believe these fundamental values are universal and encompass various religious traditions. As Dunning (2003) indicates, although Christians have a right to express views on the morality of the market system, they are on less secure ground when they try to offer professional or technical advice of how this might be improved. Religion divides the global community but common, universal moral values unify it. Moreover, social and organizational capitals and its underpinning ethical framework cannot be handed over to a country from the outside (Dunning, 2001). These three core virtues in our framework are religiously and culturally free.

Second, establishing such a moral framework requires a holistic approach, which involves all major participants in this global society, such as governments, firms, supra-national entities, and intermediate associations. Moreover, in order to move toward a truly responsible global capitalism, we also need to start from the bottom and deeply involve the entire educational system to lay a solid moral foundation for individuals as they grow. In

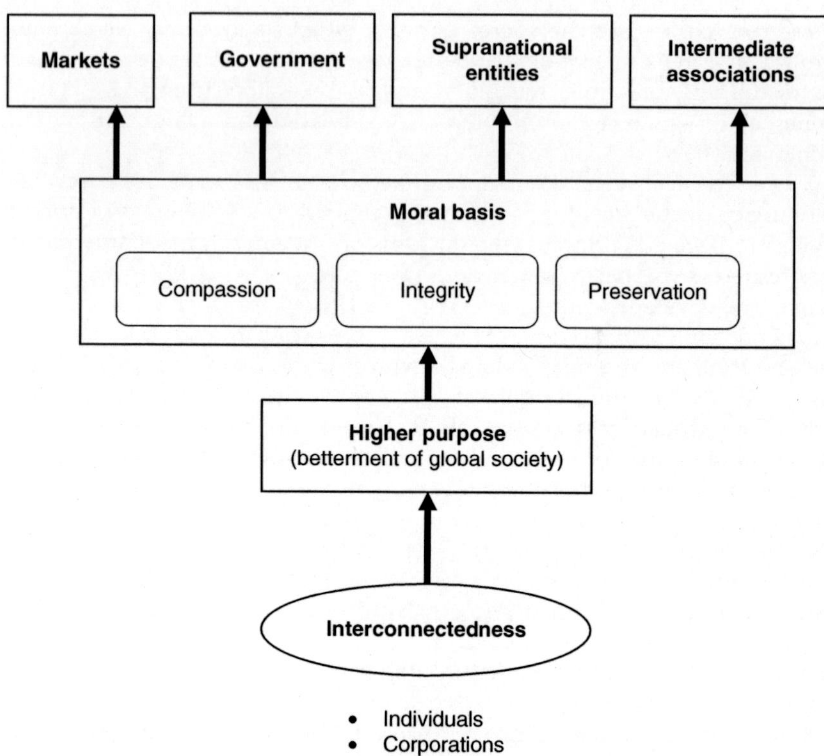

Figure 9.1 The moral framework for modern global capitalism

particular, the important role played by business schools all over the world, especially those leading institutes, in constructing such a moral basis in the minds of business practitioners cannot be ignored.

Third, establishing such a moral order is a slow process and it will certainly be an uphill battle against skepticism, cynicism, and total ignorance. At this stage of global market capitalism, it is important to demonstrate clearly that such a global moral order makes solid economic sense, that is, indicating "you can do well by doing good," and more importantly, "you can do well ONLY by doing good," to incentivize the major participants of market capitalism. As human societies and subsequently market capitalism become further developed intellectually, mentally, and spiritually, all the participants will genuinely realize that being moral and ethical is an end in itself which brings as much if not more utilities to individuals, organizations, and nations as materialistic gains and economic success.

We next argue that there is a positive relationship between a firm's *genuine* moral and ethical practices and its performance. In particular, we focus on MNEs and their performance in emerging markets. We argue that such moral values are critical for MNEs to attain enduring success in emerging markets. In those markets, not only social capital is critical in driving MNEs' success, but also *moral capital*. Moreover, a solid moral basis is the most effective and efficient way to obtain social capital through establishing *genuine* social embeddedness. In fact, social and moral capitals are the core source of MNEs' competitive advantage. Therefore, MNEs, in order to succeed in emerging markets, need a strong moral foundation for their business.

Moral basis and MNEs' performance

If rascals knew the profitability of honesty, they would be honest out of rascality.
Benjamin Franklin

As discussed before, a moral basis and a global ethic are vital for the long-term sustainability of modern global capitalism. All major participants of globalization, such as governments, supranational organizations, and MNEs, should endorse a solid moral order to ensure that globalization takes place via the form of responsive global capitalism. Among them, MNEs play a central role in global market capitalism because they are the creators and disseminators of wealth. Therefore, we focus on MNEs in this study.

Despite the fact that international business is increasingly being confronted by ethical argument (Hood, 1998), research that specifically focuses on MNEs' moral, ethical practices and their impact on firm performance has been scarce. IB research examines global ethical systems (Buller et al., 1991), the obligations of MNEs operating in other counties (Donaldson, 1989), corporate ethics in European MNEs (Langlois and Schlegelmilch, 1990), the ethical perceptions of industrial sales staff in the United States, Japan, and South Korea (Dubinsky et al., 1991), and the influence of country and industry on the ethical perceptions of senior MNEs' executives in the United States and Europe (Schlegelmilch and Robertson, 1995). None of these studies specifically investigates the relationship between MNEs' moral, ethical practices and their performance.

We argue that having a solid moral basis is vital for MNEs to improve their economic performance and achieve long-term profitability. Numerous studies in business ethics demonstrate that organizations that are moral and ethical in their business practices can obtain long-term success (Aupperle et al., 1985; Brown and Perry, 1994; Berman et al., 1999; Dunfee and Hess, 2000; Bansal, 2003). Since MNEs as a group are no more than a special case of the wider study of business ethics (Hood, 1998), there should not be any theoretical reason why this relationship regarding MNEs will be any different from that related to other firms, despite the fact that MNEs are confronted by a new set of challenges, such as practicing ethics in a cross-cultural context.

Developing countries represent the greatest growth opportunities for MNEs in the twenty-first century. In these countries where a wide range of social strata tends to be marginalized by the force of global capitalism, the need for MNEs to establish a solid moral basis is even greater if they are to successfully sustain their growth. Research indicates that social embeddedness proves to be the key driver for MNEs' enduring success in emerging markets, because it enables them to tap the mass market successfully (London and Hart, 2004). We maintain that a sound moral basis is a prerequisite for MNEs to establish such critical social embeddedness, therefore for their sustainable success. Our view is based on the following arguments.

First, organizations that operate on a moral basis besides rigorous economic rationales are by nature ethical in their business practice. Research in economics and management already indicates that moral and ethical business practices lead to better economic performance; for example, "good ethics is good business." For instance, studies show that firms benefit from socially responsible actions in terms of employee morale and productivity (Moskowitz, 1972; Parket and Eibert, 1975; Soloman and Hansen, 1985), positive perception of management skills (Alexander and Bucholtz, 1978), improved employee and customer goodwill (Soloman and Hansen, 1985), more low-cost implicit claims than other firms (Cornell and Shapiro, 1987), and improved standing with important constituencies such as bankers, investors, and government officials (Moussavi and Evans, 1986). Empirical studies also strongly support the fact that ethical practices and performance are positively correlated (Bragdon and Marlin, 1972; Bowman and Haire, 1975; Parket and Eibert, 1975).

Therefore, the general finding is that a firm's moral, ethical practices lead to its superior economic performance. Economic rationality is in no contradiction with morality and ethics even in the world of business. As a matter of fact, a truly rational economic agent tends to be moral and ethical in their business practice because trust and reputation can significantly reduce transaction cost and mitigate moral hazard (Jones and Pollitt, 1996). So, being moral and ethical in fact best serves their self-interest and firms are better off in the long run if establishing their business practices on a solid moral foundation.

Second, the key success factor for MNEs operating in emerging markets is the establishment of social embeddedness, which reflects a firm's ability to create competitive advantage based on a deep understanding of and integration with the local environment (London and Hart, 2004). We argue that a solid moral basis is the prerequisite for establishing such social embeddedness. Emerging economies have been the major target markets of modern global capitalism due to their enormous market potential. The strategies of most of these MNEs are similar in one aspect: they target the affluent segment at the top of the economic pyramid. However, as this segment becomes saturated, MNEs start to explore the untapped market segment located at the base of this economic pyramid, which in fact represents the largest and fastest growing segment of the world's market, for example, 4 billion customers and $9 trillion in hidden assets (London and Hart, 2004).

In this segment, for example, low income, high potential, MNEs' traditional methods of business practices and capabilities may not be suitable and they need to adopt a different strategy and mindset if they are to be successful due to the idiosyncrasies involved. In these markets, social contracts and social institutions dominate and relationships are primarily grounded on social, not legal contracts (de Soto, 2000). Moreover, organizations with the most expertise in serving these markets, such as government and civil society, have a strong social orientation (Aturupane et al., 1994; Chambers 1997; Sen, 1999). Therefore, successfully operating in this business environment requires the capability to understand and appreciate the benefits of the existing social infrastructure (Chambers, 1997).

Moreover, traditional partners may lack relevant experience (London and Hart, 2004). Non-profit organizations and other socially oriented institutions can play an important role in business development (Rondinelli and London, 2003). Also, societal performance matters For example, corporations are expected to address global societal issues such as eradiating poverty and environmental protection in developing countries. Global firms and institutions are increasingly being expected to consider the societal and environmental impacts of their activities (Soros, 2002).

Consequently, in low-income markets, social benefits influence economic decisions (Kennedy, 2001). The success of MNEs is no longer only driven by global efficiency, national responsiveness, and worldwide learning capabilities (Bartlett and Ghoshal, 1989), but by the firms' abilities to establish social embeddedness. Therefore, "firms without a capacity to appreciate and create social value or to become locally embedded in the social infrastructure that dominate low income markets may struggle to overcome their liability of foreignness" (London and Hart, 2004: 8). Therefore, MNEs have to possess a high degree of social embeddedness in order to be successful in tapping the mass market in emerging economies.

Although we agree that social embeddedness is a central construct in understanding the MNEs' performance in emerging economies, we believe that *genuine* social embeddedness is a more relevant concept. We then draw the link between moral basis, social capital, and social embeddedness and introduce the concept of *moral capital*. We argue that a moral basis is the key for MNEs to establish *genuine* social embeddedness. It in turn leads to the creation and generation of moral capital, which along with social capital, drives MNEs' success in emerging markets.

Social embeddedness is first used to describe the social structure of modern markets (Polanyi, 1957). Research already shows the robust effect of social embeddedness on economic action (Schumpeter, 1950; Granovetter, 1985) due to the fact that social embeddedness creates economic opportunities that are difficult to replicate via markets, contracts, or vertical integration. Social embeddedness is classified into various forms, for example, structural, cognitive, political, cultural (Zukin and DiMaggio, 1990), and institutional (Emmerik and Sanders, 2004).

In our study, we categorize social embeddedness into the following forms: pragmatic (transactional) and genuine (relational). The former can be established via common business interests of various parties involved, whereas the latter has to be built on trust, reciprocity, and mutual respect. The former is of a temporary nature, more opportunistic with limited sustainability, and tends to dissolve as the need for new business alliances emerge, while the latter is long-term orientated, genuine, and therefore more enduring. Moreover, the former has the business interest of an organization at its heart and tends to be more formal, while the latter has co-development, partnership, and mutual growth at heart and can be informal. In fact, in emerging markets where safeguarding mechanisms are not well established, informal social networks and interactions are more instrumental in facilitating business cooperation and collaboration. The former type of social embeddedness does not require a moral basis, while the latter has to be based on a moral basis.

Genuine social embeddedness demands trust and it also generates trust. Research indicates that trust and personal ties reduce monitoring costs and facilitate the exchange of proprietary and tacit knowledge, and they, rather than explicit contracts, dominate the transactions, for example, in the case of Japanese auto and Italian knitwear industries (Dore, 1983; Asanuma 1985; Gerlach, 1992), and organizational learning (Lazerson, 1995). Therefore, establishing a genuine social embeddedness in a market requires trust and moral behavior, and this type of social embeddedness is the true engine driving MNEs' enduring economic performance in emerging markets.

We further argue that a solid moral basis is the prerequisite for the establishment of genuine social embeddedness by MNEs. The reasons are as follows. First, establishing genuine social embeddedness is equivalent to obtaining a genuine membership to a community. MNEs, which are often perceived as the vanguards of Western Imperialism in developing countries due to historical reasons, have to spend extra amount of effort to break through the social barriers based on this negative perception. Domestic organizations in these markets are comfortable in establishing business-oriented alliances, but are cautious about building up relationship-oriented partnerships with MNEs because these firms are often arrogant, greedy, and irresponsible. Therefore, MNEs' membership into a local community can only be gained through trust and relationship building with the local key stakeholders. The source of such trust is MNEs' solid moral basis on which their mission, philosophy, and business practices are based. Only firms that are operated based on virtues such as compassion, integrity, and preservation can gain genuine trust from the local communities and the society as a whole, therefore establish genuine social embeddedness in these markets. Once MNEs are well established into the social network of these markets and form trust-based partnerships with local organizations, most of which may be non-traditional partners (London and Hart, 2004), they will be given access to critical resources, such as market information, tacit knowledge of local markets, government support, and so on, which are not normally available to "outsiders."

Second, genuine social embeddedness leads to the development of social capital, which is an important asset in driving a firm's performance. Social capital, defined as "a feature of successful communities, reflected in trust, reciprocity, and strong social norms that facilitate integration and cooperation and provide effective regulation of social behavior" (Putnam, 1993), has been a key concept in sociology and recently became a central notion in business research (Bourdieu, 1986; Coleman, 1990; Burt, 1997; Nahapiet and Ghoshal, 1998). Social capital reflects the potential benefits for social actors that are derived from the content of their social ties, centered on trust and trustworthiness (Putnam, 1993; Fukuyama, 1995; Tsai and Ghoshal, 1998). This leads to positive and cooperative behaviors, since they create a psychological environment conducive to collaboration and mutual support (Ring and Van de Ven, 1992, 1994; Nahapiet and Ghoshal, 1998; Zaheer et al., 1998).

It is clear that the notion of social capital centers on trust, reciprocity, and action for a common purpose, which results in collaboration and cooperation. Like physical and human capital, social capital is a productive resource (Tsai and Ghoshal, 1998), which facilitates a firm's business operations and value creation (Baker, 1990; Coleman, 1990; Burt, 1992; Nahapiet and Ghoshal, 1998), because trust, being the central element of social capital, is an antecedent of cooperation and partnership (Gambetta, 1988; Gulati, 1995; Tsai and Ghoshal, 1998; Zaheer et al., 1998). The central role played by trust in economic exchange is also recognized by theoretical work in economics (Macauley, 1963; Arrow, 1974; Granovetter, 1985).

Ample empirical evidence also indicates a positive relationship between a company's social capital and its financial performance (see Margolis and Walsh, 2003's review) and firm performance in general (Florin et al., 2003). These studies suggest that social capital brings benefits to the economy in terms of its potential to decrease transaction costs and encourage cooperative behavior and trust. Putnam (2000) observed that social capital and economic outcome go together and they tend to reinforce each other. In other words, social capital leads to better economic performance.

Research in the IB field, although acknowledging the importance of social capital, falls short in linking MNEs' social capital and their economic performance. Only one study (Kostova and Roth, 2003) discusses the need to create social capital in foreign subunits of MNCs to facilitate the coordination of cross-border activities. In this chapter, we elaborate on the relationship between the moral basis, social capital, social embeddedness, and MNEs' performance in foreign markets, in particular, in emerging markets as follows.

First, we argue that in emerging markets, due to their idiosyncratic nature, for example, non-traditional firms dominate, social contract matters, and so on, social capital is one of the most critical forms of capital. As London and Hart (2004) indicate, in these markets, social performance matters, especially when tapping into the mass market. MNEs need to work with non-traditional partners whose main mission is more social than commercial. So, in order to obtain their support and cooperation, MNEs need to establish genuine social embeddedness, through which they can obtain social capital, which can be converted into other forms of critical capitals in emerging markets where a legal and regulatory environment is not firmly established and business transaction is largely relational.

Second, in emerging markets, in order to succeed, MNEs need not only social capital, but also *moral capital*. Moral capital is defined as the accumulated stock of virtues and values which determines or influences moral behavior (Dunning, 2003; Ratnapala, 2003). It stems directly from a solid moral basis. The importance of having social capital is not new for many firms. However, the notion of moral capital (Dunning, 2001, 2003; Ratnapala, 2003) has been largely ignored by both business academics and practitioners, yet it is a critical asset for MNEs especially in emerging markets.

Compared to social capital, the impact of moral capital on MNEs' performance is much more far-reaching than that of social capital since moral capital, as a unique type of social resource, is not embedded in a specific social relationship or network. In other words, its impact on economic performance does not have to be channeled through a specific social relationship. Therefore, its influence is more widespread. Firms that operate on a solid moral basis command trust and respect at a broader societal level rather than from partners that directly interact with them. Therefore, moral capital has a wider appeal to and much stronger influence on various stakeholders in these markets.

Moreover, compared to social capital, moral capital is more enduring. Social capital as a set of social resources is embedded in relationships (Loury, 1977; Burt, 1992). If these relationships dissolve, social capital ceases to exist. However, moral capital is not relationship or network dependent. It ties to the everlasting moral and ethical concerns of human society and tends to be much more enduring as long as organizations that possess it do not damage their own moral and ethical standards. Furthermore, moral capital is the most flexible form of capital, which can be transformed into social capital and other forms of capitals. It is also by nature trust based. Therefore, moral

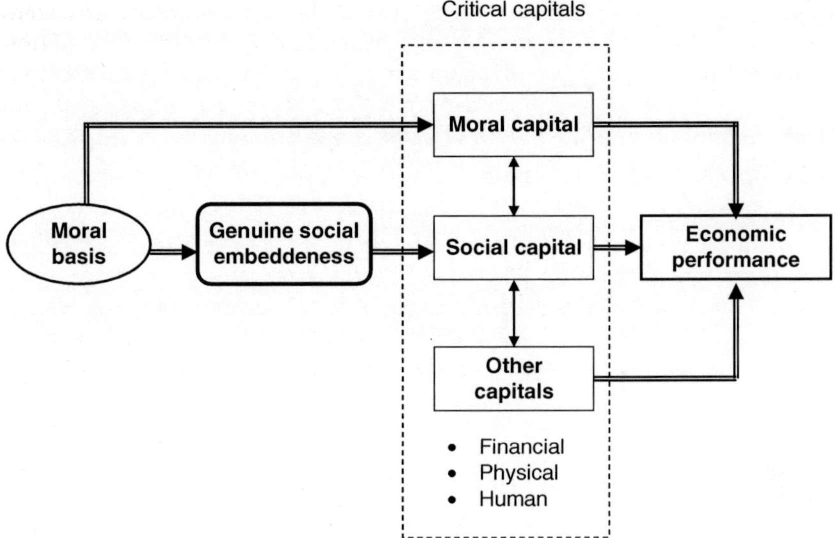

Figure 9.2   Moral basis and MNEs' performance

capital plays a key role in driving MNEs' economic success in emerging markets. In fact, moral capital can supersede social capital and be the source of social capital.

In sum, a solid moral basis not only leads to the establishment of genuine social embeddedness, it also produces moral capital. Hence, a moral basis is the source for both social and moral capitals, both of which are critical for MNEs to achieve success in emerging markets. This framework can be summarized by Figure 9.2.

We next use *Xi'an Janssen* Pharmaceutical Ltd's success story in China to further illustrate our key arguments, that is, moral basis leads to genuine social embeddedness, which in turn leads to moral capital, which along with the social capital, drives MNEs' superior performance.

Case study: *Xi'an Janssen* Pharmaceutical Ltd in China

Company background

Janssen-Cilag was established in 1953 in Belgium by Dr Paul Janssen and is a leading research-based pharmaceutical company with more than 19,000 employees worldwide and establishments in about 50 countries. In 1961, *Janssen-Cilag* joined the *Johnson & Johnson* group of companies, the world's most comprehensive manufacturer of health-care products. With more than 80 drugs to its name (five of which are featured on the World Health Organization's (WHO) list of essential drugs), *Janssen-Cilag* continues to be one of the most innovative companies in the world. *Xi'an Janssen* was established as a joint venture between China and Belgium in Xi'an, the capital city of Shanxi Province in 1985.

Moral foundation of *Xi'an Janssen's* business operations

Endorsing the value of compassion

The inception of *Xi'an Janssen* occurred three decades ago when Dr Janssen first visited China as a WHO medical expert. He soon realized the urgent need for China to develop its medical and pharmaceutical industry. With this mission in mind and a strong sense of social responsibility, he led his firm to China earlier than most other foreign firms at a time when the political and economic situation in China were uncertain. He did not choose relatively well-developed coastal cities as the location for his enterprise and instead chose Xi'an, located in the poorly developed western China. He chose this city because he saw a more urgent need for the establishment of a pharmaceutical industry in this part of the country where most people had difficulties in assessing quality medical care.

From day one, this joint venture was built on a solid moral basis. *Janssen-Cilag* genuinely wants to help the society grow. It not only produces drugs but also helps China strengthen its medical and pharmaceutical infrastructure by providing training to medical professionals and establishing various research projects. In doing so, it established a partnership with the Ministry of Public Health and the State Bureau for Drug Administration to cosponsor a large number of projects aiming at improving the overall quality of the Chinese pharmaceutical industry and public health. So far, it is the largest non-government sponsored comprehensive collaboration project, with more than 50 projects in total in China, which range from education, law and regulation, training to research and development. It also sets up various funds rewarding high achievers in medical fields.

Moreover, seeing the great shortage of blood and marrow supply in China, *Xi'an Janssen* sponsors the establishment of the first large-scale blood bank and marrow bank in China. It works with a great variety and number of non-profit local organizations, carefully balancing its efforts between activities in the fields of health, family, education, employment, environment, and culture and arts. For instance, it is involved with various charities in China, such as Helping Children with Cancer, Mental Patients Assisting Project, Help Poor Mothers, and the Hope Project aiming at helping poor children who do not have access to basic education. It also helps research for the preservation of Terracotta Soldier, the seventh wonder in the world.

Endorsing the value of integrity

Xi'an Janssen's high moral and ethical standards are also reflected by their open-minded attitude to their peers, most of which are their direct competitors. *Xi'an Janssen* is the first company in China that successfully passed all stringent international standards. Many pharmaceutical firms in China, especially the domestic ones, desperately want to learn from *Xi'an Janssen's* success. As the market becomes liberalized and China enters WTO, Chinese domestic firms are facing enormous pressure to produce products that comply with international standards. *Xi'an Janssen*, faced with numerous requests to open the door, did so at the risk of losing their business secrets just to help China's pharmaceutical industry to grow.

Furthermore, *Xi'an Janssen* is ferociously against all forms of unethical business practices to boost drug sales. At the current stage of China's pharmaceutical markets, bribery is the most commonly used selling technique for nearly all pharmaceutical firms and it becomes a norm rather than an exception. However, *Xi'an Janssen* strictly forbids its entire sales staff to engage in such unethical behavior which may put patients' health at risk, even facing tremendous competition from rivals. Despite the fact that some top salesmen resigned in protest against such an "unwise" policy, it never compromises on its moral and ethical standards.

Janssen's high moral and ethical standards are also reflected in their mission statement, which reads, "being responsible for patients, for employees, for the society, and for the shareholders" (*Xi'an Janssen's* website). Shareholder is listed last, which is quite a different business orientation compared to that of most MNEs.

Establishing genuine social embeddedness

Xi'an Janssen's involvement in numerous social projects has little connection with their core business. In fact, these involvements command a significant amount of corporate resources. However, with high moral and ethical standards, and equipped with a strong sense of social responsibility, *Xi'an Janssen* bears the need of society in mind and works for its betterment, simply because they genuinely want to help society grow rather than just focusing on their corporate profitability. In 2001, China Red Cross awarded *Xi'an Janssen* the Medal for Humanity Service. It is the first foreign enterprise that was given such a prestigious award.

With a solid moral foundation, *Xi'an Janssen* is genuinely concerned about the medical and social needs of China. It has a long-term objective which aims at helping the company grow along with the society. Through demonstrating its genuine compassion and integrity, *Xi'an Janssen* has successfully merged into the local community and become a member of the society instead of being a "foreigner." This company was so well integrated with the society that many Chinese thought *Janssen* was a domestic company.

Developing social and moral capital

Xi'an Janssen's strong moral basis and its genuine social embeddedness have earned them enormous social and moral capitals. First of all, it has developed a solid reputation as one of the most ethical companies in this industry and therefore has gained enormous support from their business partners. Their reputation has also earned them genuine respect from customers, whose loyalty to their products has been extremely strong. It is in fact the key reason why *Xi'an Janssen* has managed to maintain a rapid growth in the face of extremely stiff competition. This company, as a highly respected employer in China, has never experienced problems in attracting top talents to work for them. It is also a well-known fact that the loyalty and motivation of their employees are exceptionally high. This is quite an achievement for *Xi'an Janssen* because most other companies in the same region have been experiencing enormous difficulties in recruiting and retaining high-quality employees who tend to migrate toward the much better developed coastal cities. Moreover, *Xi'an Janssen* has been given tremendous support from the local governments due to their genuine commitments to various social projects.

Janssen's market performance

As a result of these moral and ethical conducts, *Xi'an Janssen*'s performance is nothing but phenomenal. It has been experiencing rapid growth in sales and market share for nearly ten years. Moreover, ten years in a row, it has been ranked the top pharmaceutical company in China among all joint ventures. It is also one of the 500 largest enterprises in China, and has been selected as one of the 10 Best Joint Ventures for four consecutive years, twice ranked the top of the list. In 2001, *Xi'an Janssen* was also selected as one of the 10 Most Respected Foreign Enterprises in China by the *Fortune* magazine. Besides these achievements, it has also won numerous other awards, including the Top 10 Brands in China, in which *Xi'an Janssen* is the only pharmaceutical company.

Summary

Based on our discussion, it is clear that *Xi'an Janssen*'s success is largely driven by its moral and ethical practices as its business is firmly established on a solid moral ground. Through such a basis, this company is able to establish genuine social embeddedness which allows it to accumulate enormous social and moral capitals, both of which are critical assets to obtain success in China's market. In sum, our thesis is that in emerging markets, MNEs' performance is critically dependent on their abilities to obtain both moral and social capitals. Genuine social embeddedness based on trust and respect provides MNEs with social capital. However, establishing such genuine social embeddedness requires a solid moral basis, which is also the source of moral capital. MNEs should endorse a higher purpose and establish a solid moral basis for their business if they want to achieve enduring success, especially in emerging markets, such as China.

Conclusions and future research

Global corporate scandals such as *Enron, WorldCom,* and *Global Crossing* have clearly indicated that the sustainability of global capitalism requires the establishment of a solid moral basis. As Dunning (2003) argues, it is crucial for social and moral virtues to be strengthened and reconfigured in a way which is consistent with a knowledge-intensive, alliance-based, and multicultural society, and which will best enable markets to work together to promote efficient growth and social justice. In other words, a new economy needs a new morality and there is a moral vacuum at the heart of the new economy that needs to be filled.

Achieving this goal is an extremely complicated issue and it requires all key members of modern global capitalism to work together. First and foremost, a new mindset and perspective have to be firmly established in the psyche of individuals, organizations, and society as a whole, which regards global market capitalism as a means to advance human well-being and the global society rather than as an end in itself. In other words, further movement toward globalization will require rethinking the nature and role of capitalism in meeting the goals of mankind, including its melding with both social and political objectives and institutions (Behrman, 2003). In doing so, we need a *holistic* approach to development, which embraces a social, moral, and environmental dimension as well as an economic one (Stiglitz, 2003).

Endorsing such a new perspective also requires individuals, organizations, and nations to transcend beyond the narrow "self" and embrace a higher meaning and purpose in pursuing their own objectives. This transcendence demands individuals, organizations, and nations to fundamentally revitalize their sense of genuine connection with their peers and revise their respective missions in life. Once such a strong sense of interconnectedness and subsequently profound transcendence can be experienced by all members of the global society, a solid moral framework which centers on compassion, integrity, and preservation can then be firmly established.

As we argued, a solid moral basis of modern global capitalism is the prerequisite for its long-term survival. The invisible hand that has been regulating free-market capitalism for centuries is no longer sufficient to manage an ever more complex global market system. Therefore, another invisible hand that is guided by global morality and ethics is certainly needed, because in Will Durant's words, "the health of nations is more important than the wealth of nations." We also believe that establishing a solid moral basis for the major players of the global market capitalism, that is, MNEs, has a solid economic rationale. MNEs that aspire to secure enduring success in emerging markets need to obtain social and moral capitals, both of which are intrinsically related to the moral and ethical basis of MNEs' business operations. MNEs that are based on such a solid moral foundation will be able to establish genuine social embeddedness, and therefore, genuine social and moral capitals, which are the key drivers for their economic performance.

Global business morality and ethics are topics too important to be neglected by the IB researchers. We should integrate the moral dimension in our analysis and thinking as we seek to understand and explain how modern global capitalism can benefit the global society as a whole and how MNEs should work in a holistic and cooperative manner to achieve this goal. We think that further research along this direction can be developed in several ways.

Research on global morality and its foundation

The first important task for IB scholars is to investigate the nature and the foundation of global morality. We need to develop a universally accepted moral system, which is logical, rigorous, and culture free, to quench the debate over whether such a value system does exist. Several scholars have already examined this issue, that is, hypernorms (Donaldson and Dunfee, 1999; Carroll, 2004), yet more work is needed to address issues such as how to establish a global moral standard across diverse cultural backgrounds; what insights we can draw from less economically developed cultures, such as China, India, Brazil, and Eastern Europe; what role the national culture plays in shaping the establishment of such a universal moral system, and so on.

Researchers also need to specifically define such a moral system and sketch out the practical guidance for key participants in the globalization process, especially for MNEs, namely, the implications of this global moral framework for MNEs and how those planning to endorse such a moral framework should revise their current business practices and design a morality-based business model. Furthermore, there is also an urgent need to examine the foundation of such a universal moral system. We believe that a genuine sense of interconnectedness and wholeness among all human beings, organizations, communities, and nations constituting this global society should be the ultimate foundation. Further work is required to theoretically investigate this proposition.

Research on moral and spiritual capital

Moral capital is a central construct in this study. We believe that this notion should and will gain more prominent attention from IB Scholars. Research already states that commerce is not only morally impeachable but also unsustainable without moral capital (Ratnapala, 2003). Research should investigate the nature and the sources of moral capital and its impact on MNEs' overall performance. Moreover, the concept of spiritual capital should also be examined. It is difficult to discuss genuine morality which transcends beyond our biological instinct without bringing up the notion of human spirituality. So, it would be interesting to study how spiritual capital can be developed and how it is related to moral capital.

Research on organizational moral development

Advocating the establishment of a moral basis for organizations is only the first step. Researchers also need to study how a firm should pursue its organizational moral development to truly establish a universal moral basis for its operations. Several studies have investigated this issue (Sridhar and Cambum, 1993; Moore and Beadle, 2006), but more work needs to be done in the context of MNEs, which often have a culturally diverse workforce and geographically disperse operations. Issues such as how to develop an organization-wide moral standards and practices that encompass employees from all cultural and religious backgrounds, how to maintain consistencies in the moral development for various divisions that are located at markets where the stages of economic and moral development vary significantly, and so on certainly deserve in-depth investigation.

Another area for further investigation is the impact of business education on organizational moral development. As Plato said, "Education in virtue is the only education which deserves the name," and we truly believe that business schools can play a vital role in helping organizations to endorse a solid moral basis through educating its participating members, that is, MBA students. Therefore, how to best incorporate courses centered on global business morality and ethics into MBA curriculum is an important issue for future research.

Research on the relationship between MNEs' moral basis and their performance

It is essential to develop a more rigorous theory that investigates the relationship between global morality, ethics, and the long-term success of MNEs. This study represents the first attempt along this direction. A more complete framework should be developed. It is also important to provide solid empirical evidence indicating that a global moral and ethical basis does lead MNEs to long-term economic success. In investigating the performance implications of MNEs' efforts in establishing a moral basis, researchers should also study the role of such a moral basis in shaping the global positioning of MNEs, and furthermore how such a positioning affects consumers, especially global consumers' perception and adoption of their products, given the fact that these customers themselves are at different stages of moral development.

References

Alexander, G. and Bucholtz, R. (1978), "Corporate Social Responsibility and Stock Market Performance", *Academy of Management Journal*, 21: 479–486.
Arrow, K. (1974) *The Limits of Organizations*, Norton: New York.

Asanuma, B. (1985) "The Organization of Parts Purchases in the Japanese Automotive Industry", *Japanese Economic Studies*, Summer: 32–53.

Aturupane, H., Glewwe, P., and Isenman, P. (1994) "Poverty, Human Development and Growth: A Emerging Consensus?" *The American Review*, 84(2): 244–249.

Aupperle, K.E., Carroll, A.B., and Hartfield, J.D. (1985) "An Empirical Examination of the Relationship Between Corporate Social Responsibility and Profitability", *Academy of Management Journal*, 28: 446–463.

Baker, W. (1990) "Market Networks and Corporate Behavior", *America Journal of Sociology*, 96: 589–625.

Bansal, P. (2003) "From Issues to Actions: The Importance of Individual Concerns and Organizational Values in Responding to Natural Environment Issues", *Organization Science*, 14: 510–527.

Bartlett, C. and Ghoshal, S. (1989) *Managing Across Borders*, Harvard Business School Press: Boston.

Behrman, J. (2003) "Transformation of Society: Implications for Globalization", in J., Dunning (ed.), *Making Globalization Good*, Oxford: Oxford University Press, pp. 108–142.

Berman, S.L., Wicks, A.C., Kotha, S., and Jones, T.M. (1999) "Does Stakeholder Orientation Matter? The Relationship between Stakeholder Management Modes and Firm Financial Performance", *Academy of Management Journal*, 42: 488–506.

Bourdieu, P. (1986) "The Forms of Capital", in J.G., Richardson (ed.), *Handbook of Theory and Research for Sociology of Education*, New York: Greenwood, pp. 241–258.

Bowman, E. and Haire, M. (1975) "A Strategic Posture Towards CSR", *California Management Review*, 18(2): 49–58.

Bradgon, J.H. and Marlin, J. (1972) "Is Pollution Profitable", *Risk Management*, 19(4): 9–18.

Brown, B. and Perry, S. (1994) "Removing the Financial Performance Halo from Fortune's 'Most Admired' Companies", *Academy of Management Journal*, 37: 1347–1359.

Buckley, P.J. and Casson, M. (2001) "The Moral Basis of Global Capitalism: Beyond the Eclectic Theory", *International Journal of the Economics of Business*, 8: 303–327.

Buller, P.F., Kohls, J.J. and Anderson, K.S. (1991) "The Challenge of Global Ethics", *Journal of Business Ethics*, 10(10): 767–76.

Burt, R.S. (1992) *Structural Holes: The Social Structure of Competition*, Harvard University Press: Cambridge, MA.

Burt, R.S. (1997) "The Continent Value of Social Capital", *Administrative Science Quarterly*, 42: 339–365.

Carroll, A. (2004) "Managing Ethically with Global Stakeholders: A Present and Future Challenge", *Academy of Management Executives*, 18(2): 114–120.

Chambers, R. (1997) *Whose Reality Counts? Pushing the First Last*, ITDG Publishing: London.

Coleman, J.S. (1990) *Foundations of Social Theory*, Belknap Press of Harvard University Press: Cambridge, MA, USA.

Cornell, B. and Shapiro, A. (1987) "Corporate Stakeholders and Corporate Finance", *Financial Management*, 16: 5–14.

de Soto, H. (2000) *The Mystery of Capital: Why Capitalism Triumphs in the West and Fails Everywhere Else*, Basic Books: New York.

Donaldson, T. (1989) *The Ethics of International Business*, Oxford University Press: Oxford.

Donaldson, T. (1996) "Values in Tension: Ethics Away from Home", *Harvard Business Review*, 74: 48–62.

Donaldson, T. and Dunfee, T.W. (1999) "When Ethics Travel: The Promise and Peril of Global Business Ethics", *California Management Review*, 41(4): 45–63.

Dore, R. (1983) "Goodwill and the Spirit of Market Capitalism", *British Journal of Sociology*, 34: 459–482.

Dubinsky, A.J., Jolson, M.A., Kotabe, M., and Lim, C.U. (1991) "A Cross-National Investigation of Industrial Sales Peoples' Ethical Perceptions", *Journal of International Business Studies*, 22(4): 651–70.

Dunfee, T.W. and Hess, D. (2000) "The Legitimacy of Direct Corporate Humanitarian Investment", *Business Ethics Quarterly*, 10: 95–109.

Dunning, J. (2001) *Global Capitalism at Bay*, Routledge: London, UK.

Dunning, J. (2003) *Making Globalization Good*, Oxford University Press: Oxford.

Emmerik, H. and Sanders, K. (2004) "Social Embeddedness and Job Performance of Tenured and Non-Tenured Professionals", *Human Resource Management Journal*, 14(1): 40–56.

Flack J.C. and de Waal, F.B.M. (2004) "Monkey Business and Business Ethics: Evolutionary Origins of Human Morality", *Ruffin Series in Business Ethics*, 7–41.

Florin, J., Lubatkin, M., and Schulze, W. (2003) "A Social Capital Model of High Growth Ventures", *Academy of Management Journal*, 46(3): 374–384.

Fukuyama, F. (1995) *Trust: The Social Virtues and the Creation of Prosperity*, Free Press: New York.

Gambetta, D. (1988) "Can We Trust Trust?", in D., Gambetta (ed.), *Trust: Making and Breaking Cooperative Relations*, New York: Basil Blackwell, pp. 213–238.

Gerlach, M.L. (1992) *Alliance Capitalism: The Social Organization of Japanese Business*, University of California Press: Berkeley, CA.

Granovetter, M. (1985) "Economic Action and Social Structure: The Problem of Embeddedness", *America Journal of Sociology*, 91: 481–510.

Gulati, R. (1995) "Does Familiarity Breed Trust? The Implications of Repeated Ties for Contractual Choice in Alliances", *Academy of Management Journal*, 38: 85–112.

Hinde, R. (2002) *Why Good is Good: The Sources of Morality*, Routledge: Independence, Kentucky, USA.

Hood, N. (1998) "Business Ethics and Transnational Companies", in I., Jones and M., Pollitt (eds), *The Role of Business Ethics in Economic Performance*, London: Macmillan, pp. 193–210.

Hosmer, L.T. (1994) "Strategic Planning as if Ethics Mattered", *Strategic Management Journal*, 15: 17–34.

Hume, D. (1740/1985) *A Treatise on Human Nature*, Penguin Classics: London.

Huntington, S. (1996) "The West Unique, Not Universal", *Foreign Affairs*, 75: 28–46.

Jones, I.W. and Pollitt, M.G. (1996) "Economics, Ethics and Integrity in Business", *Journal of General Management*, 21(3): 30–47.

Kennedy, R.E. (2001) *The Pharmaceutical Industry and the AIDS Crisis in Developing Countries*, Harvard Business School Publishing: Boston.

Kostova, T. and Roth, K. (2003) "Social Capital in Multinational Corporations and a Micro-Macro Model of Its Formation", *Academy of Management Review*, 28(2): 297–319.

Lal, D. (2003) "Private Morality and Capitalism: Learning from the Past", in J., Dunning (ed.), *Making Globalization Good*, Oxford: Oxford University Press, pp. 41–60.

Landes, D.S. (1999) *The Wealth and Poverty of Nations: Why Some Are So Rich and Some So Poor*, Little Brown: Boston.

Langlois, C.C. and Schlegelmilch, B.B. (1990) "Do Corporate Codes of Ethics Reflect National Character? Evidence from Europe and the United Sates", *Journal of International Business Studies*, 18(2): 17–31.

Lazerson, M. (1995) "A New Phoenix: Modern Putting-Out in the Modena Knitwear Industry", *Administrative Science Quarterly*, 40: 34–59.

London, T. and Hart, S. (2004 September) "Reinventing Strategies for Emerging Markets: Beyond the Transnational Model", *Journal of International Business Studies*, 35(5): 350–370.

Loury, G. (1977) "A Dynamic Theory of Racial Income Differences", in P.A., Wallace and A.M., LaMonde (eds), *Women, Minorities and Employment Discrimination*, Lexington, MA: Lexington Books: 153–186.

Macauley, S. (1963) "Non-Contractual Relations in Business", *American Sociological Review*, 28: 55–67.

Margolis, J. and Walsh, J. (2003) "Misery Loves Companies: Rethinking Social Initiatives by Business", *Administrative Science Quarterly*, 48: 268–305.

Moskowitz, M. (1972) "Choosing Socially Responsible Stocks", *Business and Society*, 1: 71–75.

Moore, G. and Beadle, R. (2006) "In Search of Organizational Virtue in Business: Agents, Goods, Practices, Institutions and Environments", *Organization Studies*, 27(3): 369–386.

Moussavi, F. and Evans, D. (1986) "An Attributional Approach to Measuring Corporate Social Performance", Paper Presented at the *Academy of Management Meetings*.

Nahapiet, J. and Ghoshal, S. (1998) "Social Capital, Intellectual Capital and the Organizational Advantage", *Academy of Management Review*, 23: 242–266.

Parket, R. and Eibert, H. (1975) "Social Responsibility: The Underlying Factors", *Business Horizons*, 18: 5–10.

Polanyi, K. (1957) *The Great Transformation*, Beacon Press: Boston.

Putnam, R.D. (1993) *Making Democracy Work, Civic Traditions in Modern Italy*, Princeton University Press: Princeton, New Jersey.

Putnam, R.D. (2000) *Bowling Alone, The Collapse and Revival of American Community*, Simon and Schuster: New York.

Ratnapala, S. (2003) "Moral Capital and Commercial Society", *The Independent Review*, VIII(2): 213–233.

Ring, P. and Van de Ven, A. (1992) "Structuring Cooperative Relationships Between Organizations", *Strategic Management Journal*, 13: 483–498.

Ring, P. and Van de Ven, A. (1994) "Developmental Processes of Cooperative Interorganizational Relationships", *Academy of Management Review*, 19: 90–118.

Robertson, C.J. and Crittenden, W. (2003) "Mapping Moral Philosophies: Strategic Implications for Multinational Firms", *Strategic Management Journal*, 24(4): 385–392.

Rondinelli, D.A. and London, T. (2003) "How Corporations and Environmental Groups Cooperate: Assessing Cross-Sector Alliances and Collaborations", *Academy of Management Executive*, 17(1): 61–76.

Schlegelmilch, B.B. and Robertson, D.C. (1995) "The Influence of Country and Industry on Ethical Perceptions of Senior Executives in the US and Europe", *Journal of International Business Studies*, 26(4): 859–82.

Schumpeter, J.A. (1950) *Capitalism, Socialism and Democracy*, HarperCollins: New York.

Sen, A.K. (1992) *Inequality Re-examined*, Clarendon Press: Oxford.

Sen, A.K. (1997) *Human Rights and Asian Values*, Carnegie Council on Ethics and International Affairs: New York.

Sen, A.K. (1999) *Development as Freedom*, Knopf: New York.

Singer, A. (1994) "Strategy as Moral Philosophy", *Strategic Management Journal*, 15(3): 191–213.

Skutch, A. (1970) *The Golden Core of Religion*, Goerge Allen & Unwin: London.

Small, M.W. (2002) "Practical Problems and Moral Values: Things We Tend to Ignore Revisited", *Journal of Business Ethics*, 39(4): 401–407.

Smith, A. (1776/1991) *The Wealth of Nations*, Liberty Fund: Indianapolis.

Soloman, R. and Hansen, K. (1985) *It's Good Business*, Atheneum: New York.

Soros, G. (2002) *George Soros on Globalization*, Public Affairs: New York.

Sridhar, B.S. and Cambum, A. (1993) "Stages of Moral Development of Corporations", *Journal of Business Ethics*, 12(9): 727–740.

Stiglitz, J. (2003) Towards a New Paradigm of Development, in J., Dunning (ed.), *Making Globalization Good*, Oxford: Oxford University Press, pp. 76–107.

The Economist. (2002) "Learning How Best to Behave", September, 3rd.

Tsai, W. and Ghoshal, S. (1998) "Social Capital and Value Creation: the Role of Intrafirm Networks", *Academy of Management Journal*, 41(4): 464–476.

UNCTAD (2000) *World Investment Report 2000: Cross-Border Mergers and Acquisitions and Development*, New York and Geneva: UN.

Zaheer, A., McEvily, B., and Perrone, V. (1998) "Does Trust Matter? Exploring the Effects of Interorganizational and Interpersonal Trust on Performance", *Organization Science*, 9(2): 141–159.

Zukin, S. and DiMaggio, P. (1990) *Structures of Capital: The Social Organization of the Economy*, Cambridge University Press: New York.

10

The Study of Fit in International Business Research: Methodological and Substantive Issues

Matthew B. Myers and David A. Griffith

In one stream of international business (IB) research, researchers have contended that aligning firm strategy to local environmental contexts enhanced overall firm performance. Similarly, in another stream of IB research, researchers contend that via the employment of an adaptation strategy across markets firms can more appropriately align market offerings to customer needs, thereby enhancing firm performance. Common to both of these streams is the contention that effective management in international business depends on the ability of managers to appropriately align organizational resources with environmental opportunities and threats. In other words, the basis of this idea can be explained by using a congruence approach, founded upon the concept of "fit." A congruence approach theorizes that similarities (i.e., fit) of operating components maximizes efficient operations (Tosi and Slocum, 1984; Newman and Nollen, 1996). Researchers exploring fit in organizations postulate that organizational effectiveness results from a congruence of relevant contextual, structural and/or strategic factors (Child, 1972; Doty et al., 1993; Miner et al., 1994; Newman and Nollen, 1996). Alternatively, when incongruencies exist, underlying differences in operating components create barriers to operations, thus hindering effectiveness (Doty et al., 1993; Keller, 1994; Miner et al., 1994).

Since the 1970s, difference scores and distance scores have been used in studies of congruence in organizational research (Edwards and Parry, 1993). Generally, these approaches have been used to measure the congruence, or fit, between two constructs, which is then viewed as a predictor of some outcome; for example fit between a multinational's structure and its environment influences the multinational's performance. Specifically, difference scores ($Z = a_0 + a_1X + a_2Y + a_3(X - Y) + e$), distance scores ($Z = a_0 + a_1X + a_2Y + a_3(X - Y)^2 + e$), and Euclidean distance scores ($Z = a_0 + a_1X + a_2Y + a_3(\sqrt{X_1Y_1}) + e$) are seen to indicate effects of fit on a specific outcome if a_3 is significant. Unfortunately, these approaches suffer from numerous substantive and methodological problems (Edwards and Parry, 1993), resulting in the misidentification of effects within the research efforts. These problems include (1) an inability to appropriately capture the curvilinear nature of the concept of fit; (2) an inability to differentiate the impact of two separate constructs in the fit measure; and (3) an inability to determine direction of effects, that is, positive or negative, of individual constructs. These issues are most pertinent in the field of international business where, in a critical evaluation of IB research, Sullivan (1998) states that there is a tendency to build consensus through iterative replication or trivial refinement that precludes genuine shifts in intellectual direction. Methodologically, this problem often takes form in a reliance on linear or analog models that fail to capture critical relationships. Further, linear analysis of inherently nonlinear relationships often produces illogical and oft times misleading results (e.g., Edwards, 1994; Sullivan 1998, etc.). In addition, according to Venkatraman (1989), the conceptual differences between profile deviation and matching necessitate two different forms of testing.

Given the theoretical importance of fit, either implied or explicitly stated, in models investigating IB phenomena, the purpose of this chapter is to explore the substantive and methodological issues in the measurement of fit. Specifically, we examine four alternative approaches to fit measurement, that is, difference scores, distance scores, Euclidean distance scores, and polynomial regressions. Following Edwards and Parry (1993), we demonstrate, through an illustration within the context of international business (i.e., based upon the study put forth by Griffith and Myers, 2005), that fit assessment via polynomial regression analysis and response surface maps can overcome the substantive and methodological issues with alternative fit testing approaches.[1] Our findings demonstrate the advantages of employing the polynomial regression approach for the study of fit. Implications for IB academics are then presented.

Methodological approaches

Fit is often assessed using difference scores, distance scores, Euclidean distance scores, and polynomial regression equations. Each of these methods has been used within the IB literature as a means of understanding how the congruence of two constructs, such as environment and strategy, influence a specific predictor variable, for example, performance. However, researchers have noted numerous methodological issues with each technique thus suggesting a potential for difference in outcomes given the approach utilized. Next, we will briefly review the four primary approaches used to assess fit in the IB literature.

Within managerial research, the use of difference scores has been the most popular approach for addressing a multitude of fit issues. "Typically, these scores have consisted of the algebraic, absolute, or squared differences between two component measures" (Edwards and Parry, 1993: 1577). Difference scores refer to the lack of similarity between two construct measures and can be represented as incorporated into a regression equation as in the following: $Z = a_0 + a_1X + a_2Y + a_3(X - Y) + e$. Edwards (1994) argues that difference scores are used in most cases to represent congruence between two constructs which is then viewed as a predictor of some outcome (e.g., a_3). However, Edwards and Parry (1993) note that several methodological problems, for example, an implied positive relationships between X and Z and an implied negative relationship between Y and Z, may limit the appropriateness of the use of difference scores.

Similar to difference scores, *distance* scores are measured using the squared differences between two component measures. These refer to the rating disagreement between two construct measures and can be represented as incorporated into a regression equation as in the following: $Z = a_0 + a_1X + a_2Y + a_3(X - Y)^2 + e$. Thus, a noted difference between distance scores and difference scores relates to the squared nature of the product (and therefore is also referred to as the squared difference score). Similar to the issue raised with difference scores, distance scores also imply specific relationships that may be unwarranted. For example, through the expansion of the equation one can observe that the distance score implies positive coefficients of equal magnitude on X^2 and Y^2 along with a negative coefficient twice as large in absolute magnitude on XY (Edwards and Parry 1993). Further, Edwards and Parry (1993) note that the distance approach implicitly contains curvilinear and interactive terms without appropriate lower order terms. As such, it is possible that the results obtained via distance score may not appropriately reflect the actual relationships between constructs.

Euclidean distance, by formal definition, is the straight line distance between two points. In a plane with p_1 at (x_1, y_1) and p_2 at (x_2, y_2), it is $\sqrt{((x_1 - x_2)^2 + (y_1 - y_2)^2)}$. Euclidean distance scores can be represented as incorporated into a regression equation as in the following: $Z = a_0 + a_1X + a_2Y + a_3(\sqrt{X_1Y_1}) + e$. Although overcoming some of the implied coefficient limitations of difference and distance scores, the employment of Euclidean distance scores is not without its limitations. Specifically, much as with distance scores, the Euclidean distance approach implicitly contains curvilinear and interactive terms without appropriate lower order terms. Secondly, interpretation of these results can be difficult, limiting their use in a number of research scenarios.

Polynomial regression equations refer to the utilization of component measures composing the difference and certain higher order terms, such as the squares of both component measures and their product (Edwards, 1994), and can be represented as incorporated into a regression equation as in the following: $Z = a_0 + a_1X + a_2Y + a_3(X^2) + a_4(X)(Y) + a_5(Y^2) + e$. While these equations permit a researcher to avoid the implicit limitations of difference scores, distance scores, and Euclidean distance scores, the polynomial regression approach suffers from difficulty in interpretation, particularly when the outcome coefficients differ from expectations (Edwards and Parry 1993).

As one can observe, the four different approaches to fit used in understanding profile deviation and matching each has a specific set of limitations. These limitations, when employed within a specific theoretical context, could result in differing conclusions. As such, we will next provide an empirical illustration of the four approaches and the differences in outcomes.

A global supply chain management illustration

In order to demonstrate potential problems associated with fit measures, we utilized the data presented by Griffith and Myers (2005), where the performance implications of the strategic fit of relational norm governance strategies in global supply chain relationships were investigated. Specifically, difference scores, distance scores, Euclidean distance scores, and polynomial models are specified and the resulting models are tested (cf., Venkatraman 1989; Edwards, 1994, 1996).

Griffith and Myers (2005) employ a data set consisting of 92 US firms in industrial classifications 20–39, conducting business in Japan and the Unites States.[2] The data were used to test a theoretical model of the fit of relational norm strategies of flexibility, information exchange, and solidarity across partners on firm performance, where fit to the local cultures, across strategies, was theorized to enhance performance. Firm performance (Z) was the dependent variable. Relational norm governance strategies a US firm employs in its relationships with its primary Japanese (JA) and US (US) partners were the independent variables.

Difference Scores
We began by developing an appropriate difference score equation:

$$Z = b_0 + b_1 US + b_2 JA + b_3 (US - JA) + e \quad (1)$$

Distance Scores
We next developed a corresponding distance score equation:

$$Z = b_0 + b_1 US + b_2 JA + b_3 (US - JA)^2 + e \quad (2)$$

Euclidean Distance Scores
Next, we developed a Euclidean distance score equation:

$$Z = b_0 + b_1 US + b_2 JA + b_3 (\sqrt{US_1 JA_1}) + e \quad (3)$$

Polynomial Regression Equations
Next, following Edwards and Parry (1993), we developed the appropriate corresponding constrained distance equation:

$$Z = b_0 - b(US - JA)^2 + e(4)$$

Which expanded yields:

$$Z = b_0 - b(US^2) + 2b(US)(JA) - b(JA^2) + e(5)$$

This model is equivalent to the following quadratic regression equation:

$$Z = b_0 + b_1(US) + b_2(JA) + b_3(US^2) + b_4(US)(JA) + b_5(JA^2) + e(6)$$

In this equation, *US* and *JA* are included since they are components of terms US^2, *(US)(JA)*, and JA^2 (see Cohen and Cohen, 1983; Edwards, 1996). Following Edwards (1996), the models were evaluated and a particular model was considered supported if the R^2 for the unconstrained equation was significant; significant terms existed and inclusion of the set of terms one order higher than those indicated by the model (e.g., US^3) was *not* significant (Edwards, 1996: 312). If the polynomial models were supported, then significant interaction between relational norms (interdependence) exists, demanding strategy *fit* across Japanese and US relationships for performance enhancement.

Further, response surface methodology allows description and evaluation of a three-dimensional surface by analyzing critical aspects of the corresponding quadratic regression equation (Myers and Montgomery, 1995). In order to facilitate visual exposition of the RSM models, performance was standardized to enable positive and negative interpretations (for detailed discussion of axes identification and slope measurement, see Edwards, 1996).

Results and discussion

Table 10.1 presents the results of the analysis of the four approaches. It is evident that, when testing the value of fit for each of the relational norm constructs, neither the difference nor distance approaches indicate significant relationships with performance, that is, information sharing (difference score: $B = -.07$, F-value $= .01$; distance score $B = .12$, F-value $= 1.25$), flexibility (difference score: $B = .65$, F-value $= .38$; distance score $B = .10$, F-value $= .93$), and solidarity (difference score: $B = -.06$, F-value $= .01$; distance score $B = .07$, F-value $= .42$). Furthermore, the findings conflict relative to the direction of influence. For example, under information sharing, testing of the difference scores indicated a negative relationship while the distance score testing was positive, albeit neither was significant. Furthermore, and more importantly from a methodological perspective, it is not possible to determine the influence of the Japanese or the US firms' measure

Table 10.1   Results of regression analyses for four models

Independent Constructs	R^2	*F*-value	Beta Coefficient(s)
Information sharing			
Difference scores $X + Y + (X - Y)$	.04	.01	−.07
Distance scores $X + Y + (X - Y)^2$	.01	1.25	.12
Euclidean distance $\sqrt{X_1 Y_1}$	.06	6.24*	−.25*
Polynomial $(X + Y + XY + X2 + Y^2)$	.11	2.14*	$X = 1.34$**
			$Y = .48$
			$XY = .43$
			$X^2 = .48$*
			$Y^2 = .77.$
Flexibility			
Difference scores $X + Y + (X - Y)$	.00	.38	.65
Distance scores $X + Y + (X - Y)^2$	.01	.93	.10
Euclidean distance $\sqrt{X_1 Y_1}$	.10	9.74*	−.31*
Polynomial $(X + Y + XY + X^2 + Y^2)$	.10	2.88*	$X = -.25$
			$Y = .43$
			$XY = .12$
			$X^2 = .27$
			$Y^2 = -.27.$
Solidarity			
Difference scores $X+Y+(X - Y)$	.00	.01	−.06
Distance scores $X+Y+(X - Y)^2$	.00	.42	.07
Euclidean distance $\sqrt{X_1 Y_1}$	.07	7.21*	.27*
Polynomial $(X+Y+XY+X^2 + Y^2)$	.11	2.41*	$X = -.99$*
			$Y = -.77$*
			$XY = -.46$
			$X^2 = -.67$*
			$Y^2 = 1.24$*.

Dependent variable: performance
*$p < .05$; **$p < .01$.

on relational norms, relative to its influence on performance, due to the individual coefficients offered by these methods.

Contrary to the difference and distance score testing, analysis via the Euclidean distance approach indicates significant relationships between the fit measures and performance for each of the three relational norm constructs (information sharing: $B = -.25$, *F*-value $= 6.24$; flexibility: $B = -.31$, *F*-value $= 9.74$; solidarity: $B = .27$, *F*-value $= 7.21$). Furthermore, a greater degree of variance is explained with this method, as is evident from the increased R^2s for each model (See Table 10.1). The Euclidean distance approach provides for a more sophisticated measurement of fit than simple difference and distance models and therefore is able to better capture the complex phenomena introduced when addressing profile deviation or matching. However, this method still suffers from the same shortcomings as the previous models, in that the composite nature of the fit measure prevents analysis of the constructs on an individual basis relative to their influence (positive or negative) on performance.

Testing using these three methods reveals a number of shortcomings. First, differentiation between the positive versus negative effects of fit indices on an outcome are difficult to interpret. Second, it is impossible to determine specific profiles between two constructs that maximize or minimize an outcome, that is, what is the appropriate measure of each construct for attaining a desirable outcome. This is due in part to the inability of these approaches to capture the curvilinear aspects of the fit concept, in that a certain degree of fit may be desirable, yet too much fit may be detrimental to the firm. The use of polynomial regression analysis, coupled with surface maps, addresses these concerns. Table 10.1 shows the result of this testing. For each test (information exchange, solidarity, and flexibility), coefficients for each construct in the fit testing are offered, enabling the determination of effects by individual antecedents. Similar to the Euclidean distance testing, each model was found to be significant ($p < .05$). Simultaneously, both the approaches account for greater variance as is evident in their R^2 results.

Figures 10.1–10.4 provide both the two-dimensional algebraic functions and the three-dimensional polynomial functions for the regression analyses. In Figures 10.1–10.3, results for the difference, distance, and Euclidean distance testing indicate the constraints in determining optimization points with these types of linear tests. Furthermore, examination of the X-axes illustrates how these types of composite measures lack the characteristics necessary to determine individual construct influence or interaction between performance and the other fit construct, respectively. Figure 10.4 provides the three-dimensional response surface maps from Griffith and Myers (2005) generated via polynomial analysis. By keeping the relational norm constructs independent, as opposed to creating a composite measure, it is possible to determine what levels of each construct will maximize performance. For example, for solidarity, performance is maximized when high levels of solidarity are displayed by Japanese firms and lower levels are displayed by the US firms. Simultaneously, performance is minimized when the inverse occurs. Similar findings result from the information exchange testing. However, for flexibility, performance is maximized when high levels of flexibility by US firms and lower levels of flexibility by Japanese firms are displayed. As such, consistent with Edwards and Parry (1993) we conclude that response surface maps provide considerably more insight than the two-dimensional plots, enabling the researcher to draw more meaningful conclusions from the analysis.

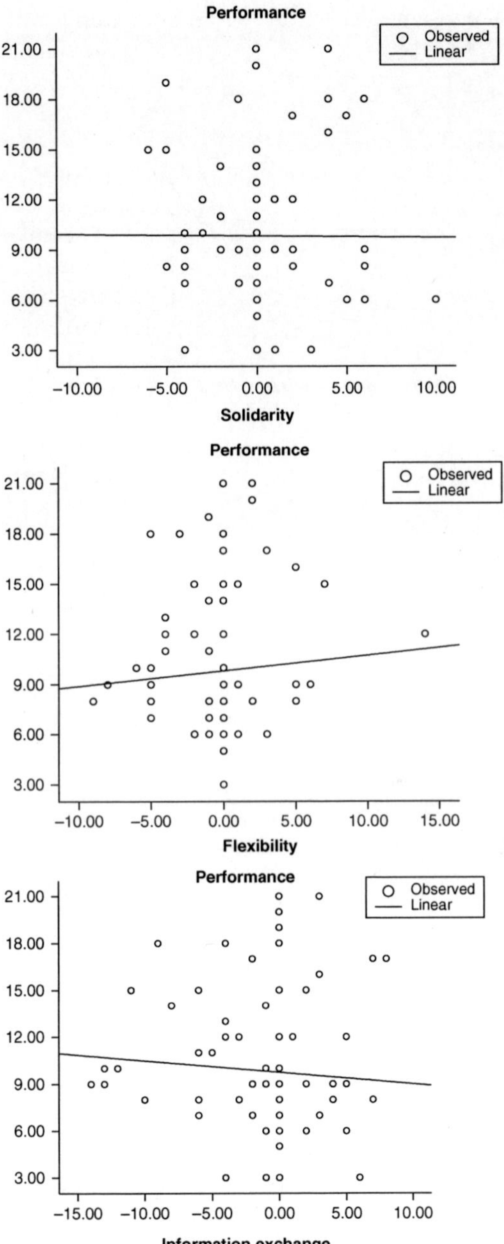

Figure 10.1 Two-dimensional algebraic difference functions $(Z = a_0 + a_1X + a_2Y + a_3(X - Y)^2 + e)$

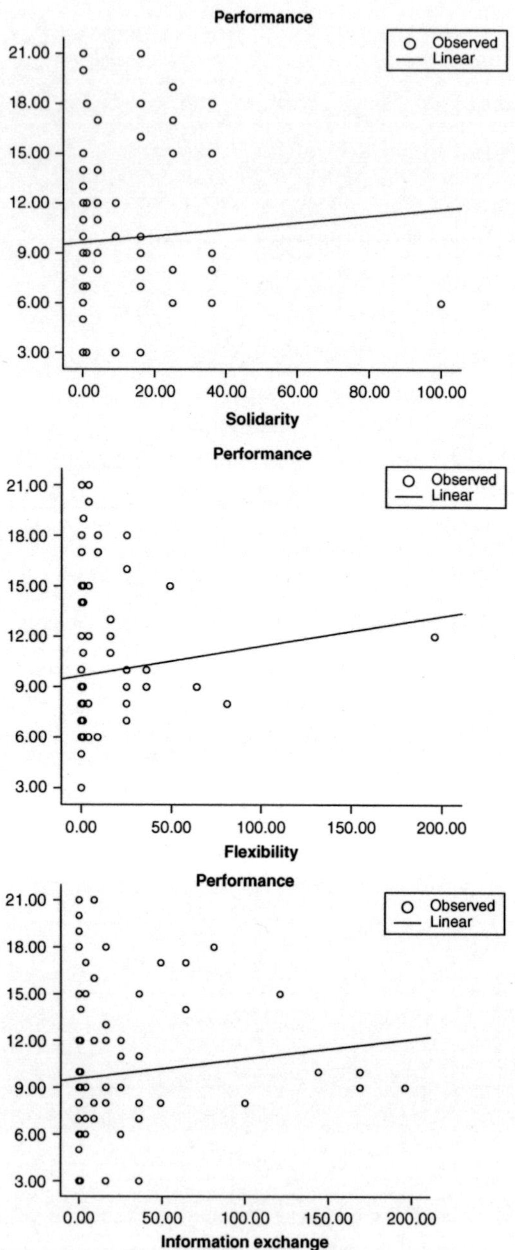

Figure 10.2 Two-dimensional algebraic distance functions $(Z = a_0 + a_1 X + a_2 Y + a_3(X - Y)^2 + e)$

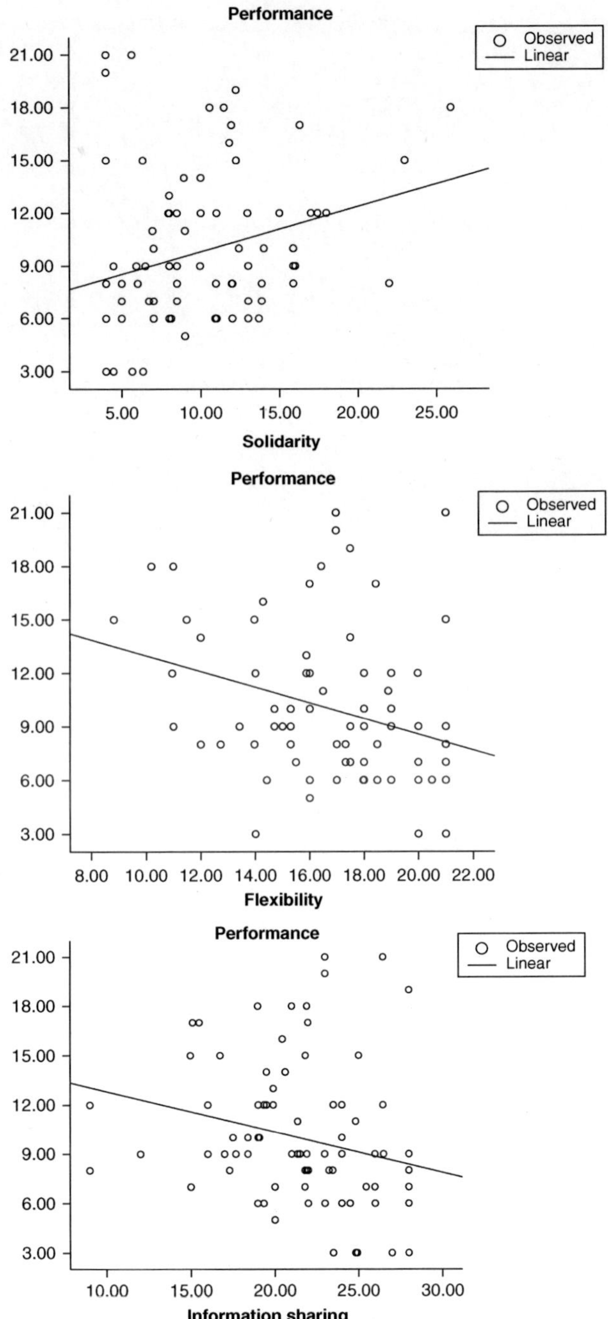

Figure 10.3 Two-dimensional euclidean distance functions $\sqrt{X_1 Y_1}$

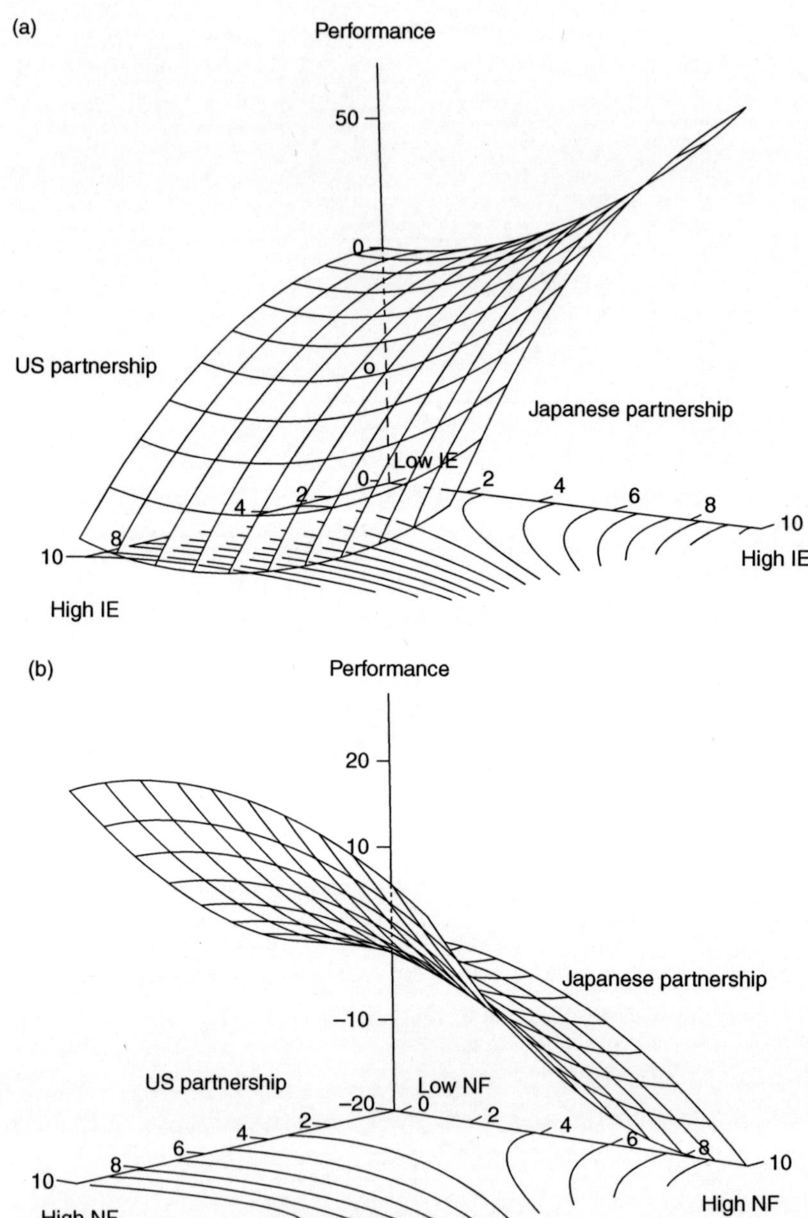

Figure 10.4 Three-dimensional polynomial functions $Z = a_0 + a_1(X), + a_2(Y), + a_3(X^2), + a_4(X)(Y), + a_5(Y^2), + e$: (a) Performance implications of information exchange fit, (b) Performance implications of norm of flexibility fit, and (c) Performance implications of solidarity fit

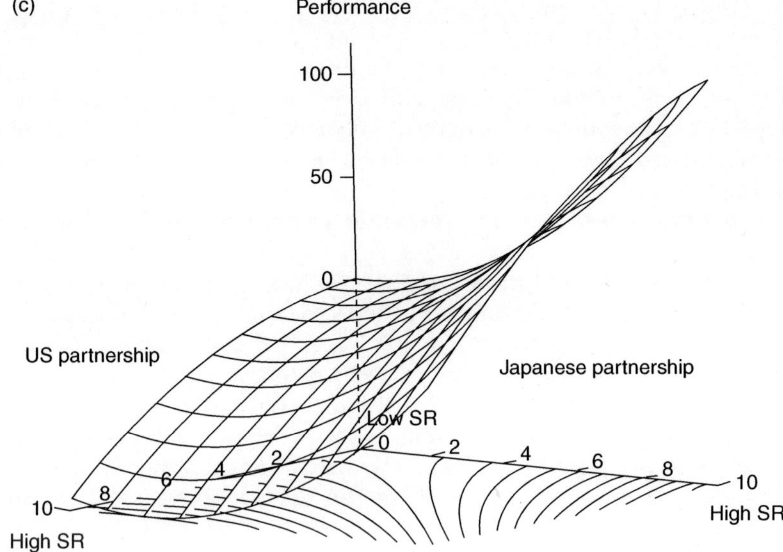

Figure 10.4   (Continued)

Implications

The purpose of this chapter was to illustrate the substantive and methodological issues in the measurement of fit within the context of the IB literature. Specifically, we examined four alternative approaches to fit measurement, that is, difference scores, distance scores, Euclidean distance scores, and polynomial regressions within the context of a recent IB study, that is, Griffith and Myers (2005). The results demonstrate the importance of appropriateness of fit measurement and interpretation. Specifically, the results suggest that the implicit assumptions and limitations of difference scores, distance scores, and Euclidean distance scores, approaches that have been used extensively in the IB literature to address the issue of fit, may have inadvertently resulted in inappropriate conclusions.

As illustrated through multiple approaches to the Griffith and Myers (2005) data, assessment of fit via either difference or distance scores resulted in substantially different conclusions than either the Euclidean distance approach or more notably the polynomial regression equations approach. It is important to note at this point that the greatest concern is not the issue of whether or not the results were significant, but rather the conceptual appropriateness of each technique, inclusive of implicit assumptions, and how these implicit assumptions influence the results and hence interpretation. Thus, these results caution researchers to question the basic manner in which fit is investigated methodologically, as each approach possesses a specific set of limitations and thus provides a unique solution.

A criticism of polynomial regression questions is often the difficulty of interpretation and the complexity of the analysis. However, we believe, as demonstrated here, that polynomial regression equations can overcome the limitations of prior approaches to fit and are more appropriate to the profile deviation and matching conceptualizations put forth in the IB literature. Furthermore, as stated earlier, Edwards and Parry (1993) argue that the use of difference and distance scores include problems such as (1) an inability to appropriately capture the curvilinear nature of the concept of fit; (2) an inability to differentiate the impact of two separate constructs in the fit measure; and (3) an inability to determine direction of effects, that is, positive or negative, of individual constructs. The results of this study demonstrate that the employment of polynomial regression equations, matched with response surface methodology, provides a more appropriate testing method for the study of fit in the field of IB research. As such, we believe that these results help to answer Sullivan's (1998) call for a genuine shift in intellectual direction in the field of IB research. Whereas Sullivan (1998) states that there is a tendency to build consensus through iterative replication or trivial refinement that precludes genuine shifts in intellectual direction, the movement from linear or analog models that fail to capture critical relationships to complex curvilinear testing provides advanced understanding of IB phenomena, which are, by their very nature, complex.

The application of this approach to the study of IB phenomena is wide ranging. For example, the effectiveness of employing a standardized global strategy has been the subject of intense academic debate and research for several decades (e.g., Brown, 1923; Samiee and Roth, 1992; Cavusgil and Zou, 1994; Zou and Cavusgil, 2002). Managers have long been interested in the standardization issue, since among other things, it suggests operational economies and the development of uniform best practices. Standardization has two fundamental aspects: program and process (Sorenson and Wiechmann, 1975; Jain, 1989; Griffith et al., 2000). In both program and process standardization/adaptation, the issue is one of fit of strategy to the firm's environment to enhance overall firm performance. As such, the issue of global strategy standardization/adaptation could be investigated through the polynomial regression equation approach. More specifically, the fact that decades of research have been conducted in the area of global strategy standardization with mixed research results highlight the implicit problems in the difference and distance score approaches to fit, that is, lack of consistent findings are likely the result of curvilinear effects which cannot be tested through a difference or distance score approach, but can be examined through a polynomial regression approach.

The environment–strategy–performance framework is another IB context that fit examined via polynomial regression equations would be appropriate. The framework theorizes that the co-alignment of strategy to environmental factors allows firms to operate effectively, thus enhancing performance (Child, 1972; Luo and Park, 2001). The foundation of the environment–strategy–performance framework is in the literatures of strategic co-alignment (Astley and Van de Ven, 1983) and strategic choice (Child, 1972, 1997). The strategic co-alignment literature argues that the alignment between a firm's strategic profile and its external environment maximizes effectiveness in operations (Child, 1972; Astley and Van de Ven, 1983; Venkatraman and Prescott, 1990). Under this perspective, operational effectiveness results from a congruence of relevant contextual and strategic factors whereas misalignments between environmental elements and firm strategy create barriers to operations, hindering effectiveness (Bourgeois, 1980; Venkatraman and Prescott, 1990; Doty et al., 1993). Given the conceptual nature of the research within profile deviation/matching, it could be argued that substantial insights could be advanced over the extant literature which primarily has relied upon difference and distance approaches.

Further, a central research stream within the IB domain that looks at profile deviation/matching is cultural distance (whether national culture, organizational culture, or professional culture). Differences in culture systems or the relative "cultural distance" between countries have been an important concern in the study of MNE strategies and organizational characteristics (Barkema et al., 1996; Brouthers and Brouthers, 2001). However, researchers have noted numerous problems with current methods of addressing this topic (e.g., Shenkar, 2001; Tihanyi et al., 2005). One criticism relates to the linear nature of the difference score method employed by Kogut and Singh (1988), a measure that has become the dominant operationalization. We offer the conceptualization of fit via polynomial regression equations as an avenue to overcome some of the limitations of existing measurement. Future methodological innovations based upon polynomial regression equations for the understanding of cultural distance could help to advance the field.

Conclusion

Overall, the purpose of this study was to illustrate the substantive and methodological issues in the measurement of fit within the context of the IB literature. Specifically, four different approaches to fit were discussed and employed. The results demonstrate the explanatory power of the polynomial regression approach over existing approach (e.g., difference scores, distance scores, Euclidean distance scores) for the study of complex phenomena such as those studied within the area of international business. Through the discussion we noted the importance of understanding the implicit elements of each fit measurement approach and its implications for substantive inference. Further, we suggested three specific IB research areas (i.e., global strategy standardization/adaptation, environment-strategy-performance, and cultural distance) in which polynomial regression equations, in the context of fit as profile deviation or matching, could enhance understanding and move the literature beyond its current state. Finally, we believe that this study can serve as a foundation for researchers to continue to explore methodological developments through a systematic comparison approach to integrate new methods into the field of international business, thus helping to overcome concerns noted by Sullivan (1998) related to iterative replication or trivial refinement that precludes genuine shifts in intellectual direction for the advancement of the field of international business.

Notes

1. Those readers familiar with Venkatraman's (1989) work in the area of fit will realize that he speaks of six types of fit: moderation, mediation, gestalt, co-variation, profile deviation, and matching. Our focus here is on the latter two types, in that these address measures between two independent variables that the researcher may wish to know the value of similarities or dissimilarities between two constructs relative to maximizing or minimizing a specific outcome. This excludes the investigation of third variable interactions (as in mediation) and focuses on the two purest forms of fit. We approach fit in this manner given that profile deviation and matching are the foundation of the seminal streams of the international business literature.
2. For a full review of the data collection, sample characteristics, measures, and so on sourced for the analysis in this study, please refer to Griffith and Myers (2005).

References

Astley, W. G. and Van de Ven, A. H. 1983. Central Perspectives and Debates in Organization Theory. *Administrative Science Quarterly*, 28(2): 245–273.

Barkema, H. G., Bell, J. H. J., and Pennings, J. M. 1996. Foreign Entry, Cultural Barriers, and Learning. *Strategic Management Journal*, 17: 151–166.

Brouthers, K. D. and Brouthers, L. E. 2001. Explaining the National Cultural Distance Paradox. *Journal of International Business Studies*, 32: 177–189.

Brown, D. L. 1923. *Export Advertising*. Ronald Press: New York, NY.

Bourgeois, L. J. III. 1980. Strategy and Environment: A Conceptual Integration. *Academy of Management Review*, 5(1): 25–39.

Cavusgil, S. T. and Shaoming, Zou. 1994. Marketing Strategy-Performance Relationship: An Investigation of the Empirical Link in Export Market Venture. *Journal of Marketing*, 58(1): 1–21.

Child, J. 1972. Organizational Structure, Environment and Performance: The Role of Strategic Choice. *Sociology*, 6(1): 1–22.

Child, J. 1997. Strategic Choice in the Analysis of Action, Structure, Organizations and Environment: Retrospect and Prospect. *Organization Studies*, 18(1): 43–76.

Cohen, J. and Cohen, P. 1983. *Applied Multiple Regression/Correlation Analysis for the Behavioral Sciences*. Erlbaum Press: Hillsdale, NJ.

Doty, D. H., Glick, W. H., and Huber, G. P. 1993. Fit, Equifinality, and Organizational Effectiveness: A Test. *Academy of Management Journal*, 36(6): 1196–1251.

Edwards, J. R. and Parry, M. E. 1993. The Use of Polynomial Regression Equations as an Alternative to Difference Scores in Organizational Research. *Academy of Management Journal*, 36(6): 1577–1613.

Edwards, J. R. 1994. The Study of Congruence in Organizational Behavior Research: Critique and a Proposed Alternative. *Organizational Behavior and Human Decision Processes*, 58: 51–100.

Edwards, J. R. 1996. An Examination of Competing Versions of the Person-Environment Fit Approach to Stress. *Academy of Management Journal*, 39(2): 392–339.

Griffith, D. A. and Myers, Matthew B. 2005. The Performance Implications of Strategic Fit of Relational Norm Governance Strategies in Global Supply Chain Relationships. *Journal of International Business Studies*, 36(3): 254–269.

Griffith, D. A., Hu, Michael Y., and Ryans, John K. Jr. 2000. Process Standardization in Inter- and Intra-Cultural Relationships. *Journal of International Business Studies*, 31(2): 303–324.

Jain, S. C. 1989. Standardization of International Marketing Strategy: Some Research Hypotheses. *Journal of Marketing*, 53(1): 70–79.

Keller, R. T. 1994. Technology-Information Processing Fit and the Performance of R&D Project Groups: A Test of Contingency Theory. *Academy of Management Journal*, 37(1): 167–180.

Kogut, B. and Singh, H. 1988. The Effect of National Culture on the Choice of Entry Mode. *Journal of International Business Studies*, 19: 411–432.

Luo, Y. and Park, S. 2001. Strategic Alignment and Performance of Market-Seeking MNCs in China. *Strategic Management Journal*, 22(2): 141–155.

Miner, J. B., Crane, D. P., and Vandenberg, R. J. 1994. Congruence and Fit in Professional Role Motivation Theory. *Organization Science*, 5(1): 86–97.

Myers, R. H. and Montgomery, D. C. 1995. *Response Surface Methodology: Process and Product Optimization Using Designed Experiments*, Wiley Press: New York.

Newman, K. and S. Nollen 1996. Culture and Congruence: The Fit Between Management Practices and National Culture. *Journal of International Business Studies*, 27(4): 753–779.

Samiee, S. and Roth, K. 1992. The Influence of Global Marketing Standardization on Performance. *Journal of Marketing*, 56(2): 1–17.

Shenkar, O. 2001. Cultural Distance Revisited: Towards a More Rigorous Conceptualization and Measurement of Cultural Differences. *Journal of International Business Studies*, 32: 519–535.

Sorenson, R. Z. and Wiechmann, Ulrich W. 1975. How Multinationals View Marketing Standardization. *Harvard Business Review*, 53(May–June) (38-54): 166–167.

Sullivan, D. 1998. Cognitive Tendencies in International Business Research: Implications of a "Narrow Vision". *Journal of International Business Studies*, 29(4): 837–862.

Tihanyi, L., Griffith, David A., and Russell, Craig, J. 2005. The Effect of Cultural Distance on Entry Mode Choice, International Diversification, and MNE Performance: A Meta-Analysis. *Russell*, 36(3): 270–283.

Tosi, H. L., Jr. and Slocum, J. W. Jr. 1984. Contingency Theory: Some Suggested Directions. *Journal of Management*, 10(1): 9–26.

Venkatraman, N. and Prescott, J. E. 1990. Environment-Strategy Coalignment: An Empirical Test of Its Performance Implications. *Strategic Management Journal*, 11(1): 1–23.

Venkatraman, N. 1989. The Concept of Fit in Strategy Research: Toward Verbal and Statistical Correspondence. *Academy of Management Review*, 14(3): 423–444.

Zou, S. and Cavusgil, S. Tamer 2002. The GMS: A Broad Conceptualization of Global Marketing Strategy and Its Effect on Firm Performance. *Journal of Marketing*, 66(4): 40–56.

Index

In this index tables are indicated by tab; figures by fig; notes by n. These are in italics, enclosed in parentheses, e.g. fit, 244*(n.1)*.